How Philosophers Saved Myths

Luc Brisson   *Translated by Catherine Tihanyi*

HOW PHILOSOPHERS SAVED MYTHS

Allegorical Interpretation and Classical Mythology

THE UNIVERSITY OF CHICAGO PRESS / CHICAGO AND LONDON

Luc Brisson is director of research at the Centre national de la recherche scientifique, France. Among his previous works published in English are *Inventing the Universe: Plato's Timaeus, the Big Bang, and the Problem of Scientific Knowledge*, with F. Walter Meyerstein (1995); *Plato the Myth Maker* (1998); and *Sexual Ambivalence: Androgyny and Hermaphroditism in Graeco-Roman Antiquity* (2002). **Catherine Tihanyi**, a research associate in the Department of Anthropology at Western Washington University, has translated a number of books, including Claude Lévi-Strauss's *The Story of Lynx* (1995) and Adam Biro's *Two Jews on a Train* (2001).

The University of Chicago Press, Chicago 60637
The University of Chicago Press, Ltd., London
© 2004 by The University of Chicago
All rights reserved. Published 2004
Printed in the United States of America
English language only
13 12 11 10 09 08 07 06 05 04   1 2 3 4 5

ISBN: 0-226-07535-4 (cloth)

Originally published in German as *Einführung in die Philosophie des Mythos*, vol. 1: *Antike, Mittelalter und Renaissance*, © 1996 by Wissenschaftliche Buchgesellschaft, Darmstadt. The present translation is based on the French edition, *Introduction à la philosophie du mythe*, vol. 1: *Sauver les mythes*, © Librairie Philosophique J. Vrin, 1996.

Library of Congress Cataloging-in-Publication Data

Brisson, Luc.
   [Sauver les mythes. English]
   How philosophers saved myths : allegorical interpretation and classical mythology / Luc Brisson ; translated by Catherine Tihanyi.
    p. cm.
   Includes bibliographical references and indexes.
   ISBN: 0-226-07535-4 (alk. paper)
   1. Mythology, Classical. 2. Allegory. 3. Philosophy—History. I. Title.

BL727.B7513 2004
201'.3'01—dc22

2004006948

To Jean Pépin
whose works on myth have been a constant source of inspiration

CONTENTS

TRANSLATOR'S NOTE

This translation has undergone a number of changes from the French original. The author has modified some sentences, made use of a recently published translation of the Derveni papyrus, and also corrected some typos and biographical errors in the original French.

I have, whenever possible, used published English-language translations to render Brisson's quotations. Occasionally I made some slight modifications, all noted in the endnotes, in order to harmonize these English-language extracts with Brisson's meaning.

I would like to express my gratitude to Luc Brisson for reading the first draft of the translation and the final proofs and for his patience in answering questions; and to Michael Chase for his thorough reading of the draft and his invaluable corrections of some errors that had crept in it. My thanks also to Gérard Naddaf for his helpful suggestions. In Chicago, I would like to thank T. David Brent for entrusting me with this project and for his kind encouragements, and Leslie Keros for very ably bringing this project to its published completion. Last but not least, my thanks to Margaret Mahan for her outstanding copyediting and her deft and sensitive solutions to a number of translation problems.

This book was begun in 1987 at the request of the Wissenschaftliche Buchgesellschaft. It is the first volume of a work titled *Einführung in die Philosophie des Mythos;* the second volume is by Christoph Jamme. Volume 1 was delayed because of health problems and then difficulties pertaining to its translation into German. The length of the delay explains a number of minor differences between the French and German versions.

I would like to thank Catherine Joubaud, Jean-Marie Flamand, and my daughter, Anne Brisson, who contributed to the realization of this work in various ways. Achim Russer, the translator of this book into German, helped to make my thinking more precise on several points; I am grateful to him for this.

Adv. math.	Sextus Empiricus, *Adversus mathematicos*
Anth. Pal.	*Anthologia Graecia ad Palatini codicis fidem edita*
CAG	*Commentaria in Aristotelem Graeca*
CO	*Chaldean Oracles*
Cod. Theod.	*Codex Theodosius*
De myst.	Iamblichus, *De mysteriis*
De Princ.	Damascius, *De principiis*
DK	H. Diehl and W. Kranz, eds., *Die Fragmente der Vorsokratiker*
DL	Diogenes Laertius, *Lives and doctrines of the eminent philosophers*
DP	Derveni papyrus
DND	Cicero, *De natura deorum*
Enn.	Plotinus, *The Enneads*
In Arist. Eth. Nicom.	Michael of Ephesus, *In librum quintum Ethicorum Nicomacheorum commentarium*
In Arist. Phys.	Simplicius, *In Aristotelis Physicae*
In Parm.	Proclus, *In Platonis Parmenidem commentarii*
In Remp.	Proclus, *In Platonis Republicam commentarii*
LP	Porphyry, *Life of Plotinus*
Od.	Homer, *Odyssey*
OF	*Orphicorum fragmenta* (Kern)
PG	*Patrologia Graeca*
PT	Marsilio Ficino, *In Platonicam theologiam*

RE	*Real-Encyclopädie des classischen Altertumswissenschaft*
SSR VA or VB	*Socratis et Socraticorum Reliquiae*
SVF	*Stoicorum Veterum Fragmenta,* ed. H. von Arnim
Theol. Graec. Comp.	Cornutus, *Theologiae graecae compendium*
Vit. Soph.	Philostratus, *Vitae sophistarum*

Introduction

Anyone conscious of being heir to a culture going back to ancient Greece would be familiar with the details of the myth of Oedipus and would be moved by the misfortunes affecting the hero and his daughter Antigone. Yet, at the same time, he or she might have trouble remembering some important political event that occurred just a few years back and was much discussed in the media.

The origins of the Oedipus narrative are impossible to trace. It was transmitted orally for generations before providing the plots for tragedies performed in the fifth century B.C. in the then tiny city of Athens in front of a relatively small audience. Now, at the close of the twentieth century, so marked by intense rational activity, particularly in the domain of science, how is it that this myth still stimulates the imagination and possesses a power of evocation giving rise to emotions and attitudes strong and deep enough to inspire new artistic works and even the foundation of psychoanalysis? This is the question I seek to answer in this book, which is firmly located on a historical plane.

The present work describes how, though we would have expected historians, philosophers, and theologians to eliminate myth, it was instead "saved" by allegory, which made it possible to associate the most scandalous of narratives and bizarre details to deep truths.

Myth did not receive its name until it underwent a radical critique by the first "historians" and especially by the first "philosophers" during the period when writing made its appearance. Myth then became the object of a progressive and increasingly broad reintegration into the frameworks of history and philosophy through the interpretive means of "allegory." Allegory was to exhibit several faces in the course of the centuries, including ethical, physical, psychological, historical, and even metaphysical ones.

Allegory was rejected by Plato, though he did not renounce myth, but it was practiced, with restraint and prudence, by Aristotle. It enabled the Stoics to associate the main figures of Greek mythology with virtues, elements (fire, air, water, earth), faculties, and even, following Euhemerus here, human beings. The Epicureans and the philosophers of the new Academy belittled this practice as it involved reducing the gods to mere human beings and even to common and trivial material realities, and they denounced the tendency to turn ancient poets into historians or philosophers unbeknownst to themselves. This hostility might have slowed down the movement, but it did not stop it.

At the dawn of the Christian era, an original allegorical current developed that was rooted in the conviction that myths and mysteries should be looked upon as two complementary means used by God to reveal truth to religious souls. Myth brought this revelation through the means of narratives, while mysteries presented it in the form of drama. In this context, poets were looked upon as initiates to whom a truth belonging to a different level of reality has been transmitted, which poets in turn transmit to those worthy of it. This mode of transmission involves the use of a coded discourse, a discourse with a double meaning, one inscribed into the action of secrecy, and in which everything is expressed through enigma and symbols. Poets were no longer philosophers in spite of themselves but theologians striving to cautiously transmit a truth to which philosophy provides a direct access.

The Neoplatonists sought to oppose the rise of the power of Christianity, and then its domination as a state religion, by establishing total agreement between Platonic doctrine they looked upon as "theology" and all the other Greek theologies that could be found in Homer, Hesiod, Orpheus, and the *Chaldean Oracles*.

The appearance of Christianity, and above all its domination, complicated the issue. Henceforth myth had to not only accord with history and philosophy but it should also not collide directly with church dogma. Thus a new effort of adaptation and hence of interpretation, was agreed to, first by the church fathers, then by thinkers and artists in the Byzantine world as well as those of the western Middle Ages.

This rescue was not easy in those troubled periods when the transmission of knowledge was a difficult undertaking. Yet it was genuine, so much so that the Renaissance inherited a treasure trove of narratives and representations whose true forms it fervently undertook to restore.

Allegory enabled the constant adaptation and interpretation of myths to fit the context in which they were received. Because of this, allegory cannot be relegated to the level of a marginal, slightly ridiculous phenomenon. It made it possible for myths to survive. This book deals with the history of this rescue, a history of extraordinary ingeniousness and amazing suppleness.

But what was the reason for this tenacity to ensure the survival of myths that were so ancient and strange in many respects? The answer perhaps lies in that neither reason nor a new faith was better able than those myths to express something very special and irreducible deep in the human heart, as one generation after another ceaselessly and imperceptibly transformed the cultural legacy of ancient Greece and thus ensured its survival.

To acknowledge the limits of reason does not lead to irrationalism. As F. Walter Meyerstein and I have sought to show in *Puissance et limites de la raison* (Paris: Les Belles Lettres, 1995), the power of reason paradoxically lies in its ability to recognize its own limits, but the transgression of these limits nonetheless leads straight to irrationalism.

ONE

Muthos and Philosophia

W hat is culture if not a specific system of communication acts? In this view, if we assume that the content of a message is to a certain extent determined by the means through which it has been communicated, we then naturally have to conclude that a change in the means of communication must lead to a change in the content of the communicated messages. Eric A. Havelock sought to confirm the pertinence of such a hypothesis in the case of ancient Greece by showing how, from the seventh century B.C. onward, the adoption of a radically new system of writing that virtually put reading within everyone's grasp led to the emergence of two new types of discourse: that of "history" and that of "philosophy." These discourses were set in opposition to poetry, which until then had maintained a monopoly in the transmission of the memorable.

I will try to briefly show how the appearance and development of what is at present called "philosophy" in ancient Greece can be linked with the introduction, a few centuries earlier, of a new system of writing. The difficulties of this project, which I do not minimize, stem mainly from the paucity of our documentation for the period preceding Plato and from the partial nature of the Platonic account, the only one which, for better or worse, we can rely on.

THE COMMUNICATION OF THE MEMORABLE
IN AN ORAL CIVILIZATION

The collapse of the Mycenaean civilization in the eleventh century B.C. marks the beginning of an obscure time in Greek history. This obscurity is due in great part to our lack of information on a period from which the works attributed to Homer and those created by Hesiod emerged. Homer and Hesiod were poets, that is, "myth makers" according to Plato, who systematically associated *poiētēs* with *muthologos* and *poiēsis* with *muthologia*.[1]

But what does myth speak of? It tells of a beyond located in a faraway time and a distant place, different from the space and time of its narrators and public. In books II and III of the *Republic,* Plato lists the five classes of individuals who partake in this temporal and spatial beyond: gods, daemons, inhabitants of Hades (the dead), heroes, and men of the past.[2]

This statement immediately raises two questions. Why should one speak of such realities, and how can one do so?

The first question is too broad to be given a satisfactory answer here as it amounts to inquiring about the causes of religious phenomena as a whole. However, it can be stated in the briefest terms that human beings almost always seem to have looked to a beyond for the principles of explanations of the sensible world. They have attributed a superior status to this beyond, and above all have sought in it the justification of their actions and the assurance that these will be crowned with success.[3] Yet this approach only makes sense if, instead of a radical separation between the sensible world and the beyond, there is but a gap that can be momentarily bridged by intermediaries such as diviners, initiators, and poets.[4]

In order to evoke the beyond, poets fashioned an image with words, but they went much farther than this. They alienated their own identities by identifying wholly with the beings they were evoking. Poets put in their own mouths words that these beings must have uttered, the sounds they must have emitted. They even became physically like them as they adopted the beings' attitudes and postures while moving to the beat of music and the rhythm of dance. In short, it was the whole of the poet's body or of that of the interpreters of the poet that was called upon to evoke the beyond.

In Plato, therefore, the critique of poetry cannot be dissociated from the critique of the fine arts—the arts dealing with painting and sculpture among others. But for the poet, visual representation was limited to illustrating and adding to the oral performance.

There is more, however, for the ultimate goal of the mimesis performed by poets or their interpreters was to lead to the audience's identification with the beings evoked. From the outset, the drive to modify the behavior of a mass of human beings posed an ethical and political challenge. This was where the real stakes were located. Poets could be looked upon as genuine educators because they strove to modify the behavior of the public they were addressing by presenting the beings evoked as models.[5]

In general terms and going beyond Plato's analysis, we could invert our approach and say that the poet was the privileged intermediary between a community and the systems of explanations and values to which this community adhered. In short, the whole of a community gave itself as a model to itself through myth. So we must avoid looking at poetic activity from an exclusively aesthetic perspective, because the myths created by poets inextricably mixed ethical values with all kinds of knowledge as well as with a religious dimension.[6] We can thus understand why, in ancient Greece until the sixth century B.C., the poet held a monopoly of the transmission of the memorable and thus of "education," this term being understood here in a particularly broad sense and placed in a specific context.

As "educator," the poet gave form and transmitted that which constituted the identity of a community, that is, in a way, its very conscience. That is why the listeners exerted a real censorship on the poets who addressed them directly or through intermediaries, a censorship all the more constraining in it that it occurred in the framework of an oral performance.

That censorship led poets to send back to their listeners the kind of images that basically fulfilled the listeners' expectation. In the context of ancient Greek civilization, where there was no priestly class invested with dual role of maintaining tradition and insuring the conformity of social behavior to this tradition,[7] such a play of mirrors could be maintained only if myth kept on adapting to public expectations.

This was possible as long as the mode of communication of myth remained exclusively oral. If we compare this mode to writing, in which it is forbidden not only to use different words from those that were finally retained but also to change the sequence of those words, the spoken word as a means of communication has a great degree of elasticity that enables a slow but constant modification of both content and form of the transmitted message. In this oral mode, the latest version of a myth is the only one available, and so it is impossible to compare the currently transmitted version with preceding ones.

THE ROLE OF WRITING AND ITS CONSEQUENCES

After disappearing for more than four centuries, the use of writing was reintroduced in ancient Greece at the beginning of the seventh century B.C. The Greeks borrowed the Phoenicians' consonant syllabary, which itself was a variant of the western Semitic systems invented in the course of the preceding millennium. The Greeks then noted vowels next to consonants and in combination with them.[8] This innovation led to a true revolution in the field of reading.[9] In contrast to a syllabic writing system, which had to be accessible only to a small group of professionals capable of making up the deficiencies of a writing system limited to consonants, reading became, at least in theory, an activity accessible to anyone with the leisure to undertake it.

The spread of an easily decipherable writing system exerted considerable change on the mental habits of a growing number of individuals, some of whom were very influential. (1) The use of prose gradually increased in a civilization where the storage of information depended less and less on individual memory, whose effectiveness depended on rhythm, particularly metrical rhythm. (2) Parallel to this, narrative was relayed or replaced by description, above all by argumentation, in which parts of a discourse can be looked at as autonomous elements whose meaning exhibits a degree of independence in relation to the whole to which they belong. (3) Hence, the criterion for the "truth" of discourse changed. While the poet claimed to transmit an oral tradition ultimately founded on the authority of the Muses, the daughters of Zeus and Mnemosyne (= Memory), a need came to be felt, particularly among "historians," to back their statements with direct or indirect eyewitness testimony. (4) Within the same movement, conceptual thought began to affirm itself. This thought no longer looked at an abstract entity, such as justice,[10] as solely a property of certain actions, or as an institutional process, or even as a divinity manifesting one of the qualities of Zeus, the king of the gods, whose daughter was Justice. Rather, conceptual thought looked upon justice as an autonomous reality, one that could be defined and could be considered an absolute norm, allowing judgment to be passed on acts carried out by a community or an individual. (5) The storage of written documents attributed by name to given individuals, which could be consulted fairly readily, favored critical thinking. In order to justify its existence, a narrative or a doctrine had to be presented by its author as superior to that which had hither to been made in the same field. This had not been the case previously. Since it had been impossible to "check" the last version of a myth, whose truth was guaranteed by the Muses, its telling unfolded in a context in which polemic was absent and even dialogue had no place. (6) Freed from the primordial and absolute constraint of memorization, the human mind acquired a freedom manifested in a dual critical movement: a critique of the status and function of the poet, and a critique of the validity of predecessors who represented the new types of discourses of history and philosophy.[11]

Writing, by freezing Homer's and Hesiod's works into standard versions, not only changed the mental habits of some individuals but gradually made most people increasingly uncomfortable with the myths evoked by those "poets." Having ceased to evolve, the myths described behavior and attitudes that were anachronistic and even shocking to a Greek of the classical period or of the end of the archaic age.

The Critique of Poetical Discourse

Only the positive aspect of poetic activity had been taken into account before the impact of writing as poets allowed what otherwise would have remained inaccessible to appear. But as soon as the poets did not completely fulfill their audience's expectation, the negative side of their activity came to be emphasized. The poet embodied false and immoral appearances. There was thus a transition from the idea of "apparition" to that of "semblance."

The most radical ancient critique that has survived on this theme is that of Xenophanes of Colophon (570?–475? B.C.), who argued that the gods have been given the physical attributes of the various human races worshiping them.

> But mortals consider that the gods are born, and that they have clothes and speech and bodies like their own.[12] The Ethiopians say that their gods are snubnosed and black, the Thracians that theirs have light blue eyes and red hair.[13] But if cattle and horses and lions had hands, or were able to draw with their hands and do the works that men can do, horses would draw the forms of the gods like horses, and cattle like cattle, and they would make their bodies such as they each had themselves.[14]

And on the moral plane, their behavior is that of the worst of men:

> Homer and Hesiod have attributed to the gods everything that is shameful and reproachable among men, stealing and committing adultery and deceiving each other.[15]

Plato was to adopt this last criticism as his own.

In their denunciation of the imitation at play in myth, Xenophanes and, later, Plato focused on only one aspect of a dual phenomenon. The spoken or acted image of a god or of any other mythical figure is a mere semblance insofar as it unavoidably makes for a considerable gap between itself and its model. Nonetheless, this image, even when reduced to a semblance, remains the only means to evoke a reality that is by nature inaccessible to both intelligence and the senses.

An ethical dimension should be associated with this epistemological one. The system of values defended by any myth features a dynamic aspect that Xenophanes and Plato refused to take into account. Myths represent good and evil from a dramatic perspective within the context of a sequence of events told in a narrative rather than from a dialectical perspective in the form of an immutable system of oppositions made explicit in an argumentative discourse.

The process of criticism of poetic discourse was slowed down by two phenomena: allegory,[16] claiming to save the explanatory value of myths and preserve their ethical validity by uncovering a deep meaning beneath the narrative fabric; and tragedy,[17] which reinterpreted myths as a function of the values of the city.

The Appearance of "History" and "Philosophy"

The deepening of the gap between stories poets such as Homer and Hesiod used to tell and the public's expectation, along with the increasingly clearer opposition between the distinctive traits of myth considered as a fact of oral communication and the new habits established through the practice of writing and reading among a certain number of citizens, all led to the emergence of other types of discourses, notably those of the "historian" and of the "philosopher"—I use quotation marks to avoid giving these terms a present-day meaning. It should not be assumed, however, that questioning the validity of poetic discourse powered by imitation implied a general questioning of the notions of "appearing" and "semblance." Until the time of philosophers such as Xenophanes and Heraclitus, all the terms grouped around *eikō, eikos* and *eikōn* and around *dokeō, dokos,* and *doxa* referred to mediate modes of knowledge. Even though these were set in opposition to a direct apprehension of objects, they were in no way considered illusions.[18]

"History"

Herodotus goes so far as to formulate the criteria that enable him to oppose his discourse to the poets' narratives. He bases the validity of his own discourse on two of those criteria: (1) that which he has observed personally, in which case he speaks of *opsis* and of *gnomē* (II 99, 1), and (2) that which he knows through his chosen informants, in which case he speaks of *historiē* (I 5, 3), a word involving the idea of a question put to an eyewitness, even if his informants happen to depend exclusively on oral traditions. Thucydides is more demanding in his choice of sources, still without radically separating *akoē* from *opsis* (I 20–22). He takes as certain only events witnessed personally by himself or by those of his contemporaries whose accounts have stood up to close examination. In contrast, he considers as uncertain those facts that have come to him through hearsay, inasmuch as he was not able to collect them from qualified informants to whom he could have put direct questions. Yet this did not prevent him from viewing Minos as a "historical" personage (I 4).

"Philosophy"

"Philosophers" too favor sight; but, for them, and even for the Eleatics, who were more inclined to re-question the status of the sensible world, image and semblance describe a legitimate approach and an indispensable path of access to what otherwise would remain hidden. This is well illustrated by Democritus's statement, reported by Anaxagoras: ὄψις γὰρ τῶν ἀδήλων τὰ φαινόμενα. I would risk the following paraphrase for this almost untranslatable statement: "Appearances allow the unseen to show itself."[19]

But everything changed with Plato, for he radically challenged the status of appearing. Before him, the world of sensible things had been looked upon as the only one accessible directly, and thus as providing the obligatory path for apprehending the beyond. In Plato, the sensible is assimilated to a world of images whose models are intelligible forms. However, the nouns that designate intelligible forms and the verbs that describe their apprehension through the intellect all pertain to sight. *Eidos* and *idea* derive from the root *weid,* which expresses the idea of seeing; and most of the terms describing the activity of the intellect pertain to this vocabulary of the gaze.[20] Plato thus transposes this favoring of sight by the "historians" and "philosophers" who preceded him from the level of the sensible toward that of the intelligible.

We can thus understand why the conflict between "myth" and "philosophy" reaches its apex with Plato. But in order to oppose in such a radical manner "myth" and "philosophy," the two terms at the poles of this opposition must be precisely defined. Plato was the first to do this, as we can see when looking at the terms *philosophia, philosophos,* and *philosophein.*[21] The term *muthos,* along with its derivatives and the compounds in which it appears, will be the first term examined in chapter 2.

Before Plato's time, these three terms seem to have been very rarely used,[22] though we must recognize that only a small number of surviving texts predate the fourth century B.C. This would not matter much if, as some have believed and some others keep on believing, we possessed the birth certificate of the word *philosophos.* It is thought that the moment of birth lies in an anecdote about Pythagoras told by Heraclides of Pontus, who is said to have almost become leader of the Academy upon Plato's death. The story is told in his Περὶ ἄπνου ἢ περὶ νόσων:

> Pythagoras was the first to call himself a "philosopher" (*philosophos*). He not only used a new word but he taught an original doctrine. He came to Phlius, he talked at length and learnedly with Leo, the tyrant of Phlius. Leo, admiring his mind and eloquence, asked him what art pleased him the most. But he answered that he didn't know art, but that he was a "philosopher." Surprised by the novelty of the word, Leo asked him what philosophers were and what distinguished them from other men.
>
> Pythagoras answered that our passage in this life resembles the crowds that one meets at the great festivals. Some go there for the glory earned by their physical strength, others for gain from exchanging merchandises, and there is a third sort of persons, who goes there to see the sites, art works, exploits, and virtuous speeches that are usually given during great festivals. Likewise, as one goes from one town toward another market, we have left another life and another nature to go to this one. Some are slaves to glory, others to riches. On the contrary, few are those who have received as their lot the contemplation of the most beautiful things, and it is they who are called "philosophers" (*philosophoi*), and not "wise men" (*sophoi*), because only God can be wise.[23]

However, the interpretation of this text led to a controversy which is far from being settled. Its more recent developments have pitted Robert Joly,[24] who leans toward the authenticity of the anecdote, against Walter Burkert,[25] who, following Werner Jaeger,[26] thinks that the theme of this anecdote reveals the Platonic view of Pythagoras held in the Academy shortly after Plato's death.

The decisive argument in favor of rejecting the anecdote's authenticity resides in its final statement: "and it is they who are called 'philosophers' and not 'wise men,' because only God can be wise." This statement echoes the following two passages from the Platonic corpus: "None of the gods devote themselves to philosophizing (*philosophei*), none wish to become wise (*sophos*) because they are so already."[27] And: "To call him wise (*sophos*), Phaedrus, would, I think be going too far; the epithet is proper only to a god. A name that would fit him better and have more seemliness would be 'philosopher' (*philosophos*)."[28] The meaning given to the terms *sophos* and *philosophos* in these passages is based on the opposition between being and appearing, between model and image, between the intelligible and the sensible, oppositions that mesh with that between god and man.

Until Plato, the term *sophia* could be applied to any sort of content insofar as it is not linked in the sensible world to any specific content. To be *sophos* in this context is to dominate one's activity, to dominate oneself and to dominate others.[29] This is why a carpenter, a doctor, a diviner, a poet, a rhetor, a sophist, and the like, could be labeled *sophoi*. Later on, *sophia* became synonymous with "civilization," a position adopted by Aristotle in his Περὶ φιλοσοφίας.[30] Thus anyone completing the apprenticeship of a *sophia*, regardless of the nature of the activity involved, could be called *philosophos*. And once this *sophia* is acquired, this same individual could thus be referred to as *sophos*.

It is also in this broad sense that Isocrates uses the terms *philosophos* and *philosophia*.[31]

In contrast, in Plato, the term *philosophia* no longer designates the apprenticeship of a human *sophia*, whose content can be infinitely varied. It becomes the aspiration to a *sophia* transcending human possibilities in that its ultimate goal is the contemplation of a domain of objects, the world of intelligible form, of which the world of sensible things—into which the human soul has temporarily fallen—is only a reflection. As Socrates explains in *Phaedrus*, the knowledge to which the philosopher aspires is "not the knowledge that is subject to becoming, nor that which varies with the various objects that we find real at present, but the knowledge of that which is truly being (ἀλλὰ τὴν ἐν τῷ ὅ ἐστιν ὂν ὄντως ἐπιστήμην οὖσαν)."[32] The opposition between being and becoming is formulated here with extreme clarity. Since sensible things are only the images of intelligible forms, this first opposition is the equivalent of another, being versus appearing, whence the inferiority of the status Plato attributes to poets, and indeed to imitators in general, whom he looks upon as makers of images of images.

Plato rejects the mediation of the sensible to evoke the beyond, even though he does have the greatest respect for rites and sacred places.[33] A philosopher is a man whose way of life enables a detachment from the sensible and a striving toward a direct contemplation of the beyond. This contemplation will be truly effective and complete only after his death, when his soul will be separated from his body. Plato stated this fundamental position fairly early in his work, and he maintained it to the end, even though he responded with increasing interest and veneration to the sensible world, which he conceived as an orderly whole under the direction of "reason."[34]

This position was so radical and paradoxical that it was not taken up as such by any other philosopher, not even by the Neoplatonic thinkers. Plato questioned the status of the sensible world, which then falls from its status as ultimate point of reference for human beings and as access to the beyond, to the rank of an image, and is reduced to being only an obstacle on the path to the beyond. Such an attitude toward the sensible world involves a new definition of human beings, who are no longer perceived as bodies animated by obscure forces but defined as souls fallen into a piece of matter. Hence the discrediting of imitation, which had previously been considered the only means of apprehending that which otherwise would have remained inaccessible but which henceforth comes to be seen as an image of an image, as an appearing, both misleading and immoral.

To a philosopher such as Plato, representing the beyond by means of imitation is something degrading. This beyond can be apprehended directly at the end of a conversion of the soul made possible by proper teaching and a demanding way of life. Yet such an attitude is not without serious consequences. While poetic representation is within everyone's reach, philosophical experience is reserved for an elite. The use of allegory by some philosophers will tend toward a reappropriation of the collective memory; yet in order to accomplish this goal they will have to start by giving more value than Plato did to the opinion of the majority.

TWO

Plato's Attitude toward Myth

The word "myth" comes from a transcription of the ancient Greek *muthos*. This is the case in most of the modern European languages: for instance, *mythe* in French, *Mythos* in German, *mito* in Spanish and Italian, and *mif* in Russian.[1]

Consequently, when the predicate "myth" is attributed to a different subject than it would have been in ancient Greece, we are setting up a comparison between two cultural facts pertaining to two different civilizations, one of which will always be that of ancient Greece. Thus, to say "*x* is a myth" amounts to saying "*x* is a myth (as *z* is in ancient Greece)." The Hellenocentric attitude, of which a pragmatic analysis of the use of the term "myth" makes us aware, brings out the need for research into the origin of this term.

In ancient Greece, the meaning of *muthos* changed as a function of the transformations that affected the vocabulary of "saying" and of "speech"[2] in the course of a historical evolution ending with Plato when the meaning of *muthos* became fixed once and for all.

When Plato uses *muthos* in a nonmetaphorical way, he does two things: he describes and he criticizes. With the help of this term, he describes a certain type of discursive practice while expressing his judgment on its status in relation to that of another discursive practice he considers superior.

PLATO THE ETHNOLOGIST

From the perspective of ethnology, myth appears as a message through which, from one generation to the next, a collectivity transmits what it keeps in memory of what it considers its past. The starting point of this past blends in with the origin of the gods and its lower temporal limit consists of a time that is still distant enough to make it impossible for narrators to verify the validity of the discourse they are producing, both because they did not experience the events they are telling and because their narratives are not based on eyewitness accounts. Thus Plato often wrote of the Persian wars and the Peloponnesian wars without ever using the word *muthos* or one of its derivatives or compounds. He did, however, make use of them in book III of the *Laws* to designate the life style of the Cyclops (680d3) and the foundation and fall of Troy (682a8), as well as the foundation of the Dorian cities of Argos, Messene, and Sparta (682e5, 683d3). But when he moves on to the description of the establishment of these same cities, he notes that he is on a different level (683e10–684a1).

Myth as Communication

The information to be remembered was transmitted in ancient Greece exclusively by word of mouth.[3] Even when Solon went to Egypt to refresh the Greeks' failing memory, he was informed by a priest of Sais, who didn't have to decipher the sacred hieroglyphs on the temple of Neith because he knew by heart the message he was transmitting.[4] For Plato, writing could only play the role of "control copy" (as in the etymological sense of "control" meaning the keeping of a duplicate register to check accounts).[5] This was nonetheless an important function, as the catastrophes that periodically befell ancient Greece were leading to the progressive impoverishment of information that was transmitted only orally.

Things were further complicated by another means of maintaining the quality of the oral transmission of the memorable—namely, poetry. The poet's work pertained as much to the form as to the content of a myth.[6] These specialists of the collective communication of the memorable reorganize an oral tradition so as to fashion a narrative adapted to the context of enunciation. Moreover, with respect to the form of the narrative, they use technical mnemonic procedures such as meter and formulaic repetitions that add to its efficaciousness.

In an oral civilization, the making of a message cannot be separated from its emission, but these two aspects become differentiated in a written civilization. The ambiguity of the Platonic vocabulary on this point reveals the gradual passage of ancient Greece to writing around that time, although Plato often and quite clearly differentiated the making of a myth from its narration.

The narration of a myth as distinguished from its making became the purview of either professionals such as poets[7] and their subordinates— rhapsodists, actors, and choral dancers[8]—or of nonprofessionals. Professionals performed mostly on the occasion of festivals, notably in the framework of contests.[9] Rhapsody contests were held at Athens during the

Panathenaia, and tragedy contests during the urban Dionysia festivals. Yet most myth tellers were nonprofessionals, who always expressed themselves outside of any competitive context. In Plato, these nonprofessionals have two characteristics: old age and being female. Why is this so?

In a written civilization, the accumulation of messages does not depend on individuals, for it amounts to the preservation of material traces on material supports. In an oral civilization, on the other hand, messages can be accumulated only by individuals. Hence, advanced age appears as the necessary, albeit not always sufficient, condition for breadth of knowledge in a given individual. Moreover, the narrator's advanced age helps minimize the degradation of messages transmitted exclusively by word of mouth for a long period of time, a degradation stemming from the transformation undergone by all narratives in the course of each stage of their transmission. When told by grandparents to grandchildren, the narrative skips a stage.

As to the second characteristic—that of being female—mothers,[10] wet nurses,[11] and old women[12] are the primary myth tellers simply because of their relationship with the audience at whom myths are primarily aimed, children. Thus, in terms of the present discussion, old women obviously present the most interest as they combine both traits mentioned above.

In an oral civilization, the reception of a myth cannot be separated from its emission and thus its making. So hearing was a fundamental element in the reception of a myth by an audience of both professionals and nonprofessionals. The professionals, that is poets, rhapsodists, actors, and choir dancers, addressed themselves to an audience gathered on the occasion of a contest during major festivals. For the dramatic contests held during the urban Dionysia for instance, the audience included rich and poor Athenians along with their children, as well as foreigners, and perhaps even slaves. In contrast, when nonprofessionals told myths, their audience was much more limited and consisted mostly of children younger than seven years old,[13] an age when boys usually began to attend the gymnasium in ancient Greece.

Myth and Imitation

According to Plato, regardless of how it was narrated, the activity involved in communicating a myth always belonged in the realm of imitation (*mimēsis*). Imitation first manifests itself in discourse in general. In relation to the reality to which it refers, discourse is merely an imitation, or a copy[14] that it is akin to a painting. Like painting, which uses forms and colors, language uses sounds and makes reality appear, but this in the ambiguous mode of the presence of absence. This affective absence is attached to every representation of reality through discourse (oral and, more particularly, written), but the poet seeks to make his or her audience forget it by using a series of procedures belonging to the realm of imitation.

The imitation that occurs at the level of *logos,* or "that which is expressed in discourse," involves, as we have just seen, a relation between copy object and model object. But the imitation that functions at the level of *lexis,* or "the way of expressing the content of this discourse," pertains to the relation between a subject, the poet, and the object of which the poet is making a copy. The exposition / imitation opposition can be defined in terms of enunciation as follows: as long as the statement reveals its author, there is exposition; in contrast, when the author alienates his "I" in favor of another instance of enunciation, to which he gives a status of reality and behind which he disappears, there is imitation.[15] Plato finds this last mode of expression unacceptable because, at the level of the subject, it generates illusions by the confusion it creates between discourse and reality. Plato's exasperation increases when he reminds us that it is possible to express oneself in a way that imitates not only the discourse of wicked or inferior men but also the cries of animals and the sounds of nature.[16]

On this point, poets themselves were necessarily imitated, not only by those who recounted the myths they fabricated in this way, but, as we will see below, even more by the addressees of these myths. A myth is a discourse that can be made in prose or in verse. When a myth is narrated, it can be recited with or without musical accompaniment, or it can be sung. In the course of its interpretation, a choreographic arrangement can come into play. When a myth is sung, it is through a melody consisting of three elements: speech, harmony, and rhythm. In this context, harmony and rhythm are not autonomous, for they have to illustrate speech.[17] In other words, harmony—that is, the strictly musical aspect of the spectacle—also takes up in its own domain the imitation at play in speech and thus adds to its effectiveness.[18] The same holds true for rhythm, that is, dance.[19]

Yet the imitation at play in myth truly reaches its goal only when it moves the audience to which poets and interpreters address themselves. Regardless of the technique used, there must be a passage from senders to receivers. The imitation employed by senders affects receivers, who seek to make themselves, in effect, similar to the beings evoked by the narrative.[20] This gives rise to an ethical issue. Through the process of communication of the myth, the reality that is the object of the communicated message becomes present for the receiver in a manner so intense that its actual absence is forgotten, and thus it triggers a process of identification that modifies the physical and, more particularly, the moral behavior of the receiver.

Myth and Persuasion

Plato presents this emotive fusion as the effect of an incantation[21] affecting the soul as would a drug[22] or a charm,[23] or, more simply, as the effect of persuasion.[24] It is triggered by the pleasure given by the communication of the myth to the lowest part of the soul (the *epithumia*), the part that craves food and drink and is the seat of sexual appetite.[25] We can understand then that myths are aimed primarily at children.[26] In Plato's eyes, childhood and youth are the untamed portion of human existence[27] because, at that age, the appetitive part dominates the human soul.[28] And since the word *paidia,* "game," derives from the word *pais,* "child," Plato naturally looks upon myth as a game.[29]

In short, myth is a discourse through which all the information on the distant past is communicated. This information is thus preserved in the memory of a given collectivity, which transmits it orally from one generation to the next, and it does so regardless of whether mythical discourse was elaborated by a poet, that is, a technician of the collective communication of the memorable, or by a nonspecialist.

Imitation comes into play at all stages of this process of communication. It manifests itself during the making and the interpretation of a myth in words as well as in gestures, and leads listeners to adopt or modify their physical and moral behavior as a function of the model proposed by the performance.

PLATO THE PHILOSOPHER

Plato is so interested in myth because he wants to break its monopoly and impose instead a type of discourse he intends to develop, that is, the philosophical discourse for which he claims a superior status.

The Inferiority of Myth

In order to set up this opposition and name its terms, Plato has to reorganize the vocabulary of "speech" and of "saying" in ancient Greece. We must first look at this group of terms from a diachronic perspective, since it results from a process of semantic transformation affecting a certain number of greatly interdependent vocables.

Myth as a Discourse

The meaning of *muthos,* a word of unknown etymology, underwent profound modifications between the time of Homer and that of Plato as a function of the increasingly important place of *logos* in the vocabulary of "speech."[30] Indeed, *logos* is heir to *epos* and *muthos*. This explains why Plato can assimilate *muthos* to *logos* in its sense of "discourse" in general. However, the values attached to the root *leg-* and the semantic evolution of *logos* not only make it impossible to fully identify *muthos* with *logos* but also lead to a great number of oppositions. The main opposition will be explained below. It contrasts *muthos,* a discourse that cannot be verified and is nonargumentative, and *logos,* an argumentative and verifiable discourse.

Myth as an Unverifiable Discourse

In Plato, *logos* designates language not only as performance, that is, discourse in general, but, above all, as verifiable discourse. Hence, it is clear that the relation of *muthos* and *logos* taken in this sense can only be one of opposition.

In the *Sophist,* Plato defines *logos* as "verifiable discourse,[31] a definition that, *mutatis mutandis,* serves as model for a definition of myth as unverifiable discourse since his definition makes it possible to answer the following three questions: What classes of subjects and verbs are at play in this type of discourse called myth? What are its referents? What truth value and/or falsehood can be assigned to it?

According to the Stranger from Elea, the definition of discourse at the level of its most basic elements comprises three elements, the third being the equivalent of the relation between the first two: (1) a statement is a weaving together of names and verbs; (2) it always applies to something; and (3) consequently, it must be true or false.

A statement is, essentially, composed of nouns and verbs.[32] A verb (*rhēma*) can be defined as "an expression which is applied to actions";[33] and a name or noun (*onoma*) is defined as "the spoken sign applied to what performs these actions." But a succession of verbs ("walks," "runs," "sleeps") or of names ("lion," "stag," "horse") strung together will never make a discourse.

Further, to be a discourse, there must be a weaving together of name(s) and verb(s).[34] As a result of this weaving together, a statement can be made whose proper function is to refer to an extralinguistic reality situated in the present, past, or future, where the present may also indicate atemporality.[35] It is this referentiality that determines the truth or falsehood of a statement.[36] Herein lies the third element of the definition of speech.[37]

Any weaving together of name(s) and verb(s) is true if its relation to that upon which it bears is adequate; and any weaving together of name(s) and verb(s) is false if its relation to that upon which it bears is inadequate.

Hence, false discourse does not refer to nothing, as was claimed by some Sophists in denying the possibility of false statements, but rather to something other than what it states.

Finally, it is important to note that for Plato the domain of discourse and that of thought are homogenous: "Well, thinking (*dianoia*) and discourse (*logos*) are the same thing, except that what we call thinking is, precisely, the inward dialogue carried on by the mind with itself without spoken sound."[38] Hence, everything that has been stated of discourse also applies to thought.

The analysis of the passage from the *Sophist*[39] proposed above is, of course, superficial in that it retains only what is essential. Moreover, within these limits, a number of problems are not confronted. Plato defines discourse at the level of its basic constituents without distinguishing between grammar and logic. By defining a sentence as the weaving together of verb(s) and name(s), Plato is also defining a proposition as the attribution of one or more predicate(s) to one (or more) subject(s). Moreover, Plato discusses too briefly and too vaguely what we now call "referent," a particularly difficult topic, on which there is still no consensus because of the complex logical and ontological difficulties it raises. Finally, the question of the truth or falsity of discourse presents a degree of complexity well beyond what has just been said about it here.

Nonetheless, the consequence of this long development is clear. The definition of verifiable discourse, which limits and specializes the meaning of the term *logos,* allows us to distinguish between the sophist and the philosopher.

The Sophist is characterized by false discourse, that is, a discourse that bears upon something other than what it states. False discourse gives an unfaithful image of the reality which it claims to depict. And since the Sophist's falsity is voluntary, he is defined, at the end of the dialogue bearing his name, as a human illusion maker in the realm of discourse.[40]

In contrast, the philosopher is characterized by true discourse. However, there is still the need, within the framework of Platonic doctrine, of distinguishing between discourse bearing upon intelligible forms and that which deals with sensible things. One of the most explicit texts in this regard is found in 29b3–c3 of the *Timaeus*.

This passage is supplemented by another,[41] in which the intellect, whose object is intelligible forms, is contrasted with true opinion, whose object is sensible things perceived by the body. This epistemological opposition is further developed by a sociological one: "Every man may be said to share in true opinion, but mind is the attribute of the gods and of very few men."[42] This tiny class of men is obviously that of the philosophers.

So, how can we define *muthos* if we take the definition of *logos* in the *Sophist* as our model?

At the level of its basic components, myth, like verifiable discourse, amounts to an interweaving of name(s) and verb(s).

Books II and III of the *Republic* focus on the role of music in the education of the guardians and use "music" in its broad sense of "everything pertaining to the muses." In the section devoted to the type of discourse proper to music,[43] Plato gives a list of the five classes of names into which the subjects of mythical discourse are divided: gods, daemons, heroes, inhabitants of Hades, and men of the past. All the names pertaining to each of these five classes share an essential characteristic: they are all proper names. Hence they do not refer to concepts ("gods, heroes etc.") but to individuals ("Zeus, Oedipus, etc.") or to groups considered as individuals ("Muses, Trojans, etc."); that is, in general they refer to animate beings endowed with a rational soul, including animals, plants, and inanimate objects playing a role on the model of rational beings. The result is generalized anthropomorphism.

Why, then, does Plato, who carefully lists the subjects of mythical discourse, not do the same thing for the verbs describing the actions performed by these subjects? As a philosopher, Plato has something to say about gods, daemons, heroes, the inhabitants of Hades, and the men of the past, but only from his own viewpoint. But the actions described by the verbs used in the type of discourse called myth unfold in the sensible world, which, for Plato, exists only through its participation in the world of intelligible forms.

According to Plato, the philosopher's discourse bears upon the intelligible forms apprehended by the intellect. These intelligible forms, which constitute true reality, are immutable. Thus both the act of intellection enabling their apprehension and the discourse externally expressing this act of intellection exhibit an absolute stability. They are always true because, like their referents, which are situated outside of time, they are indifferent to time.

In contrast, sensible things, whose reality depends on their participation in intelligible forms, are immediately situated in time. Consequently, both the act of sensation, which enables the apprehension of sensible things, and the discourse that externally expresses this act of sensation are characterized by instability. For what is true at time t can become false at time $t + 1$, as, for example, in "it is raining." Contrary to the discourse focusing on intelligible forms, the discourse bearing upon sensible things is not indifferent to time, because its referent is located in a world subject to becoming. Such a situation therefore sets limits to the verification of this type of discourse.

Indeed, the adequacy or inadequacy of such a discourse to its referent can be verified only if this referent is in the present or in a recent enough in past relation to the speaker for that speaker to have experienced it or to have been informed of it by someone who has had a direct experience of it.

The distant past, the knowledge of which rests exclusively on tradition, and the entire future therefore cannot be considered valid referents for a discourse susceptible to verification.

Yet Plato obviously did not himself lock up his own discourse within the limits set in the *Sophist.* Indeed, he mentions events that unfolded in a distant past, events he could only know through the intermediary of tradition. This is reflected principally in one of the most important components of his philosophy, that of the realm of the immortal soul,[44] which is situated at an intermediate level between the world of forms and the world of sensible things.

The five classes of names—gods, daemons, heroes, inhabitants of Hades, and men of the past—listed in books II and III of the *Republic* refer precisely to these two types of referents. Myth recounts extraordinary deeds accomplished in a very distant past by people living in the sensible world and of which tradition has kept the memory. The gods, daemons, heroes, and inhabitants of Hades are situated between the intelligible world and the sensible world, at the level of the soul in all its diversity. Gods, daemons, and heroes are either full-fledged immortals or the offspring of immortalized mortals, while human beings are endowed with souls that are partly immortal, which in this respect makes them akin to gods, daemons, and heroes. Consequently, it is necessary to describe the soul's destiny before it descends into a body and particularly after it leaves this body—in other words, according to ancient Greek popular belief, when it finds itself in Hades. Ultimately, the domain of myth covers roughly the same territory that later came to be claimed by history and mythology, mythology perpetuating itself in history, which is merely one of its avatars.

Two consequences follow from this, the first entailing the second. One is concerned with the relation that mythical discourse maintains with its referent. The other deals with the self-referential character of this type of discourse.

Myth is an unverifiable discourse because its referent is located either at a level of reality inaccessible both to the intellect and to the senses, or at the level of sensible things, but in a past of which the speaker of the discourse can have no direct or indirect experience.

However, we need to determine the nature of this inaccessibility. To hold that a referent is accessible to the intellect and the senses is, on the one hand, to indicate that it is a particular thing. In contrast, to say that a referent is inaccessible to the intellect and the senses indicates that it is not possible to determine precisely what this referent is, even if taking its existence for granted. In short, in the first case, the referent in question does exist and can be definitely described, while in the second case the referent in question cannot give rise to any definite description, even if its existence is taken for granted.

It is just as futile to list all the passages in which Plato takes for granted the existence of gods, daemons, heroes, and an immortal part of the human soul, or to note all the other passages where he demonstrates the existence of these same realities against all those who, in one way or another, raise doubts about them. One could mention, among other passages, book X of the *Laws* for the existence of gods, daemons, and heroes, and the *Phaedo* in support of the existence of an immortal part of the human soul. Moreover, Plato does not seem to doubt the existence of facts dating back to a very distant past, whether these concern the state and government of the world and of men under the reign of Kronos[45] or the war between primeval Athens and Atlantis.[46]

But, although he does not doubt the existence of these referents, Plato has to concede that there cannot be any definitive description of the soul in all its immortality nor of most of the extraordinary events that happened in the past. This is simply because these referents are accessible neither to the senses nor to the intellect, assuming of course that the debate is not situated at the level of the intelligible in an attempt to define the intelligible form of a god, a daemon, a hero, or the soul.

How can one make up for this lacuna at the level of definitive description? It can be done only through a certain use of imitation that cannot be separated from a generalized anthropomorphism, as Xenophanes so well understood.[47] In other words, human traits and behavior are attributed to mythical figures, be they gods, daemons, heroes, inhabitants of Hades, or even an animal, a plant, or an inanimate object.

A discourse can be deemed verifiable only if its referent, which is either in the world of intelligible forms or in that of sensible things, is accessible either to the intellect or to the senses. In this case, truth or falsity is defined respectively as the adequacy or inadequacy of the discourse to its referent. But the referents of the mythical type of discourse are, by definition, accessible neither to the intellect nor to the senses; thus is it impossible to ascertain whether there is adequacy between the mythic type of discourse and its referent. Hence, myth should be situated beyond truth and falsehood; yet this does not seem to be the case since Plato presents myth at times as a false discourse[48] and at times as a true one.[49]

This can be explained by a change in perspective. Truth and error no longer depend on the correspondence of a discourse with its supposed referent but on the correspondence of a discourse, in this case myth, with another discourse held up as norm. Here, it no longer matters whether this discourse—that of the philosopher and, of course more specifically that of Plato—pertains to the world of intelligible forms or to that of sensible things. Epistemology then gives way to censorship. The truth of a myth thus depends, in the final analysis, on its conformity with the philosopher's discourse on the intelligible forms in which the individual entities that are the subjects of this myth participate, and this is true as much in the religious, ethical, and political[50] domains as in that of cosmology.[51]

Myth as a Nonargumentative Discourse

The *muthos/logos* dichotomy can be interpreted not only as the opposition between verifiable and unverifiable discourse but also as the opposition between narrative discourse (or more simply narratives) and argumentative discourse. While the first opposition is based on an external criterion, namely the relation of the discourse with its supposed referent, the second depends on an internal criterion: the organization of its development. It must be noted that this last opposition only makes sense in a philosophical context, as both history and myth partake of the narrative form.

A narrative relates events as they are supposed to have happened, without giving an explanation. Consequently, the link between its parts is contingent, at least from a superficial viewpoint, for several attempts have been made, beginning with Propp's,[52] to uncover the logic of the narrative. Moreover, the sole aim of the narrative, at least on the surface, is to realize, through the intermediary of the story maker or teller an emotive fusion between the intended audience and the hero of the narrative.

In contrast, argumentative discourse follows a rational order (regardless of how reason is defined). The sequence of its parts is constructed on the model of mathematics, according to rules aiming to make the conclusion necessary. The speaker of this discourse seeks rational agreement with regard to this conclusion.

The opposition between myth and argumentative discourse is admirably illustrated by the structures of the dialogues *Protagoras* and the *Statesman*.

The principal character of the *Statesman* is a Stranger from Elea, in Southern Italy. The dialogue's aim is to elaborate a definition of the royal and political man. To this end, the Eleatic Stranger relies on an argumentative discourse that has recourse to one of the methods proper to dialectic, that of division. This method consist in dividing, according to certain rules defined in the *Statesman*,[53] each intelligible form into two parts, one of which is in turn submitted to the same process of division, and so forth, so as to obtain all the constituent elements of the sought-for definition. At one point a definition of the royal and political man as shepherd to his people is proposed. However, the Stranger from Elea rejects this by invoking a myth showing that this definition applies to a very distant past and not to the present, as the Stranger explains after narrating the myth in question.[54] This same idea is taken up and developed later with the help of an enlightening comparison to painting.[55]

In the dialogue bearing his name, Protagoras narrates a myth[56] and then develops an argumentative discourse[57] so as to propound the same thesis with different means: virtue can be taught, and it is the sophist who is best qualified to teach it. However, at three decisive moments of this dual development, at the beginning[58] and at the end[59] of this myth, and at the end of the argumentative discourse that follows it, Protagoras takes up the opposition between myth and argumentative discourse. The myth Protagoras tells refers to a very distant past, set at the time of the appearance of mortal beings, beasts and humans, to whom the gods allocated different qualities. In contrast, the argumentative discourse that follows describes certain social and political practices of Greece around the fifth and fourth centuries B.C.

For Plato, therefore, myth presents two defects. It is an unverifiable discourse that can often be assimilated to a false one. And it is a narrative whose elements are linked contingently, in contrast to an argumentative discourse whose internal organization manifests necessity.

The Usefulness of Myth

Yet Plato does not renounce traditional myths, to which he makes many allusions in his work.[60] What is more, he adapts traditional myths and even creates new ones when necessary. He does so basically for two reasons. On the one hand, Plato can speak only about certain referents in mythical terms. These pertain to everything having to do with the soul and with the distant past, which accordingly remains inaccessible to both the senses and the intellect. On the other hand, he recognizes the efficacity of myth in the field of ethics and politics for most of those individuals who are not philosophers and in whose souls the desiring (*epithumia*) part predominates.

Even though myth is an unverifiable discourse and lacks an argumentative character, it is all the more effective in that it transmits a basic knowledge shared by all the members of a given community, which makes it a formidable instrument with universal impact. As the sole alternative to violence, myth makes it possible for reason to prevail over the mortal part in the human soul, and it ensures, in the city, the submission of the multitude to the prescriptions of the philosophers who founded the city or are its legislators. In both cases, myth plays the role of a paradigm according to which, by means of persuasion rather than education, all those who are not philosophers—that is, the majority of human beings—are led to model their behavior.

Yet the necessity of having recourse to myth, as well as its usefulness, cannot result from an allegorical interpretation,[61] which Plato refuses to use both in the *Republic*[62] and in the *Phaedrus*,[63] each time giving a different reason: the inability of children, for whom the myths are mainly intended, to distinguish between allegorical and nonallegorical interpretations, and the overwhelming scope of the task. But the reason for Plato's rejection of allegory lies elsewhere and might very well be as follows.

A myth's truth value or lack of it is secondary only insofar as the myth is true or false according to whether or not it accords with the discourse conducted by the philosopher on the same subject. Why, then, try to transform the falsity of a myth into a truth? Truth must rather be sought where it lies, that is, in philosophical discourse. Above all, that knowledge or science which appears in ancient Greece in the sixth century, which Plato calls by the name of "philosophy," must not be used to transform the falsity of myth into truth. Such a practice would reverse the order of status by making philosophy an instrument of the interpretation of myths, which in turn would be the genuine locus of truth.

Other Types of Discourse That Plato Calls Myths

At times, Plato uses *muthos* in a derivative or figurative sense to evoke types of discourse other than the one usually called "myth." Two of these instances refer to rhetorical discourse,[64] the first discourse where, in the *Phaedrus*, Socrates imitates Lysias. Plato makes a figurative use of the other occurrences of *muthos* in a philosophical context. Five of these derivative occurrences refer to philosophical doctrines Plato criticizes.[65] Yet he does not limit his use of the term to the doctrines he is opposing. In eleven other cases, he uses this same term to characterize his own discourse. Seven of these occurrences pertain to the political domain. Of this group, two[66] are references to the description of the city made by Socrates in the *Republic* and by the Athenian Stranger in the *Laws*. The other five occurrences of *muthos* in *Laws*[67] belong in a category of their own, which can be explained only by means of the role that Plato assigns to myth as a preamble to laws in this dialogue, thus reactualizing the ancient sense of *muthos*.

But at once the richest and the most difficult to explain is Plato's use of *muthos* to help describe the origin, the constitution, and the organization of the sensible world in the *Timaeus*.[68] In three of these cases[69] he uses the expression *eikōs muthos*. As Gregory Vlastos so rightly notes,[70] the fundamental element in this expression is the epithet *eikōs*. In seven passages in the *Timaeus*, Plato presents Timaeus's discourse on the constitution of the sensible world as an *eikōs logos*.[71] Moreover, *eikōs* and *eikotōs* are used with a similar meaning in six other passages in the *Timaeus*.[72] And this is because the dialogue is a discourse on the constitution of the sensible world, that is, on the "image" or "copy" of the intelligible world.

The meaning of this last comment is explained by a passage in the *Timaeus* (29b3–c3) in which two types of discourses, true discourse, stable and invincible, and credible discourse are set in opposition by virtue of the nature of their objects. They are, respectively, the model (*paradeigma*) and its copy (*eikōn*).

What is more, the falsity of the mythical traditions evoked in the myth in *Statesman* (269b5–c3), along with that of the myth of Phaethon in the *Timaeus* (22c3–d3), is denounced in the name of an astronomical hypothesis, that of alternation (*parallaxis*), which thus pertains to *eikōs muthos* since it deals with cosmogony and cosmology. Here we find a surprising pitting of myth against myth. But isn't this the price of the rejection of all recourse to allegory?

THREE

Aristotle and the Beginnings
of Allegorical Exegesis

Myth was given a name when its status came to be contested and its function questioned. The challenge began during the sixth century B.C. and very soon brought about a twofold response from those who wanted to preserve a place for myth. On the one hand, tragedy reinterpreted the old versions of myths in terms of the new ideals of the city, and, on the other, allegory claimed to uncover under the disconcerting surface of the narrative a deep truth in harmony with new ideas.

While Plato attacked tragedy and condemned allegory, Aristotle proposed a remarkably subtle analysis of tragedy and adopted a conciliatory attitude toward allegory. This can probably be explained by the close relation Aristotle established between myth and philosophy:[1]

> For it is owing to their wonder that men both now begin and at first began to philosophize; they wondered originally at the obvious difficulties, then advanced little by little and stated difficulties about the greater matters, e.g. about the phenomena of the moon and those of the sun and the stars, and about the genesis of the universe. And a man who is puzzled and wonders thinks himself ignorant. Whence even the lover of myth is in a sense a lover of wisdom (φιλόμυθος φιλόσοφός πώς ἐστιν), for myth is composed of wonders.[2]

To wonder is to admit one's ignorance, and those who admit their ignorance have the desire to acquire knowledge. Myths are full of surprising things. Thus an interest in myth implies a desire to acquire wisdom. So philosophy no longer implies, as it did in Plato, a radical rupture with tradition. Rather, it is equivalent to a reappropriation of that tradition, of the memory shared by all Greeks, and in particular all Athenians.

TRAGEDY

Tragedy is indissolubly linked to myth, much more so than comedy and satyrical drama. Tragedy, we could say, reinterprets myth in terms of the ideals of the city.³ The tragic poet reuses the great myths evoked by Homer, Hesiod, and others but transforms their meaning so that they serve to illustrate and defend the new values of the city. All tragic heroes are mythical figures, and "we can say that classical tragedy died even though it survived as a literary form when Euripides' contemporary, young Agathon, who embodies tragedy in Plato's *Symposium,* wrote for the first time a tragedy whose characters were of his own making."⁴ This comment fits with the analysis of tragedy Aristotle proposes in his *Poetics,*⁵ except that Aristotle, recognizing the success of Agathon's innovations, refrains from condemning them.⁶

According to Aristotle,⁷ every tragedy is made up of six parts: "myth (*muthos*), characters (*ēthē*), expression (*lexis*), thought (*dianoia*), spectacle (*opsis*), and melody (*melopoiia*)."⁸ In his *Poetics,* he provides a detailed description, if not a definition, of these six parts.

He begins by evoking myth, whose import is due to the partial overlap of its definition with that of tragedy as a whole:

> We maintain that tragedy is primarily the imitation of an action and that this action is performed by actors who of necessity must be what they are in terms of character (*ēthos*) and thought (*dianoia*). . . . It is myth that is the imitation of an action. This because I call "myth" the arrangement of actions into a system . . . , while character is that which enables us to state that the actors are such or such, and thought is all that which is used to demonstrate something or to state a maxim.⁹

A characteristic of myth is its ability to insure order, organization, arrangement, and system in the domain of action. And yet, much more than that, this order must permeate all the other elements of the tragedy: the staging, the coherence of thoughts, and, finally, the arrangement of the verses.

Character (*ēthos*) is that which confers coherence to the arrangement of the actions through a sort of unique choice that underlies each action.¹⁰ Thought (*dianoia*) corresponds to the arguments the characters use to justify their action.¹¹ Character and thought reveal something of the person and of the situation: these are thus elements belonging to the content of language. In contrast, when it comes to expression (*lexis*) we are dealing with a means of manifesting this content. Expression is indeed "the manifestation of meaning through words,"¹² in verse as much as in prose, even though

Aristotle has just defined expression as the "arrangement" of verses into a "system."[13] Finally, with respect to singing (*melopoiia*), Aristotle says merely that it is "the greatest of the pleasurable accessories of tragedy."[14]

Since tragedy is defined as "an imitation of agents' actions,"[15] and since myth makes this imitation possible by organizing actions into a system, it follows that "the first principle (*arkhē*) and, so to speak, the soul (*psukhē*) of tragedy is myth."[16] We also get a better understanding of why *Poetics* opens up with the following statement of intent: "I propose to speak not only of poetry in general but also of its species and their respective capacities, each considered in function of the effects it produces, and the manner that myths have to be composed for poetry to be good."[17] Thus it follows that the poet should be looked upon as a myth maker rather than a verse maker.[18]

The ability of myth to introduce order also enables it to produce imitation (*mimēsis*), a word that should not be understood here in Plato's sense of "copy." Rather, because its form is an arrangement of actions within a system, myth can be looked upon as an imitation, one that universalizes and elevates. For Aristotle, poetry is "something more philosophical and of graver import than history."[19] History remains at the level of the particular, limited to description as faithful as possible, while poetry rises from the particular to the universal, which can be defined as follows in this context: "What a certain kind of man will probably or necessarily say or do."[20] Within this perspective, a particular action becomes the illustration of paradigmatic behavior that instantly gets understood in function of a system of preestablished values. But that's not all. In contrast to what happens in comedy, the imitation of human actions at play in tragedy magnifies them: "the one [comedy] would makes its personages worse, and the other [tragedy] better than the men of the present day."[21] In short, myth reorganizes human actions not only to give them a coherent form that enables them to reach universality, but also, and more especially, to elevate these actions to the rank of positive models. The imitation at play in myth gives back to human traits their universal characters only to make them greater and nobler.

Because myth draws on the particularly powerful and universal feelings of fear and pity,[22] it is a formidable instrument of consensus, since all human beings without exception are sensitive to fear and pity.

ALLEGORY

Aristotle's remarkable analysis of myth as the soul of tragedy was to have no legacy as such, probably because, as a literary genre he described in *Poetics*, tragedy fell out of favor at the end of the fifth century B.C. As Aristotle shows,[23] some of the new tragedies were written to be read, but most were aimed primarily at providing material for actors, who, to his chagrin,[24] had become the dominant element of the theater.[25] In contrast, allegory, whose origins long preceded Plato and Aristotle, was to have an immense and multiform legacy.

A Short History of the Origins of Allegory[26]

The word "allegory"[27] derives from the ancient Greek *allēgoria,* which later came to be used to designate the practice that in Plato's and Aristotle's time was called *huponoia.* In terms of etymology, *huponoia* is a noun corresponding to the verb *huponoein,* literally "to see under, to understand under," that is, to make out a hidden (deep) meaning beneath the manifest (superficial) sense of discourse.

It is practically impossible to ascertain the origins of allegory because, as we will see, the accounts of its first supposed practitioners came much later than the period they evoke. It is nonetheless true that sixth-century criticisms of Homer and Hesiod gave rise to a defensive reaction that led to a specific hermeneutic practice powered by two sets of motivations. First, the deep attachment people still had for Homer and Hesiod led their admirers to defend them in the face of the criticism directed at them. These defenders even tried to rediscover in Homer and Hesiod the very rationales at the basis of the criticisms leveled against them. Thus, beneath the literal meaning of these Homeric poems, their defenders claimed to make out a deep meaning, which made it possible to see gods and heroes as representing either the elements (physical allegories) or dispositions of the soul (psychological allegories) or even virtues and vices (moral allegory). Second, these three types of allegory were rooted in the common practice of applying etymology to proper names, a practice of which there is a remarkable example in Plato's *Cratylus.* Socrates too shared the widespread belief according to which, as evidenced by etymology, words do not come from a purely arbitrary convention but, rather, have been instituted by legislators on the basis of their analogy to the nature of the things they were intended to express.

We now have at our disposal a document that makes it possible for us "to see" how this worked in reality. The Orphic theogony preserved in the Derveni papyrus is an excellent example of allegory of the physical type based on the etymology of divine names. The archeological context[28] shows that this burned roll of papyrus, of which only twenty-three columns and a few fragments have been restored, couldn't have been set on fire later than 300 B.C.[29] Its content includes allusions notably to Diogenes of Apollonia,

Anaxagoras, Leucippus, Democritus, and Heraclitus.[30] The commentary, which contains no trace of Platonic influence, cannot date from earlier than 400 B.C., even thought the Orphic theogony commented on may well be older, probably dating from the fifth or even the sixth century B.C.

The following is what M. L. West[31] has been able to reconstitute of this Orphic theogony. In a short poem, Orpheus announces that he is going to sing, for initiates, about the deeds of Zeus and the gods born with him. His narrative begins at the moment when Zeus is about to seize royal power and asks Night's opinion. Zeus swallows Protogonos, the "Firstborn." There is then a flashback evocation of the divine line into which Zeus was born: Night, Protogonos, Ouranos (Gaia), Kronos (who castrates Ouranos). After swallowing Protogonos, the "Firstborn," Zeus becomes the beginning, the middle, and the end of everything. He then proceeds to a new creation described in the verses that follow. The narrative stops with Zeus's desire for his own mother.

The author of the commentary, who in fact tries to translate this Orphic theogony into a cosmogony, expresses himself in an Ionian dialect that also includes a number of Atticisms possibly due to the intermediaries who ensured its transmission. He maintains that the poem he comments on is allegorical.[32] He presents his work as a continuous discourse.[33] His citations from the Orphic theogony are introduced by preliminary formulas, but he uses the Orphic text to illustrate his own ideas rather than slavishly expressing its content.

Let us try very briefly to reconstruct the main lines of the cosmological model on which the allegorical commentary preserved in the Derveni papyrus is based.[34] The cosmos presents two distinct states: an anterior state,[35] from which the present state originates,[36] and the present state of things,[37] resulting from a long process comprising the following stages.

1. First, the realities that existed at the origin were set in motion[38] by the heat dispensed by the sun, which at this stage is Ouranos's sex;[39] they collided with each other[40] and then underwent a process of division.[41]

2. The separated particles had to clump together[42] to form compact masses.[43] In order for this process to occur, the sun had to be rendered less active.[44] That is why Ouranos is castrated by Kronos.

3. Inside the masses thus constituted, a separation took place that enabled the formation of distinct objects in the air assimilated to Zeus after he had swallowed everything.[45]

4. Finally, these distinct objects were maintained in a state of immobile suspension[46] at a certain distance from each other.[47]

The boundary between the old and the new order of things is represented in the poem by the reign[48] of Kronos,[49] who caused the particles to collide[50] and also controlled the rest of the process, even though, on completion of the third stage, he received the new name of Zeus. The commentator stresses that, in accordance with this principle,[51] only the name of the demiurge changes and not his identity. Ouranos is Kronos[52] and is replaced by Zeus.[53] However, the demiurge seems to take on a new identity with each new name: Ouranos is the sky,[54] Kronos the sun,[55] and Zeus the air.[56]

In order to gain a direct and concrete view of this commentary, let us read the five most significant columns[57] of the Derveni papyrus.

So (Orpheus) is stating that this "Kronos by Earth was born" to the sun, because (Mind) caused the elements to be "thrust" (*krouesthai*) against each other on account of the sun. This is why (Orpheus) says "he who did a great deed."

The next verse: "Sky son of Night, he who first was king." After (Orpheus) has named Mind (*Nous*) "Kronos" because he "thrust" (*krouonta*) the elements against one another, he states that he "did a great deed" to Sky: for he states that (Sky) had his kingship taken away. (DP XIV)

. . . them from thrusting against each other, and make the things that exist, once they had been separated, stand apart from each other. For as the sun was being separated and isolated in the centre, (Mind) fixed both the elements above the sun and those below and holds them fast.

Next verse: "From him in turn came Kronos, and next contriving Zeus." (Orpheus) means that his rule has existed since (Mind) became king. But his rule is explained because, by thrusting the things that exist against each other, he caused them to stand apart and created the present transmutation, creating not different things from different ones, but different ones from the same.

The phrase "and next contriving Zeus" reveals that he is not different (from Mind), but the same. (Orpheus) gives the following indication: ". . . contrivance, he held kingly honour . . . sinews. . . ." (DP XV)

. . . and the elements that are borne downwards; in mentioning these (Orpheus) meant that the vortex and all the other elements are in the Air, it being "breath." So Orpheus named this "breath" "Fate." But the rest of mankind say "Fate spun" for them, as the saying goes, and "what Fate spun will be"; for this appeared to him to be the most apt of the names that all mankind had given him. For before being called "Zeus," Fate was the wisdom of God forever and always. But because (Fate) was called "Zeus," he was thought to have been "born," although he had also existed before but was not named. This is why (Orpheus) says "Zeus first was born," as he existed first . . . then . . . those people who do not grasp what is meant (suppose that) . . . Zeus . . . (DP XVIII)

... the things that exist, each individual thing has been called after that which is dominant in it. All things were called "Zeus" by the same principle; for Air dominates all things to the extent that he wants. When people say "Fate spun" (*epiklōsai*), they mean that the wisdom of Zeus "sanctioned" (*epikurōsai*) that what exists, has come to be, and will come to be, must have come to be, exist, and will cease to be.

(Orpheus) likens him to a "king"—for this, among the names that were current, appeared to him to be apt—when he says as follows: "Zeus the king, Zeus ruler of all, he of the shining bolt." (Orpheus) said that he is "king" because, although there are many rulerships, one rule dominates and brings all things about . . . for not one . . . to bring about . . . "ruler" . . . (the world) is ruled . . . (DP XIX, trans. slightly modified)

. . . not the cold with the cold. By saying "mounting" (Orpheus) reveals that the elements, separated into little bits, moved and "mounted" in the Air, and by "mounting" were put together with each other. They kept "mounting" until the point at which each had come to its like.

"Heavenly Aphrodite," "Zeus," "Persuasion" and "Harmony" are conventional names for the same god. A man uniting with a woman is said to "aphrodize" or "mount," as the saying goes. For when the things that now exist were united with each other, (Zeus) was named "Aphrodite," but (he was named) "Persuasion" because the things that exist "gave way" to each other—"to give way" is the same thing as "to persuade"—and (he was named) "Harmony" because he "harmonised" (*hērmose*) together many elements with each of the things which exist. For he had existed even before, but was thought to have been "born" when they were separated. By the fact of their separation (Orpheus) reveals that (Zeus) kept pursuing and overcoming their unions, with the result that they were separated . . . now . . .

(the verse:) "he contrived the Earth (*Gē/Gaia*) and broad Sky above" . . . (DP XXI)

Whatever his presuppositions may be, the author of this commentary on the Orphic theogony is clearly heir to an interpretive tradition pertaining primarily to the *Iliad* and the *Odyssey*. According to Porphyry, this interpretive tradition goes back to Theagenes of Rhegium:

Homer's doctrine on the gods is usually concentrated on what is useless, or even improper, as the myths he tells about the gods are unseemly. In order to counter this sort of accusation, some people invoke the manner of speaking (ἀπὸ τῆς λέξεως ἐπιλύουσιν); they feel that all was said in an allegorical mode (ἀλληγορίᾳ πάντα εἰρῆσθαι) and has to do with the nature of the elements, for instance, as is the case of conflicts between the gods. Thus, according to them, dryness struggles against humidity, heat against cold, and light against heavy; water extinguishes fire, but fire dries out air; this applies as well to all the elements making up the universe; there is a fundamental opposition between them; they incorporate once and for all corruption at the level of individual beings, but they last eternally as a whole. These are the struggles that Homer depicted by giving to fire the names of Apollo, Helios, and Hephaistos, to water those of Poseidon and Scamander, to the moon that of Artemis, to air that of Hera, etc. In the same way, he sometimes gave names of gods to dispositions of the soul, to thinking that of Athena, to madness that of Ares, to desire that of Aphrodite, to beautiful speaking that of Hermes, all faculties to which these gods are linked. This mode of defense is quite ancient and goes back to Theagenes of Rhegium, who was to first of write about Homer; its nature is thus to take into account the manner of speaking.[58]

It is doubtful that, on the basis of Porphyry's sole account (second half of the third century A.D.), we can attribute to Theagenes of Rhegium (first half of the sixth century B.C.) the invention of physical and moral allegory. Yet it would not be surprising if this *grammatistēs* who undertook the study of Homer's work had sought to justify, in any way he could, all of its details by seeking a deep sense under the apparent meaning of certain passages that were under attack on account of their immorality. Whatever the case may be, the practice of allegory was rapidly adopted by those who, after Plato, were referred to as philosophers.

Toward the middle of the fifth century, Anaxagoras, whom Pericles himself is supposed to have invited to Athens, elaborated an allegory of the moral type: "Anaxagoras seems to have been the first to state that Homer's poetry had to do with virtue and justice."[59] His disciples followed his example. Some found a psychological kind of teaching in Homer: "Anaxagoras's disciples submit the gods, as they are presented in the myths, to interpretation: for them, Zeus is reason, Athena art—which justifies Orphic thinkers' speaking of Athena as having a manifold *mētis*."[60] As to Diogenes of Apollonia, who saw physical allegories in the *Iliad* and the *Odyssey,* he seems to have interpreted Zeus in the same way as the commentator of the Derveni Papyrus: "Diogenes praises Homer for having discussed divine questions, not in the form of myth but according to the truth (οὐ μυθικῶς, ἀλλ' ἀληθῶς). Air represents Homer's Zeus, since the poet himself states that Zeus knows everything."[61] Even Democritus adhered to this interpretation, if we are to believe Clement of Alexandria: "Democritus not unreasonably says that a few men of reason raise up their hands toward that which we Greeks now call air and speak of it as Zeus. He knows all, he gives and takes away all, and he is the king of all things."[62] Democritus was also thought to have practiced psychological allegory. Was this not the way he justified adding the epithet *Tritogenia* to Athena's name because she represents reason, which is the mother of the three essential actions of the mind: reflection, speech, and action?[63]

Allegory was also practiced by the Sophists, a practice rooted in the conviction expressed by Protagoras:

> Personally I hold that the Sophist's art is an ancient one, but that those who put their hand to it in former times, fearing the odium which it brings, adopted a disguise and worked under cover. Some used poetry as a screen, for instance Homer and Hesiod and Simonides; others religious rites and prophecy, like Orpheus and Musaeus."[64]

The Sophists thought of the poets' works as the condensed sums of all technical and ethical knowledge. By interpreting these allegorically, the Sophists were simply revealing the doctrine that the poets had purposely hidden in them. For instance, Prodicus of Ceos saw in Homer's gods the personalization of natural substances useful to human beings' lives: bread was Demeter; wine, Dionysos; water, Poseidon; fire, Hephaistos; and so forth.[65] Furthermore, a long paraphrase of Prodicus in Xenophon's *Memorabilia*[66] proposed a moralizing interpretation of Heracles. He developed the following theme in it: virtue and the happiness that comes from it can be reached only as the result of an arduous effort. In contrast, vice starts out as easy and attractive but inevitably brings unhappiness and shame. Of the two women that appear before Heracles, Virtue has a modest and stern demeanor, while the other has all the traits that seduce the senses and provoke desire. Yet it is Virtue who has the last word.

But, it is with the Cynics, Plato's and Aristotle's contemporaries, that allegory reaches one of its peaks.

Antisthenes,[67] whom Plato supposedly represented as Cratylus in the dialogue so titled, is thought to have devoted a very large part of his work to Homer and his characters, as can be seen by a glance at the list of the titles listed by Diogenes Laertius.[68] If we are to believe Xenophon, he was even the inventor of a distinction that was to have a great future: "The distinction between a poet speaking from opinion and one speaking from truth (τὰ μὲν δόξῃ, τὰ δὲ ἀληθείᾳ) goes back to Antisthenes, but he didn't pursue it as far as he could have."[69] His two favorite heroes were Heracles and Odysseus. In his eyes, Heracles was a fine pedagogue;[70] he was interested in educational problems[71] and enjoyed scholars' respect.[72] Odysseus saw him as a model in the domain of morality. His self-control enabled him to escape Circe's spells and to prefer Penelope over Calypso.[73]

Diogenes the Cynic, who was Antisthenes' disciple, continued this moralizing allegory. He applied it to the legend of Medea, a legend whose point of departure can be read in Hesiod's *Theogony* (965ff.). Rather than being the magician responsible for Pelias's horrible death, Medea becomes a Cynic dietician using scientific means to become young again.[74] Medea's aunt or sister, Circe, embodies pleasure, an enemy all the more dangerous in that he attacks treacherously.[75]

Plato reacted vigorously to the rise of allegory in book II of the *Republic* (378d–e) and again in the *Phaedrus* (222b–230a), where he was perhaps targeting Antisthenes.

Aristotle's Attitude toward Allegory

Paralleling his interest in tragedy, Aristotle was interested in allegory and even practiced it.

In a passage from the *Metaphysics,* there is a clear formulation of the two postulates on which his practice is based: (1) there is continuity between the tradition concerning the gods and what philosophy has to say about them; (2) nonetheless, the philosopher must distinguish the narrative from its initial basis:

> Our forefathers in the most remote age have handed down to us their posterity a tradition, in the form of a myth, that these first substances are gods and that the divine encloses the whole of nature. The rest of the tradition has been added later in mythical form with a view to the persuasion of the multitude and to its legal and utilitarian expediency; they say these gods are in the form of men or like some of the other animals, and they say other things consequent on and similar to these which we have mentioned. But if we were to separate the first point from these additions and take it alone—that they thought the first substances to be gods—we must regard this as a truly inspired utterance, and reflect that, while probably each art and science has repeatedly been developed as far as possible and then has each time been lost, these opinions are, so to speak, like relics of ancient wisdom preserved until the present. It is thus only with these reservations that we accept the tradition of our fathers and our earliest predecessors.[76]

In this perspective and with certain reservations, metaphysics constitutes the essence of Greek mythology; therefore Aristotle anchored metaphysics into the most distant past. While the various branches of knowledge, including philosophy, had to be learned anew after the recurring destructions suffered by humankind, perceptions of the gods, conveyed by myths, had been maintained without interruption from their beginning to the time of Aristotle.

Aristotle wasn't satisfied with declarations of principles. He also practiced allegory. He uncovered a crucially important allegorical description in book VIII of the *Iliad* in which the Prime Mover, Zeus, sure of his power, challenges the gods. From heaven he would dangle a golden chain,[77] which they would grab and pull their way. All of their joint effort would not make Zeus fall to earth, but instead, if he chose, he would be able to pull them all up to him, along with the earth and the sea, tie the chain to Olympus, and let this mass float in the ether, so much greater was his power than that of the gods as well as that of men. For Aristotle, this being who can move everything without moving himself is the primordial Mover who remains immobile outside of the universe he set in motion.[78]

Elsewhere in the *Politics,* when he evokes the forms of government favoring the warrior function, Aristotle sees in the love of Aphrodite and Ares sung by Demodocus in book VIII of the *Odyssey* (266ff.) the proof that warriors are inclined to love: "The old mythologer would seem to have been right in uniting Ares and Aphrodite, for all warlike races are prone to the love either of men or of women."[79] Elsewhere, Aristotle proposes what he thinks is the correct interpretation of a well-known myth, that of Athena, who, after inventing the flute, neglects it:

> There is wisdom in the myth of the ancients, which tells how Athene invented the flute and then threw it away. It was not a bad idea of theirs that the Goddess disliked the instrument because it made the face ugly; but with still more reason may we say that she rejected it because the acquirements of flute-playing contributes nothing to the mind, since to Athene we ascribe both knowledge and art.[80]

What can we conclude from all this?

In contrast to Plato, Aristotle did not adopt an attitude of radical rupture with myth. While he looked upon tragedy as the poetic genre par excellence, he was forced to admit that myth was its soul. This led him to propose a particularly original analysis of this type of discourse, an analysis that unfortunately was hardly ever pursued by later writers, linked as it was to an obsolete view of tragedy. Furthermore, Aristotle wanted to take popular traditions into account by dissociating the instruction they carried from the narrative in which this instruction was expressed. Such an attitude led him to justify allegory and to practice it. Yet he only occasionally relied on this practice. It was the Stoics, claiming to be the successors of the Cynics in their allegorical practice, who were to give to allegory its definitive thrust.

FOUR

Stoics, Epicureans, and the New Academy

The Stoics appear on the scene as the successors of the Cynics, at least on the moral plane. They were to continue the allegorical interpretation of Homer, Hesiod, and even Orpheus and increase its import. Stoic allegory, however, generated lively responses from the Epicureans and the philosophers of the New Academy.

Since only fragments of the works of the Stoics, the Epicureans, and the philosophers of the New Academy have survived, I am forced to base my analyses on *De natura deorum,*[1] in which Cicero systematically covered what the three predominant philosophical currents of the time had to say on the various gods and on the interpretations that each of these figures generated. My discussion of Cicero's account will be backed by systematic recourse to pertinent fragments.

OUR SOURCE: CICERO'S *DE NATURA DEORUM*

De natura deorum (*DND*) was written in between the *Tusculan Disputations* and *De divinatione,* that is, between June 45 B.C. and March 44 B.C. Cicero places the scene in Cotta's villa around 76 B.C. The three protagonists are spokespersons of the three philosophical systems vying with one another at the time: C. Aurelius Cotta[2] represents the Academy, C. Velleius[3] is the Epicurean, and Q. Lucilius Balbus[4] represents Stoicism.

The organization of *De natura deorum* is simple. The first book opens with an introduction (*DND* I 1–17) pertaining not only to the first book but also to the other two.

After this introduction, Cotta, who was already engaged in a discussion with Velleius (*DND* I 16), invites the latter to continue it so as to inform Cicero, who had just arrived (*DND* I 16–17). Then Velleius, the Epicurean, heatedly attacks Plato's system along with that of the Stoics (*DND* I 18–24). He goes on to a doxographical retrospective exposition of the opinions of twenty-seven Greek philosophers, from Thales to the Stoics (*DND* I 25–41), on the existence and the nature of the gods. Velleius continues this exposition by briefly evoking the absurdity of poets' narratives, the superstitions circulated by eastern religions, and the ignorance of the masses (*DND* I 42–43). Then, praising Epicurus, he describes the positive doctrine of the Epicureans on the existence of the gods, their form, their nature, and their happiness (*DND* I 43–56). In the last part of the first book (*DND* I 57–124), Cotta criticizes the positions that Balbus has just presented.

The second book, the most "scientific" of the three, pertains to cosmology, astronomy, zoology, anatomy, physiology, and so forth. It features Balbus's exposition of Stoic theology. After a brief introduction (*DND* II 1–3), Balbus broaches the following four themes: the existence of the gods (*DND* II 4–44), their nature (*DND* II 45–72), providence (*DND* II 73–153), and divine intervention in human affairs (*DND* II 154–167). The whole ends on a sort of Stoic credo.

The third book opens with an introduction, which works as a transition between the two books (*DND* III 1–5) and contains Cotta's refutation of the Stoic doctrine on the gods. This third book must have followed the same organization as the second, but because parts of the manuscript have been lost, the third and the fourth parts as well as a large section of the first part are missing. After developing proofs of the existence of the gods (*DND* III 6–64), Cotta evokes the issue of providence (*DND* III 65–93). The dialogue closes on an exchange of friendly comments between Cicero and the participants in the discussion (*DND* III 94–95).

Cicero's ideas, particularly those pertaining to knowledge about the gods, are fairly syncretistic. In 87 B.C., Cicero, who was nineteen at the time, came to Rome to attend the lectures of the Epicurean Phaedrus[5] and those of Philo of Larissa,[6] who had been the leader of the Academy in Athens. Later on, in 79, the twenty-eight-year-old Cicero attended the lectures of Phaedrus and of Zeno[7] the Epicurean, but he listened mainly to Antiochus of Ascalon.[8] His subsequent stay in Rhodes probably enabled him to become familiar with the great cosmological doctrines of Stoicism.

What were the works that Cicero might have used to write *De natura deorum?* In a letter to Atticus (XIII 39, 2) sent from the Arpinum estate and dated August 16, 45 B.C., Cicero requests a work by Phaedrus titled *On the gods* (Περὶ θεῶν). Moreover, a text with that same title[9] was found on one of the Herculaneum papyri. It is attributed to Philodemus,[10] and on several points it gives the Greek counterparts to some of the passages in the exposition of the Epicurean doctrine in book I of *De natura deorum*. Finally, Cicero's text exhibits troubling resemblances with another of Philodemus's works, *On piety* (Περὶ εὐσεβείας).[11] That said, it is not possible to know whether Cicero drew his inspiration from Philodemus or whether both Philodemus and Cicero were getting their information from a common source. Furthermore, when still writing *De natura deorum,* Cicero, in a letter to Atticus (XIII 8) sent from the Tusculum estate on June 9, 45 B.C., requested a work by Panaetius of Rhodes,[12] *On providence* (Περὶ Προνοίας). It must be remembered, however, that while writing *De natura deorum,* Cicero was also working on *De divinatione.* In *De natura deorum* (I 123), Cicero admits also having made use of a work by Posidonius.[13] But since he never states that he borrowed from Posidonius's exposition, it is impossible to know what Cicero might have adopted from him.

Faced with all these uncertainties, it is better to maintain reservations and to limit oneself to the following general point. Cicero always proclaimed his loyalty to Platonic ideas. He refered to Plato as "deus philosophorum, deus ille noster." However, Cicero's Plato was the one introduced to him by two members of the New Academy, Philo of Larissa and Antiochus of Ascalon. While Philo of Larissa was a probabilist, Antiochus of Ascalon showed more eclecticism by attempting to harmonize Platonic philosophy with Stoic doctrines. Cicero takes pains to differentiate himself from Cotta in an exchange occurring at the beginning of *De natura deorum* (Balbus is the first speaker; the narrator is Cicero):

"Let us concentrate at present . . . on the subject on which we have already embarked."

"That suits me," said Cotta, "but we mustn't keep our new arrival in the dark about the topic." He looked over at me. "We were discussing the nature of the gods, a question which as always I find extremely opaque; so I was sounding out Velleius on the views of Epicurus. So, Velleius, if it is not too much trouble, recapitulate your initial remarks."

"I'll do that," he replied. "Mind you, his arrival is a reinforcement of you rather than me, since both of you" (this he added with a grin) "have been taught by the same teacher Philo to know nothing."

Then I interposed. "That was teaching I leave to Cotta to explain; please don't think that I'm here as his second; I shall listen impartially and without prejudice. No compulsion binds me to defend any particular view willy-nilly." (*DND* I 17)

In the controversy between Antiochus of Ascalon and Philo of Larissa, Cicero sided with Philo because Cicero was particularly interested in skepticism in the Academy, except when it came to ethics.[14]

STOIC-INSPIRED ALLEGORICAL INTERPRETATION AND ITS CRITIQUES

The exposition that follows will not respect the order Cicero used in *De natura deorum.* I will start with a presentation of the Stoic doctrine on the gods. This doctrine was the object of the lengthiest discussion as well as that of lively attacks by Epicureans and Academicians.

The Stoic Doctrine on the Gods in *De natura deorum*[15]

In the second book of *De natura deorum,* Balbus, the representative of Stoicism, wonders about the origins of the gods of the popular religion. He explains their origins by evoking four causes. (1) Since people believed that any useful thing could have come only from the benevolence of a god, they linked each of these benefits to a divinity. That is why Ceres stands for wheat and Liber for wine (*DND* II 60–61). (2) Many immaterial values were also elevated to the rank of divinities as for instance, Fides (= Faith), Mens (= Spirit), and Virtus (= Virtue). People have even gone so far as to turn lower appetites into gods, as for example Cupido (= Desire), Voluptas (= Pleasure), and so forth (*DND* II 61–62). (3) And then certain individuals who had performed great services to humankind were also sent to heaven, such as Hercules, Castor and Pollux, Asclepius, Liber (son of Semele), and Romulus-Quirinus (*DND* II 62). (4) However, it is mainly the world of nature that explains the origin of most of these gods who "have been clothed in human form and have provided fables for poets, cramming our lives with every kind of superstition (*DND* II 63–64)."

Balbus illustrates his argument with several examples. Hesiod (*Theogony* 159ff.) tells how Caelus (= Ouranos) was mutilated by his son Saturn (= Kronos), who himself was bound in chains by his son Jupiter (= Zeus). These sacrilegious narratives make a mockery of a profound physical doctrine. The celestial and ethereal substance that engenders everything by itself has no need of any organ dependent on copulation in order to engender. Furthermore, Caelus's son is called Saturn in Latin because he is "gorged with years" (*saturetur annis*); that is why he is identified with time (on the basis of the assimilation in Greek of Kronos to Khronos). And since time keeps on devouring the years, which are its children, Jupiter (the brilliant firmament) must put him in chains in order to force time into a regular flow measured by the movement of the heavenly bodies (*DND* II 63–65). The great gods are anthropomorphic transpositions of the forces of nature. This can be demonstrated by studying their respective names in Greek and in Latin. Air was deified under the name of Juno (= Hera), water under the name of Neptune (= Poseidon), and earth was identified with Dives, Ditus, or Dis Pater (in Greek *Ploutōn*), as *ploutōs* in ancient Greek and *dives* in Latin evoke the idea of wealth. The wife of Dis Pater, Proserpina (= Persephone) is the seed hidden in the earth that her mother Ceres (= Demeter) is searching for. Ceres' name is explained by the fact that she is "producer of fruits (*a gerendis fructibus*), like its Greek equivalent (Dēmētēr = Gēmētēr = Mother Earth) (*DND* II 66–69).

This, then, is how Balbus explains the origin of the gods. He has recourse to an allegorical interpretation and concludes with the necessity of differentiating between superstition and religion (*DND* II 69–72). In his view, genuine religion consists in uncovering, behind the gods of the myths, the natural facts they represent.

All this should be placed into a much broader context, that of Stoic doctrine. According to this doctrine, the universe is a living being, possessing reason, and arranging all things on the basis of the best aims. This universal intelligence, even while animating the whole of the universe and circulating in all of its parts, becomes self-conscious and concentrated into a divine figure called Zeus, Jupiter, or simply God. And since this God is manifested in a multitude of different aspects, notably that of fire, one can give him as many names as the forms he assumes. The names are those of the mythical divinities. In short, etymology enables the Stoics to reappropriate the gods of popular religion for their own system. Balbus's argument is a good example of this practice.

Balbus places his exposition under the joint patronage of Zeno, Cleanthes, and Chrysippus.

The Antecedents of This Doctrine

Zeno of Citium (335–263 B.C.), who is thought to be the founder of the Stoic School, is supposed to have devoted five books of Προβλήματα Ὁμηρικά (*SVF I* n° 41 = DL VII 4) to Homer's poems. In this work, we are told Zeno made the most of the distinction propounded by Antisthenes according to which Homer spoke sometimes in terms that were within the grasp of the masses, and at other times in terms of the truth that was known by only a small number of people, and in particular by philosophers (*SVF I* n° 274 = Dio Chrysostom, *Orationes* 53, 4). From this perspective, Zeno is said to have interpreted the myth of the Titans as follows:

According to Zeno, the Titans have always stood for the elements (*stoikheia*) of the world. He interprets Koios (*Koion*) as a quality (*poiotēta*) and relies for this interpretation on the Eolian linguistic turn that led to replace *p* with *k*. Krios is the royal and dominant element (*hēgemonikon*);[16] Hyperion (*Huperiona*) designates the ascending movement because of the expression "to go higher" (ὑπεράνω ἰέναι); finally, because all light things that are let loose naturally fall upwards (πίπτειν ἄνω), this part of the universe was called *Japet* (*Iapeton*).[17]

Here we find an interpretation of the physical type based ultimately on the etymological analysis of divine names.

Cleanthes (311–232 B.C.), Zeno's disciple and successor, appears to have been obsessed with etymology. In particular, Cleanthes applied his etymological virtuosity to Apollo's name: "Cleanthes said that Apollo represents the sun because he rises at times at one place and at times at another (ἀπ᾿ ἄλλων καὶ ἄλλων τόπων)."[18] Cleanthes also applied etymology to Apollo's cult epithets, as for instance Loxias.[19] Cleanthes again had recourse to allegory to explain that the sun was called Dionysus because, in its daily course from east to west, which produces night and day, it completely travels (*dianusai*) the circle of the sky.[20]

Chrysippus (280–207 B.C.), who succeeded to Cleanthes as the leader of the School, also based allegory on etymology to explain several divine names. He thus explained the names Rhea[21] and Ares[22] and drew upon an etymological explanation harking back to Plato's *Cratylus* (396b) to explain the names Apollo[23] and Zeus.[24] Nevertheless, it must be noted that Chrysippus was interested not only in Homer and Hesiod but also in Orpheus and Musaeus.[25]

Even though the positions adopted by Zeno, Cleanthes, and Chrysippus toward mythology differed in details, they all agreed on these three points: (1) Allegorical interpretation deals with the nature of the gods, so it accepts their existence from the outset. (2) Only a careful study of divine names makes it possible to apprehend the nature of the gods who bear them. (3) A rigorous description of their nature bases mythology on the Stoic system, and this the more easily in that a Stoic sees gods not as elements or natural forces but as the manifestation of divine reason in these elements and natural forces.

The Extensions of This Doctrine

Such an allegorical orientation could not be stymied by criticisms from the Epicureans or from the members of the New Academy. It was to give birth to two great currents of thought in the Stoic tradition, of which Cicero gives an account in *De natura deorum.* One of these currents focused on the metaphysical and cosmological manifestation of traditional myths, while the other, much more realist, saw Homer in particular as a pioneer of history and of geography.

The first proponent of a metaphysical and cosmological allegory was Crates of Mallos, a grammarian of the School of Pergamon, who in the second century B.C. wrote a *Rectification of Homer* (Ὁμήρου διόρθωσις), which included both a correction of the text of the poems and suggestions, illustrated with examples, of how to interpret them allegorically.

According to Eustathius,[26] Crates interpreted the description of Agamemnon's fighting equipment at the beginning of book XI of the *Iliad* (32–37) as a description of the world whereby, Crates claimed, Homer imparted in a hidden form the main part of his astronomical and cosmological knowledge. The shield envelops the warrior as the universe envelops mortals; the circles are those described by the celestial bodies, while the bumps on the shield represent the stars. In the passage where Hephaistos reminds Hera (*Iliad* I 589–593) of the ill-treatments Zeus made him endure, notably by hurling him down from Olympus, Crates uncovers an allusion to the myth of the celestial trajectory of Helios.[27] He sees these two mythical episodes as the means Homer used to measure the universe: having departed from the same point and with the same speed, Hephaistos and Helios ended up at the same time the same place. Pseudo-Heraclitus,[28] who reported this interpretation, called it "bizarre" (*terateia*).

It is practically impossible to assess the extent of Crates' influence on the allegorists of the Stoic tradition who followed him. These allegorists probably drew from several sources, one of which was Crates. As for Crates, he practiced a type of allegory that can be found in an attenuated form in Apollodorus of Athens, Cornutus, and Pseudo-Heraclitus.

Apollodorus was born in Athens around 180 B.C. He was a disciple of the Stoic Diogenes of Seleucia (or of Babylon)[29] and of the Pergamon grammarians. Apollodorus, to whom a manual of mythography has been erroneously attributed,[30] is the author of a lost treatise *On the Gods* (Περὶ θεῶν), in which he developed several etymologies of the Stoic type. The reason the sun is called Ἰήϊος is that "he springs up and circulates (ἴεσθαι καὶ ἰέναι)"[31] Likewise the red mullet was consecrated to Hecate because the Greek name of this fish (τρίγλη) includes the prefix τρι-, and this goddess appears under the sign of the number three and its multiples. She has three forms and three eyes and is honored at crossroads where three roads meet, as well as on the thirtieth day of each month.[32] Nevertheless, there is general agreement that Apollodorus of Athens was the immediate source for Cornutus[33] and Pseudo-Heraclitus.[34]

This type of allegorical interpretation, which poets turned into metaphysical and cosmological teachings, paralleled another type, which saw Homer as a historian and geographer. For the allegorists belonging to this current, gods and heroes correspond to concrete beings deified on account of the great services they rendered for the human species, and it is possible to uncover a historian, a naturalist, and a geographer in Homer.

Euhemerus can be seen as the initiator of realist allegory. This Sicilian from the middle of the third century B.C. became the confidant of King Cassander, who entrusted him with exploring the Red Sea. Euhemerus took this opportunity to write a sort of geographical novel combining the fabulous with the real, which included a description of Panchaie, an imaginary island off the coast of Arabia. This island was long covered with water, and it emerged shortly before the arrival of the traveler who discovered in it a temple of Triphyllian Zeus "in which there was a golden column with an inscription indicating it had been erected by Zeus himself. On this column the god had inscribed the detail of his exploits so that posterity would remember his deeds."[35] That is why Euhemerus gave the title *Sacred Inscription* (Ἱερὰ ἀναγραφή) to the work in which he claimed to have written the narratives told by Zeus and Hermes themselves, and to which he was adding commentaries. This work has been lost, but its substance has been reported by several doxographers, including Diodorus of Sicily in his *Historical Library* (V 41–46). Moreover, Cicero (*DND* I 119) informs us that Ennius,[36] who greatly admired Euhemerus, had translated or at least adapted this work, and some fragments of this translation or adaptation were preserved by Lactantius.

Before civilization, the shrewdest and most powerful chiefs claimed divine attributes, which the crowd accepted.

> And Euhemerus, nicknamed "The Atheist,"[37] says: "When the life of mankind was without order, those who so far excelled the rest in strength and intelligence that all men lived subservient to their commands, being intent to gain for themselves more admiration and veneration, invented for themselves a kind of superhuman and divine authority, and in consequence were by the populace accounted Gods."[38]

Furthermore, nations willingly granted divine status posthumously to their bravest kings and to the inventors who bettered their living conditions:

There is no doubt that those who are worshiped as gods were first human beings; this was the case for the first and the greatest of kings; but this was also the case for those whose courage had served the human species, and who, once they were dead, were given divine honors; or of those whose . . . inventions had bettered human lives and who left behind an undying admiration. Who can ignore this? . . . This is particularly Euhemerus's and our Ennius's theory.[39]

Euhemerism was to acquire another dimension, this time political, as soon as it could be used to justify the divine status given to the emperors. Having served to explain how the gods had been men, this doctrine was then used to justify how men could be gods. Euhemerism was to be one of the pillars of imperial ideology.

On a strictly intellectual plane, Euhemerus's realist and historical interpretation was to be immensely successful and to have a deep and lasting influence. It was practiced by Palaephatus, an Alexandrian grammarian of the second century B.C., the author of a treatise *On Unbelievable Things* (Περὶ ἀπίστων); by Diodorus of Sicily, a contemporary of the emperor Augustus and the author of a general history to which the title *Historical Library* was given; and by Strabo, who lived at the beginning of the Christian era and who, in the first book of his *Geōgraphica,* introduced Homer as the founder of geography based on experience.[40]

In *De natura deorum,* the criticisms of Velleius, the representative of Epicureanism, and those of Cotta, the representative of the New Academy, are directed to the whole of the Stoic-inspired allegorical interpretation. Cicero's account of this polemic no doubt corresponded to reality.

Epicurean Critique

As we have seen above, Velleius, in the first book of *De natura deorum* (36–41), makes a heated indictment of Stoic inspired allegory. He successively attacks Zeno (36–37) and then his disciples—Ariston (37), Cleanthes (37), Persaeus (38), and Chrysippus (39–41), the last of whom he considers "the craftiest interpreter of the Stoic dreams" (*stoicorum somniorum vaferrumus interpres*) (*DND* I 39)—and finally Diogenes of Babylon (*DND* I 41). This attack unfolds in three directions.

Velleius first attacks Persaeus, who held that "those men have been considered gods who have devised some great and useful contribution to civilized life" (*DND* I 38) and who argued that "such useful and beneficial contributions have themselves been accorded the status of gods. He did not even qualify this by calling them discoveries by the gods, but maintained that they were themselves divine" (*DND* I 38). Velleius gives an ironic retort: "What could be more stupid than to attach the dignity of gods to mean and ugly objects, or to grant a place in the company of gods to men already obliterated in death, so that worship of them would consist of nothing but lamentation?" (*DND* I 38) In his *De pietate* (c. 9), Philodemus, who was to be followed in this by Minucius Felix (*Octavius* XXI 2), attributed to Prodicus of Ceos[41] the first of these two stances (*DND* I 118), probably because he also attributed the first one to Euhemerus (*DND* I 119).

Velleius then confronts all the other Stoics (*DND* I 39–41), whom he presents as adhering to a metaphysical type of allegorical interpretation aimed at reconciling the poets' narratives (Homer, Hesiod, and even Musaeus and Orpheus in Chrysippus's case) with Stoic doctrine. He criticizes this doctrine for its tenet that the universe is the sensible manifestation of universal reason, which is identified with the ether and then referred to as Zeus. Velleius argues that this practice flagrantly lacks historical credibility, so that "even the remotest poets appear to have been Stoics, even though they had never dreamed of such doctrines" (*DND* I 41). This criticism was much less superficial than those evoked above. It was to be taken up again later on and still retain its validity today.

Another Epicurean criticism is expressed in chapters 17 and 18 of Philodemus's *De pietate*. Here the author accuses the Stoics of impiety and even likens them to Diagoras[42] for abandoning traditional polytheism and anthropomorphism and believing the gods to be mere natural forces and the simple manifestations of a unique divinity.

These sorts of criticism make sense only when they are related to the philosophical context to which they belong. Epicurean philosophy is based on the atomistic mechanism of Leucippus and of Democritus, which had several consequences for theology. Since the precipitating activity of atoms has no beginning and no end, the totality of combinations of agglomerated atoms is realized at all times. It follows that no new figure or god can appear. In this perspective, any explanation pertaining to the origin of a given divinity is meaningless. The question is whether this view fixes the divine image into a unique type—which seems to be Velleius's and Cicero's interpretation—or, alternatively, whether one can accept the existence of two kinds of gods, which fits in better with Philodemus's interpretation.

That said, the Epicureans were atheists neither in practice nor in theory. They participated in religious ceremonies and only placed their god outside of earthly affairs to mark their greater respect for his definition. As Velleius explains, evidence and reason confirm that gods do exist as individual beings, that they are eternal, and that they are absolutely happy, since they have no cause to be troubled by the world or by human beings, whence it follows that they receive the worship of men because of their transcendence (*DND* I 43–57). Thus it is not surprising that Epicureans often wrote works of the *On piety* type. Philodemus's Περὶ εὐσεβείας is an excellent example.

The Critique of the Academicians

In the third book of *De natura deorum,* Cicero reproduces a long exposition by the academician Cotta of the New Academic critique of Stoic allegorical practices, in particular the critique developed by Carneades,[43] who disputed point by point the Stoic doctrine on the gods: he denied finality, contested the proofs for the existence of the gods, held that the idea people had of the divinity was contradictory, and, above all, reduced the partisans of popular religion to absurdity. It is thus not surprising that in spite of the somewhat incoherent nature of his composition, this third book should respond point by point to the doctrine formulated by Balbus in book II (60–62).

Cotta, a pontifex, just as Cicero is an augur,[44] speaks not with the aim of destroying religion but rather to reclaim ancestral opinions beyond Stoic interpretations:

> "Fine," said Cotta, "so let us proceed as the discussion leads us. But before I broach the topic, let me say a word about my own position. I take considerably to heart your authority, Balbus, and the comments at the close of your discourse, in which you urged me to remember that I am not just Cotta, but also a priest. The point you were making, I imagine, was that I should defend the beliefs about the immortal gods which we have inherited from our ancestors, together with our sacrifices, ceremonies, and religious observances. I shall indeed defend them, and I have always done so; no words from any person, whether learned or unlearned, will ever budge me from the views which I inherited from our ancestors concerning the worship of the immortal gods. In any discussion of religion, my guiding lights are Tiberius Coruncanius, Publius Scipio, and Publius Scaevola, all of whom were chief priests, and not Zeno or Cleanthes or Chrysippus, and my inspiration is Gaius Laelius, augur and a philosopher to boot; I would rather lend an ear to him, in that celebrated discourse of his on religion, than to any Stoic authority.[45]

We must reposition Cotta's philosophical critique of the allegorical interpretation of gods and myths developed by the Stoics in this semisociological framework.

Cotta begins by attacking the conventional origin of the gods, whether conceived as deriving from the identification of a benefit with a benevolent divinity, or from the posthumous divinization of the benefactors of humankind.

> When we label the harvest as Ceres, and our wine as Liber, we are of course using a familiar turn of speech, but do you imagine that anyone is so mindless as to think that what he eats is a deity? As for those who you say have advanced in status from humans to gods, I shall be delighted to learn how this could have occurred, and why it no longer does so, if only you explain it. But as things stand, I do not see how, as Accius puts it, the man beneath whom "The funeral-torch was lit on Oeta's mount" survived that burning to attain "His father's home that stands for ever,"[46] when Homer recounts how Ulysses encountered him among the others who had departed this life in the world below.[47]

Cotta does not develop the argument further and keeps it at the level of mockery.

The case is quite different for the other two kinds of divinities, whether these be values raised to the ranks of divinities, or the traditional divinities whose human appearances stand for natural realities.

Cotta broaches the question from a logical view point with an evocation of Carneades' sorites. This type of reasoning consists in drawing from one point to another the consequences of an initial proposition whose falsehood one wishes to demonstrate, ending up with a sequence of such points with a consequence known to be false. Here is an example:

> If the gods exist, are the nymphs likewise goddesses? If nymphs are divine, then so are Pans and Satyrs. But Pans and Satyrs are not deities, so neither are nymphs. Yet temples have been solemnly dedicated to nymphs by the state, so it follows from this that the rest who have had temples dedicated to them are not deities either.
>
> Take the argument a step further. You count Jupiter and Neptune as gods, so Orcus their brother is also a god, and so are the rivers which are said to flow in Hades, namely Acheron, Cocytus, and Pyriphlegethon; then too Charon and Cerberus are to be regarded as gods. But the notion that these five are gods must be rejected, so it must follow that Orcus is no god either, so what have you Stoics to say about his brothers? These issues were raised by Carneades not to dispose of the gods, for this would be wholly unworthy of a philosopher, but to demonstrate that Stoics have nothing plausible to say about the god (*sed ut Stoïcos nihil de diis explicare convinceret*).[48]
>
> He uses the same type of reasoning for the values elevated to the ranks of divinities: "Well then," he [Carneades] would say "if these brothers are members

of the Pantheon, their father Saturn can surely not be denied a place, for he is popularly worshiped in the lands of the west.[49] But if Saturn is a god, then we must grant that his father Caelus is one as well, and if this is the case, the parents of Caelus, Aether, and Dies, must be reckoned as gods, and so must their brothers and sisters. These are named by genealogists of old as Love, Guile, Sickness, Toil, Envy, Fate, Old Age, Death, Darkness, Wretchedness, Lamentation, Partiality, Deceit, Obstinacy, the Fates, the Daughters of Hesperus, and Dreams. They say that all these are the children of Erebus and Night. So we must either admit that these monstrous entities are gods, or hold that the first four we mentioned are not gods.[50]

As we will soon see, Sextus Empiricus cites very similar types of arguments.

After vituperating against the unbridled proliferation of divinities implied by the Stoic interpretation, Cotta challenges the analytical tool—etymological analysis—used by the Stoics.

Why do you Stoics take such pleasure in rationalizing fables, and in pursuing the etymologies of names? You defend the castration of Caelus by his son, and the shackling of Saturn also by his son, and stories of this kind, so enthusiastically that those who originated them are regarded not merely as sound in mind, but even as philosophers! As for your delving into the meaning of names, your strained interpretations are quite pathetic. Saturn is so called because "he is sated with years,"[51] Mars because "he overturns might (*magna vertit*)"[52] . . .[53]

And then Cotta continues by attacking the most famous Stoics by name:

First of all Zeno, followed by Cleanthes and then by Chrysippus,[54] landed themselves in great and wholly unnecessary difficulties in seeking to make sense of lying fables, and in seeking to explain the reasons for the names of individual gods. By so doing, you Stoics are surely admitting that the facts are at odds with popular beliefs, for figures dignified with the title of gods turn out to be properties in nature, and not personal deities at all.[55]

Like Carneades' critique (*DND* III 4), that of Cotta is aimed not at traditional religion but at Stoic theology in its most dogmatic aspect.

Cotta does not question the existence of the gods. He contests the Stoic interpretation of their nature, based as it is on the etymological analysis of their names. In the main, his criticism parallels Socrates' criticisms at the beginning of the *Phaedrus*.

At the end of the second century A.D., four centuries after Carneades, we can still hear the echo of this attack against Stoic allegorism in the work of Sextus Empiricus.[56]

The philosopher can take pleasure in poetry, but he fails in his duties if he calls on poets to take up rational demonstration. Further, "it is not the genuine philosophers who make use of testimonies from the poets, because for them [philosophers] first reason is sufficient in itself to carry conviction, but those who humbug the vulgar crowd."[57] As a good Skeptic, Sextus Empiricus notes that the very diversity of opinions on the divine and on the different gods shows their common error.[58] But to believe that Homer's gods can be identified with elements of the physical world is a grotesque notion:

> Those who say that the ancients supposed that all the things which benefit life are gods—such as the sun and moon, rivers and lakes, and the like—are not only defending an improbable view but also convicting the ancients of the utmost stupidity. For it is not likely that they were so foolish as to imagine that things they saw perishing before their eyes are gods, or that they attributed divine power to things which were being devoured by themselves and dissolved. For some things, perhaps, are reasonable, such as believing the Earth to be divine—not that substance which is plowed into furrows or dug up, but the power which pervades it and it is fruitful, and really most divine, nature. But to suppose that lakes and rivers, and whatsoever else is of a nature to be useful to us, are gods surpasses the height of lunacy. For, on this showing, one ought also to believe that men, and especially philosophers, are gods (for they help to benefit our life), and most of the irrational animals (for they co-operate with us), and our domestic furniture and whatsoever else there is of a still more humble kind. But all this is extremely ludicrous; so that one must declare that the view set forth is not sound.[59]

Sextus Empiricus echoes most of the arguments Cotta used against Balbus and Stoic allegorism, which in the meanwhile had been practiced by such authors as Cornutus and Pseudo-Heraclitus.

What can we conclude from this all too cursory reading of Cicero's *De natura deorum?* None of the philosophical currents—Stoicism, Epicureanism, and Academy—raises the least doubt about the existence of the gods. But in no way do they agree on the nature of these gods.

The doctrine against which the attacks of the Epicureans and the Academicians converge is that of the Stoics, which is characterized by two traits: the acceptance of the existence of all the traditional divinities, and the allegorical justification of their nature; they are benefactor deities, immaterial values, and beneficent and natural realities. This justification is always made with the help of etymology.

The Epicureans raise two types of criticism against Stoic practice. One mocks the practice of reducing the divine to common and trivial material realities. The other denounces the tendency to make the poets Homer and Hesiod as well as Orpheus and Musaeus into Stoic precursors. As to the philosophers representing the New Academy, they show the contradictions stemming from multiplying the number of divinities almost ad infinitum. They denounce the etymological torture that the Stoics perpetrate on the names of the gods, torture aimed at identifying these gods with creations or inventions of benefit to humankind, or with individual benefactors to the species, or again with values as well as material realities.

Despite all these attacks, the allegorical interpretation advocated by the Stoics remained predominant for centuries.

FIVE

Pythagoreanism and Platonism

A new type of interpretation of myth was to be developed during the very first centuries of the Roman Empire. Platonic philosophers who believed that Plato was inspired by Pythagoras saw myth as "symbol" and "enigma." It was the task of philosophers to unveil its true meaning, after an initiation in which purification and teaching were inextricably intertwined, just as they were in the mysteries. Thus the aim was no longer the compilation of as complete as possible a list of correspondences between mythical figures and the elements of a philosophical system incapable of reaching beyond a universe within which the divine manifested itself. Rather, philosophers now aimed to accede, through the intermediary of myths properly interpreted, to a level of reality in which a philosophical truth that was in some ways a revealed truth was rooted.

HISTORICAL CONTEXT

From the first century B.C. on, the methods of interpreting myths underwent a radical transformation, linked to the methods of teaching philosophy.[1]

The Transformation of the Teaching of Philosophy

The period spanning the fourth to the first centuries B.C. presents two characteristics: the existence of philosophical institutions in Athens, and teaching aimed at the arts of speaking and living. The great schools, Platonic, Aristotelian, Epicurean and Stoic, were set up in different areas of the city of Athens. Teaching consisted in dialectic exercises and in discussions aimed at training students for political action enlightened by science (in Platonism), for scientific life (in Aristotelianism), or for moral life (in Epicureanism and Stoicism).

There is strong evidence that these philosophical institutions did not survive the taking of Athens by Sulla in 87 B.C. Already on their last legs during the final years of the Republic, they were practically nonexistent during the first years of the Principate.[2] A new phase in the history of philosophy opened up with the disappearance of the philosophical schools at Athens and the establishment of numerous philosophical institutions scattered around the whole of the Mediterranean basin.

The four philosophical schools were now spread throughout various eastern and western cities and could no longer affirm their loyalty to their respective founders by drawing on the Athenian institutions that had been created by them and that had perpetuated oral traditions. As a result, philosophical courses became primarily commentaries on texts.

Philosophical commentaries had existed for a long time. It seems that Crantor commented in one form or another on Plato's *Timaeus,* around 300 B.C.[3] But the systematic character of this practice was new at the beginning of the Empire. Previously, you learned to speak, and while learning to speak, you learned to live. Now, however, you learned not so much to speak as to read, though while learning to read, you still learned to live. Philosophical thought was thus becoming exegetical. The sort of questions raised involved the relations between the "living-in-itself," the intelligible forms, and the intellect in the following sentence "the mind contemplates intelligible forms in that which is the "living-in-itself" (*Timaeus* 39e).[4] Reflection no longer bore directly on problems themselves but on problems as they were dealt with by Aristotle and by Plato. But the true sense of Plato's and Aristotle's texts was no longer a given. They now had to be interpreted: hence the notion of double meaning.

This was the time when the Pythagorean influence, which was so strong in the ancient Academy with Speusippus and Xenocrates, became a deciding factor in Platonism. The historical modes of this influence remain obscure. It is apparent in Eudorus, who is thought to have lived in Alexandria during the first century B.C. and who commented on the *Timaeus,* and also apparent in his compatriot Philo. This trend became very strong in Thrasyllus, Tiberius's astrologer and philosopher at Nero's court, and became dominant as one of Plutarch's philosophical presuppositions.[5]

The influence of Pythagoreanism on Platonism took on a number of aspects. Yet one of them, secrecy,[6] acquired fundamental importance. Secrecy pertains to two elements at play in communication: the means of transmission and encoding.

The privileged means of transmission of fundamental truths had to be the spoken word, since writing puts information within everyone's reach, at least in theory. Whence the use of the term *akousmata* to designate Pythagorean doctrines in which writing is used only for the writing of notes (*hupomnēmata*). The problematic nature of the relationship with writing in the Platonic tradition facilitated its links to Pythagoreanism. This first restriction pertaining to the mean of transmission was complemented by another, pertaining to the mode of expression of these doctrines. These were expressed in a symbolic and enigmatic manner, which is why they were referred to as *sumbola* and as *ainigmata*.

The word most commonly associated with the oral doctrines of Pythagoreanism is *sumbolon*. Etymologically, the Greek term, of which our word "symbol"[7] is only a transliteration, is a combination of a nominal derivative of the verb *ballō* (to throw, to place rapidly) and of the prefix *sun* (together). It designates, in its first sense, an object cut in two; putting the object back together constitutes a sign of recognition. In a second sense, any object or any message capable of a double level of interpretation is called "symbol." While the deepest level of meaning was reserved to a very small number of initiates, the superficial sense was within anyone's reach.

At any rate, their double meaning explains why the oral doctrines of the Pythagoreans were also labeled *ainigmata*, that is, "enigmas." By definition, an enigma is an element of discourse or a statement generating an ambiguous or obscure meaning in the form of a description or a definition, and of which the sense has to be uncovered. Formulating a profound doctrine in a language unintelligible to the noninitiate involved expressing oneself through enigmas.[8] Speaking δι᾽ αἰνιγμῶν, meant to speak *more pythagorico*.[9]

A New Way of Interpreting Myths

The interpretation of myths that were increasingly associated with the mysteries underwent a similar evolution. This decisive choice became apparent in the use of new technical terms to designate the interpretation of myths.

As we have seen,[10] the oldest term to designate the interpretation of myths is *huponoia*, of which we find two occurrences in Plato. This term was to give up its place, in the first century B.C., to the term *allēgoria*, an evolution of which Plutarch was the critical witness:

> Some commentators forcibly distorted these stories through what used to be termed "deeper meanings" (ταῖς πάλαι μὲν ὑπονοίαις), but are nowadays called "allegorical interpretations" (ἀλληγορίαις δὲ νῦν λεγομέναις).[11]

In its narrow sense, allegory designates the stylistic device that makes it possible to express something while appearing to say something else. In its broad sense, allegory is the mode of interpretation consisting in uncovering in a text an allegory in the narrow sense of the term.

In his *Moralia,* Plutarch uses the noun *allēgoria*[12] only once, and the verb *allēgorein*[13] only twice. The terms he prefers are *ainigma, ainigmatōdēs,* and *ainittesthai.* These are derivatives of *ainos,* which is used to refer primarily to words, of stories laden with meaning,[14] an instructive fable,[15] or even a compliment.[16] But something much more important is at play here: from Plato on, *ainigma, ainigmatōdēs,* and *ainittesthai* referred to the mysteries.[17]

Eleusis[18] comes to mind here, for it highlights this aspect. In the *Hymn to Demeter,* dating from the end of the seventh and the beginning of the sixth century B.C., we read that the rites the goddess herself has just revealed are "impossible to transgress, or to pry into, or to divulge: for so great is one's awe of the goddesses that it stops the tongue."[19] The same idea is expressed in the famous description of the Eleusinian plain, which Sophocles included in *Oedipus at Colonus:* "by the torch-lit shore where the divine ladies nurse the august rites for mortals on whose tongues rests the golden key of the attendant sons of Eumolpus."[20] A scholium[21] explains that these verses contain an allusion to the fact that Demeter's mysteries are ineffable (ἄρρητα τὰ μυστήρια), and that they must not be divulged.[22] It might be useful at this point to give some information of the sequence of the Eleusinian mysteries.

Initiation was individual. It was made up of two stages: the preliminaries during the "small mysteries," and the initiation itself in the course of the "great mysteries." The initiate, referred to as *mustēs,* was guided by the *mustagōgos.*

The "small mysteries" were celebrated at the beginning of spring at Athens, more specifically at Agra, on the eastern bank of the Ilissos. These ceremonies brought large crowds together, but we don't know exactly what they were. The "great mysteries" were celebrated in the fall at the end of September and the beginning of October. They lasted ten days. The day preceding the beginning of the ceremonies, sacred objects (*hiera*) were carried from Eleusis to Athens. These sacred objects, kept in the Anaktoron, in the heart of the Telesterion, were carried in baskets in a procession to the Eleusinion, at the foot of the Acropolis.

The first day must have been devoted to the examination of the candidates. On the second, those who had been admitted went to purify themselves in the sea and offered a small pig as sacrifice. Sacrifices were offered on the third day. It seems that the fourth day was a day of rest. On the fifth day, the sacred objects were brought back to Eleusis, where they were placed again in the Anaktoron in the center of the Telesterion. On the sixth day, after the candidates had fasted and had drunk *kykeion,* a "sacred" drink of which nothing is known at present, the initiation itself, called *teletē,* was held.

We are almost certain that the initiation rites included three elements: the *drōmena,* dramatic representations; the *deiknumena,* a display of sacred objects; and the *legomena,* commentaries on the *drōmena.* What were each of these three elements?

The *drōmena* must have been a theatrical representation of Kore's abduction and Demeter's quest to find her daughter. We don't know if the *legomena* consisted of short commentaries on the *drōmena* or of myths featured in the *drōmena.* In any case, they were essential, for the initiation would be voided if the initiate did not understand them. The *deiknumena,* or the displayed sacred objects, played an essential role. The most important priest of the Eleusinian mysteries was the Hierophant, "the one who shows the sacred objects." What could these sacred objects have been? We cannot be certain, but they were probably small Mycenaean relics passed down from one generation to the next in the families of the Eumolpides and the Kerykes, the two families claiming the honor of having first established the mysteries.

On the seventh day, the close of the ceremonies was declared. On the eighth day, libations were offered, and rites in honor of the dead were performed. On the ninth day, everyone returned to Athens, but this time not in a procession. On the tenth day, the Council of the Five Hundred gathered in the Eleusinion of Athens to hear the king archon's report of the ceremonies.

One year after the initiation itself, some initiates were admitted to a higher rank, that of *epopteia.* Some of the sacred objects were then shown to those who wished thus to complete their initiation.

Not much is known about these ceremonies. From the start, secrecy was rigorously maintained. Nevertheless, the little we do know about the Eleusinian mysteries makes it possible to understand how myths and mysteries came to be identified with each other, all the more easily because Plato had used the vocabulary of the mysteries to describe philosophical experience.[23]

The basic idea is that sacred objects could be shown to chosen individuals who had completed a twofold preparation aimed at making them worthy of seeing them: purification and a "learning" that enabled them to grasp the true meaning of "symbols" that referred to a divine drama capable of radically changing the initiates' lives.

In this perspective, myths and mysteries were looked upon as two parallel paths leading human beings to the divine, or, if we start from the other

end of the chain, as two complementary means used by the divinity to reveal truth to religious souls. Myths bring this revelation in an envelope of
legendary dramas, while mysteries present it in the form of ritual enact-
ments. The Homeric myth of Hera and Zeus uniting with each other on
Mount Ida, and the "hierogamic" or "sacred marriages" represented in the
mysteries, offered the same doctrine to the faithful: the myth in an inspired
narrative, the "sacred marriage" in a liturgical production. In spite of essential differences there is a major resemblance between the two forms of revelation in that both saw truth as accessible only to a small number of initiates. Greek authors from Plutarch's[24] time on frequently expressed an idea
that went back much farther: that Homer purposely used the arcana of his
myths to hide the gods' message his narratives brought to human beings.

THE MYSTAGOGIC INTERPRETATION OF MYTHS IN
PLATONISM IN THE FIRST CENTURIES OF THE EMPIRE

The Platonists had the means of reconciling the two interpretive traditions
during the first centuries of the Empire. The *Phaedrus* enabled them, by
means of the concept of madness,[25] to establish a relationship between philosophy on the one hand, and divination, mysteries, and poetry on the
other. In this perspective, philosophy, divination, mysteries, and poetry expressed the same truth, one that stemmed, in this Pythagorean-Platonist
context, from a renewal of truth emanating directly from the gods. And it
is precisely because it came directly from the gods that this truth was transmitted by poets like Homer and Hesiod, and by philosophers like Pythagoras and Plato, in a ciphered form that prevented it from being divulged and
made it exclusive to a very small number of human beings capable of thinking like gods.

Let us look at how this type of interpretation evolved from Philo of
Alexandria to Porphyry, by way of Numenius, Cronius, and Plotinus.

Philo of Alexandria

Philo must have enjoyed high esteem in the Jewish community of Alexandria since he was one of the group of ambassadors sent to Caligula in A.D.
39 to plead the cause of the persecuted Jews of Alexandria.[26] Philo's close relationship with Greek culture and his desire to give Judaism an attractive
representation were so great that he came close to dissolving the specificity
of Moses's revelation by blending it with the Homeric narratives.

Philo practically never wonders in his writings about the theological
foundations of his interpretive practice. Still, *On Providence,* a work that

is attributed to him,[27] contains an explicit mention of the different levels of meaning in Homer and in Hesiod and of their relative importance. The context is a conversation between Philo and his nephew Alexander. Alexander is attacking the idea of providence that Philo is defending. In his attack, Alexander makes a certain number of comments on the obscenity of certain myths told by Homer and by Hesiod. This is Philo's response:

> Don't you know, you lover of wisdom who through your words just accused the whole of mankind of madness, don't you know that things are not the way you say? If the glory of Hesiod and Homer have spread throughout the whole world, it is thanks to the meaning hidden beneath the words. Their many exegetes are filled with admiration for this, and from their time to ours they have not ceased to be an object of admiration. . . . The passages you just mentioned do not contain any blasphemy against the gods, but show the presence of a hidden physical theory of which it is forbidden to reveal the mystery to those whose heads have not been anointed. But I will give you some examples in passing, to the extent that this idea can be illustrated even while respecting the law; because the law forbids explaining these mysteries to those who are not prepared (*siquidem vetat lex mysteria iis qui inhabiles sunt ad mysterium exponere*).
>
> What is told about Hephaistos under the cover of a fable pertains to fire. What is said about Hera pertains to the nature of air. What is said about Hermes pertains to the logos, and so forth with the other gods, according to the method of theology. Thus, it is certain that the poets whom you just accused will receive your praises for having truly and with dignity celebrated the divinity. If you did not admit the rules of allegory and their interpretations, you would be like those children who, in their ignorance, neglect the authentic paintings of Apelles[28] in favor of the effigies struck on coins, admiring that which is derisory and disdaining that which merits unanimous approval.[29]

Philo thus begins by identifying myths with mysteries. This enables him to emphasize the need for an interpretation of myths which alone enables their hidden meaning to be brought to light. The examples Philo gives evoke Stoic interpretation, but the allusion to the mysteries positions his interpretation in a radically different context. Poets are not precursors of Stoicism but are genuine theologians, who have reserved the revelation of truth which has been granted them to a small group of initiates, who alone can receive it.

Yet looking at poets as theologians leads Philo to ask why were those who truly practiced theology—that is, the philosophers—were not also poets.

And why did Empedocles, Parmenides, Xenophanes, and their many students not receive the inspiration of the Muses when they practiced theology? It is, my dear Alexander, because it is not right for a man to be a kind of god, having in himself all the perfections; he must remain a man, a member of the human species, for whom error and faltering are congenital. They finally had to be content with the search for truth, but they were not supposed to strain for something they had not been made for. And it would have been better for them, as it was likewise for philosophy, if they had renounced poetry and oriented themselves toward diatribe and dialogue. That is precisely what the great Plato did: even though he was attracted to poetry, he was not as gifted in it as he wished; so he followed the call of his own nature and wrote down in his dialogues the questions and responses of Socrates as well as the more ancient wisdom of Pythagoras, and these writings, by their elegance and their elevated style, come fairly close to the majesty of poetry. Plato went even so far as to belittle . . . those who write in verse without having any poetic talent.[30]

Here Philo uses the *Phaedrus* not in order to establish a link between poetry and philosophy but to explain why philosophers are not poets.

Yet nothing prevents philosophers from being inspired the way poets are, even if this inspiration takes them in another direction. In any case, Plato is considered the spokesperson of Socrates and especially of Pythagoras, which orients the exegesis of his work in a specific direction: one that unearths "symbols" and "enigmas" so as to interpret them.

The above discussion of Philo of Alexandria is partial in both senses of the term.[31] Its sole aim is to introduce Plutarch's practice of myth interpretation.

Plutarch of Chaeronea

Plutarch was born in Chaeronea, a town in Boeotia, around A.D. 45, during the reign of Claudius. When about twenty, he went to Athens, then to Alexandria. Upon his return to Chaeronea he was entrusted by his fellow citizens with various missions, first to Corinth, then to Rome toward the end of Vespasian's reign. He remained in Rome from 69 to 79. After a new stay in Rome and in Italy during the reign of Domitian (81–96), he returned definitively to Chaeronea around 90. Plutarch became the eponymous archon of Chaeronea and Boeotarch, and then, in addition, priest of Apollo at Delphi. The Pythian sanctuary was only at one day's travel on horseback or muleback across Parnassus. At Delphi, Plutarch took on additional positions: that of "epimelete" of the Amphictyonic council as well as that of agonothetes. In the meanwhile he also wrote his *Lives* and his *Moralia*. He died around 126.[32]

Plutarch notes with satisfaction, in his dialogue *The Oracles at Delphi*, the changes in the Pythia's modus operandi that occurred while he was priest of Apollo at Delphi. The Pythia no longer expressed herself in imagery and adopted a clear language, directly accessible to all, thus rendering useless the interpretation of her words by the priests assisting her.[33] This change in the Pythia's language corresponded to a change in the public's taste.[34] Moreover, the giving up of poetic obscurity also occurred outside the domain of divination in history and philosophy as both these fields turned away from the attraction of myth and toward a more didactic mode of expression.[35] As a known opponent of Stoicism, Plutarch could only rejoice at this trend and mock those who regretted the abandonment of the previous practices.[36] Nonetheless, Plutarch did recognize that everything was not negative in allegorical divination.[37]

Principles of Myth Interpretation

Plutarch's attitude towards the allegorical interpretation of myths reflected a similar ambivalence. Heatedly rejecting the Stoic exegesis of the historical and physical type,[38] he practiced an exegesis of the metaphysical and mysterial type, which he applied to daemonology and Platonic dualism. He can therefore be considered as representing a transition between the Stoic type of allegory and the Neoplatonic type of allegory.[39]

Plutarch was aware of the originality of his stance. As we have seen above, this originality was already apparent in his comments on the changing vocabulary used by the Delphic oracles. He rejected the terms *huponoia* and *allēgoria,* preferring the terms *ainigma, ainigmatōdēs,* and *ainittesthai* to define his position on myth interpretation, for all myths, including those of non-Greek peoples.

Such a stance was based on the following postulate. Secrecy is an ever present requirement in religious as well as in philosophical matters. As the most famous Greeks had been witness, secrecy was practiced in Egypt, a land that could be looked upon as the source of all civilization. Pythagoras was one of those Greek thinkers, and he even introduced this practice in philosophy:

> Great was the concern of the Egyptians for secrecy in religion. This is attested
> by the wisest of the Greeks, Solon, Thales, Plato, Eudoxus, and Pythagoras, and
> Lycurgus as well, according to some; they came to Egypt and were in touch with
> the priests. . . . Pythagoras in particular enjoyed a state of mutual admiration
> with these people, imitated their symbolism and mysterial ways by incorporat-

ing enigmas in his doctrine (ἀπεμιμήσατο τὸ συμβολικὸν αὐτῶν καὶ μυστηριῶδες ἀναμείξας αἰνίγμασι τὰ δόγματα).[40]

Thus, if myths are ciphered, knowledge is needed to decipher them.[41]

Myths can be deciphered only on condition that an interpretative practice of the Stoic type is rejected at the outset.

> Thus, whenever you hear the myths told by the Egyptians about the gods, those, for instance, which tell of their wanderings, mutilations, and many other such tales, you should remember what was said above and not think that any of these things is said to have actually happened so or to have been enacted so.[42] . . . If you hear the matters pertaining to the gods in this way, receiving the myth from those who interpret it reverently and philosophically (παρὰ τῶν ἐξηγουμένων τὸν μῦθον ὁσίως καὶ φιλοσόφως),[43] and if you perform and observe constantly the accepted rites, considering that nothing is more pleasing to the gods, whether sacrifice or ritual enactment, than the true belief about them, thus you will avoid superstition, which is no less an evil than atheism.[44]

For Plutarch, an allegorical interpretation of myths, inspired by Euhemerus among others, led directly to atheism and superstition. Hence it was contrary to piety and philosophy.

An interpretation that assimilated myths to mysteries had to be preferred over the allegorical type of interpretation. In Plutarch's case, this theoretical position was backed by a matching religious practice, since he and his wife had been initiated into the mysteries of Dionysos:

> [You hear][45] the statement of that other set of people who win many to their way of thinking when they say that nothing is in any way evil or painful to what has undergone dissolution. But you are kept from believing them by the teaching of our fathers and by the mystic symbols of the Dionysiac rites (καὶ τὰ μυστικὰ σύμβολα τῶν περὶ τὸν Διόνυσον ὀργιασμῶν), the knowledge of which we who are initiates share with each other.[46]

In *De Iside and Osiride,* which will be discussed below, Plutarch addresses himself to Clea, a "Thyiad," that is, a priestess of Dionysos, herself initiated into the Osirian mysteries.[47]

An Example: *De Iside et Osiride*[48]

As its title indicates, *De Iside et Osiride* deals essentially with the Egyptian myth of Isis and Osiris, which Plutarch interprets in the "mysterial" sense by relating it to some Greek myths: those in Hesiod's *Theogony;* the story of the birth of Eros in Plato's *Symposium;* that of the dismemberment of Dionysos in Orphism; and particularly the "incredible myth" that makes up Plato's *Timaeus,* the cornerstone of Plutarch's whole construction.

Plutarch narrates the Egyptian myth[49] at length and establishes systematic correspondences between the names of the Egyptian and the Greek divinities.

Rhea (= Nout) secretly couples with Kronos (= Geb). Five divinities are born from this union: Osiris; Aroueris (whom some consider as Apollo); Typhon (= Seth), who from the time of his birth, which happened on an ill-omened day, manifested his violent and malevolent character; Isis, who was to become Osiris's spouse; and Nephthys, who, along with Seth her husband, forms a symmetrical and antithetical couple to the Isis/Osiris couple.

Osiris succeeds his father Geb on the throne of the two Egypts. He thus becomes the main benefactor of humankind, bringing civilization to it. Isis appears to be the ideal queen, the worthy female replicate of the beneficent god. In the course of a feast, Seth, with the help of accomplices, succeeds in locking up Osiris in a chest, which is thrown into the Nile and carried toward the sea. Osiris's death leads to great mourning, especially for Isis, who sets out in search of Osiris's body. She finds the chest in Byblos, puts the chest-coffin on a ship, and brings it back. In the first deserted place she comes across, and after making sure she is completely alone, Isis opens the chest, presses her face to Osiris's, and embraces his body, weeping.

Horus was to be born from this union. An omission in Plutarch's text obliges us to reconstitute the narrative from other sources. Seth discovers Osiris's body and splits it in pieces, which he disperses. Isis, however, manages to reconstitute Osiris's body except for his penis, which had been thrown into the river and immediately devoured by fish. She replaces it with a fake one.

The last part of the myth tells how Osiris was avenged by his son Horus, who confronted Seth several times and definitely vanquished him in a fight held in the context of a judicial trial. Once Horus's victory was certain, Osiris avenged, and his eternity assured, Isis wanted to perpetuate the means she had used to save Osiris and Horus in order to help humankind. This is the origin of the Osirian initiation and mysteries, which Plutarch relates to the mysteries of Dionysus.

In Hesiod's framework, Isis corresponds to the Earth (= Demeter), Osiris to Love (= Eros), and Typhon to Tartarus.[50]

In addition, according to Plutarch, this myth evokes the story of the birth of Eros as rendered by Socrates through Diotima's words in the *Sym-*

posium.[51] Poverty (Penia = Isis), who wants children, lies down next to Wealth (Poros = Osiris). Eros is born of this union.[52]

Clea, however, whom Plutarch addresses in *De Iside et Osiride,* is no more able than is Plutarch to overlook the notion that Dionysos and Osiris are one and the same. The myth of Dionysos put to death and dismembered by the Titans occupied a central place in Orphism. According to Plutarch, this was the most remarkable similarity between the fates of Dionysos and Osiris: "Further, what is told about the Titans and the Nyktelies[53] [Night festivals] agrees with the rites 'of dismemberment,' 'the resurrection,' and 'new life of Osiris.'"[54] This is a key allusion in spite of its cryptic aspect.

But it is the *Timaeus* that provides the philosophical framework in which all these elements are given a place, and we need to remember that Plato himself describes the *Timaeus* as *eikōs muthos*[55] and that Plutarch does not hesitate to interpret myth in a very narrative manner. Plutarch establishes a clear distinction between a transcendent divinity and totally indeterminate matter. Because of this, he accounts for chaos and the irregularity of the movement that permeates corporeal nature by hypothesizing existence of a world soul, which was at first irrational but was then, as far as possible, set in order by the demiurgic intelligence.[56]

After narrating the myth of Osiris and seeking to establish its connections with as many mythic Greek and barbarian elements as possible, Plutarch recognizes the necessity of deciphering it and then resorts to a comparison that is not without beauty:

> You know yourself [Clea] that all this [the narrative that has just been told] does not at all resemble the flimsy and inconsistent stories that are carried by myths (μυθεύμασι ἀραιοῖς καὶ διακένοις πλάσμασιν) and that poets and prose writers (ποιηταὶ καὶ λογογράφοι) weave and spread out before us, like spiders creating from themselves arbitrary notions, but rather it takes into account troubles and passions, that you [Clea] would be the first to admit. Just as scientists tell us that the rainbow is an image of the sun made brilliant by the refraction of its appearance into a cloud, so the present myth is the image of a reality which refracts our mind toward realities belonging to another realm.[57]

The very absurdity of certain mythic details shows the need to uncover their deeper meaning. This is worthwhile because, unlike other myths, the myth of Osiris is not pure fiction. It reflects a *logos* that is objectively true.[58] Yet like all myths, this one leads to the truth indirectly, through alternate paths, just as in the case of the rainbow the eye reaches the sun only through re-

fraction. Myth thus can lead into error, which is why it needs to be interpreted or to be deciphered according to well-defined rules.

Plutarch lists five methods of deciphering.

1. *Realist* (or Euhemerist). Plutarch[59] first proposes a clear and precise
definition, which he illustrates with the help of several examples. Then he
refutes it, but without giving many arguments. The Euhemerist mistake
essentially consists in accepting an inadmissible consequence, namely, that
the gods are human.[60]

2. *Daemonological.*[61] Plutarch accepts this method[62] and relates it to the
totality of philosophical trends of which he is aware.

> Better, therefore, is the view of those who take the stories about Typhon, Osiris,
> and Isis to be the experiences neither of gods nor of men but of great daemons.
> These are said by Plato, Pythagoras, Xenocrates and Chrysippus, following the
> early theologians, to be stronger than men and in power to surpass greatly our
> nature, although they do not possess the divine element in a pure and unadul-
> terated form, but joined in one with the nature of the soul and the perception
> of the body. This perception is susceptible to pleasure and pain and to whatever
> experiences are inherent in changes, experiences which disturb some more than
> others; for daemons, like men, vary in virtue and vice.[63]

We are here at the heart of Plutarch's religious thought in which daemonology plays such an important role. Daemonology had several elements
in its favor.

(a) It made it possible to reconcile traditional polytheism with the increasingly pressing needs of monotheism, the ancient gods becoming daemons under the authority of a supreme god.

(b) It made it possible to explain those rites and myths offensive to
morality and religious feelings. Gods were washed clean of all those indig-
nities by attributing them to daemons who had received the name of a god
and were dependent on that god. These daemons were the ones really
responsible for struggles, adulteries, and metamorphoses wrongly attributed to gods, since with daemons the divine principle is neither pure nor
without admixture. These intermediary beings do experience passions as
they partake at once of the spiritual nature of the soul and of the sensible
faculties of bodies. This introduces a disturbance, which explains why vices
and virtues exist in daemons.[64] So they bear the punishment for their sins
of commission or omission and undergo successive purification.[65]

(c) Finally, daemonology provided an explanation for divination.

3. *Physical.*[66] This is the type of interpretation that should be called "al-

legorical" inasmuch as it corresponds fully to Stoic practice. Plutarch distinguishes three main currents that fit under this label.

(a) Geographical and meteorological. Osiris is the Nile, Isis is the valley of the Nile, and Typhon is the sea.[67]

(b) Physical (in the narrow sense of the term). Osiris is the principle of humidity; Isis is that of the earth thirsting for water; and Typhon is that of everything arid or dry, everything opposed to humidity.[68]

(c) Astronomical. Typhon is the solar world; Osiris is the lunar world; and Isis is the terrestrial world, though she can also be identified with Sirius.[69]

Plutarch rejects all of these Stoic interpretations for two reasons. Without denying the relationship between the gods and geographical, physical, and even astronomical realities, Plutarch believes this relationship is not equivalent to identifying one with the other but must be understood as implying a metonymy, in the way one can say "acting Menander" or "buying Plato."[70] Moreover, the identification of the gods with the type of realities listed by Plutarch leads straight to superstition.[71]

4. *Dualist.* Plutarch, who spontaneously locates the origin of dualism with the Chaldeans, links it with the exegesis of the *Timaeus.* The cosmological scheme that Plutarch uncovers in the Osiris myth is binary. It is explained by the antagonism between the opposite forces in the world's soul. The second scheme is triadic, in which the principle of evil does not appear as a constitutive force but only as a recurring,[72] adverse one. Let us look at both these schemes.

(a) The binary scheme. Plutarch reminds his readers of Plato's thought on the origin and constitution of the universe. He briefly discusses the opposition and the complementarity of the Same and the Other described in the *Timaeus* (35 a–b) and insists on a certain interpretation of a passage in book X of *Laws,* in which Plato described the world as moved by two souls: one being the source of good, the other the source of evil, even while admitting the existence of a third, intermediary nature, dependent on the gods but tending to follow, desire, and pursue the better of the other two.[73]

(b) The triadic scheme. The binary scheme does not exhaust cosmic reality and, furthermore, fails to fully account for it. Taking a text from the *Timaeus* (49e–50a) that takes these three elements into account, Plutarch adapts it to the Osirian triad: "Plato," he writes, "is wont to call what is intelligible 'form,' 'model,' or 'father'; and to call matter 'mother,' 'nurse,' 'seat' or 'place of generation'; while the fruit of both he calls "descendance' and 'becoming.'"[74] Plutarch attempts to base these relationships on etymological considerations.[75]

This, ultimately, is what Plutarch is driving at. Even if the myth of Osiris can leave us perplexed, even if it shocks us, it does contain a profound truth. Yet it does not convey this truth directly, which is why the Egyptian narrative has to be deciphered. Of course, the Stoics propose a method of deciphering that assimilates the gods to human beings or that identifies them with geographical, physical, and astronomic phenomena. But this method must be rejected since its first current leads to atheism and superstition, while the second confuses metonymy with synonymy. So what method should be used? It should be the one that looks upon myths as "symbols," as "enigmas"—a formulation both ambiguous and obscure, allowing for a double level of interpretation to be applied to profound doctrines that would be impossible to express adequately and must not be divulged to all comers.

Such a conception of myths and even of the rites based on them sends us back not only to the mysteries, those of Eleusis, of course, and of Dionysos, but also to (neo-)Pythagoreanism, whose oral doctrines were described as "symbols" and in which secrecy played an important role. This kind of Pythagoreanism corresponded to a certain form of Platonism.

The point of departure of Plutarch's thought is thus the totality of the myths and rites established by tradition, particularly in their unexpected and paradoxical aspects. The variety of religious customs should orient the philosopher's gaze toward the pure light of knowledge,[76] while those who are not philosophers remain at the level of appearances,[77] but appearances which, if properly interpreted, let the truth shine through.[78] These appearances, varying from one people to another,[79] constitute the first stage toward knowledge. Let us reread what Plutarch has to say about the sphinx of the Egyptians:

A king chosen from among the warriors instantly became a priest and shared in the philosophy which is hidden for the most part in myths and stories that show dim reflections and insights of the truth, as the Egyptians themselves suggest when they place sphinxes at the entrances of shrines: places well chosen to mesh with the idea they have of their theology as containing an enigmatic wisdom (αἰνιγματώδη σοφίαν).[80]

In order to be initiated to "enigmatic wisdom," philosophical reasoning must be used as a mystagogue.[81] All initiations involve the death of a former life and rebirth to a new one. This is true of philosophy, which involves a kind of death in the realm of opinion and, thanks to reason, a rebirth in that of the immaterial. From this viewpoint, initiation and philosophy enable us to transcend appearances and to reach the true reality of which myths speak, this at times under disconcerting surfaces. Furthermore, philosophers such as Plato and Aristotle have become actual "epopts."

> Thus Plato and Aristotle call this branch of philosophy "epoptic" because those who escape from the domain of opinion, of mixtures, and of variety, to spring up toward the primordial, the indivisible, and the immaterial by making total contact with the pure truth belonging to that domain, have the impression of possessing, just as at the close of an initiation, the supreme achievement of philosophy (ἐν τελετῇ τέλος ἔχειν φιλοσοφίας νομίζουσι).[82]

It is surprising that Plutarch invokes Aristotle at this point, for the reference to epoptic corresponds perfectly to Plato's description of the contemplation of truth in the *Symposium,* the *Phaedrus,* and even the *Seventh Letter.*

Numenius and Cronius

The systematization of the point of view discussed above seems to have been undertaken by Numenius, a (neo-)Pythagorean philosopher thought to have lived in the second half of the second century A.D., a date deduced from a hypothesis pertaining to his associate disciple (*hetairos*).[83] We know next to nothing about this person, except that he had some sort of link with Apamea in Syria.[84]

Numenius's work is lost, except for sixty fragments[85] transmitted by various authors ranging from Clement of Alexandria (A.D. 150?–215?) to John Lydus (sixth century A.D.). But the only transmitter of the allegorical interpretation of Homer proposed by Numenius and by Cronius was Porphyry in his the *Cave of the Nymphs.* In his work on *On the Good,* Numenius wrote:

> With respect to this matter [the problem of God], after citing Plato's account and using it as his seal (σημηνάμενον), he will have to go back further and link it with Pythagoras's teachings, then call upon peoples of renown, comparing their initiations, dogmas, and cultural foundations inasmuch as they agree with Plato, and all that was established by the Brahmins, the Hebrews, the Magi, and the Egyptians.[86]

Numenius's point of reference was Plato, but a Plato inseparable from Pythagoras. Moreover, Numenius did not limit himself to the Greeks, for he established connections between the doctrines of Plato and Pythagoras on the one hand and Indian, Jewish, Persian, and Egyptian wisdom on the other.

Numenius interpreted all of these doctrines so as to bring out their figurative meaning. Following Origenes, he wrote,

> The Pythagorean Numenius, who . . . in the first book of his treatise *On the Good* also mentions, among the nations that believed God was incorporeal, the Hebrews, not scrupling to quote the expressions of the prophets, and expounding them figuratively (χρήσασθαι καὶ λόγοις προφητικοῖς καὶ τροπολογῆσαι αὐτούς).[87]

A passage in Porphyry's *Cave of the Nymphs* yields more details on the nature of this interpretative practice:

> In the stricter sense it is the powers presiding over waters that we call naiad nymphs, but they [the Pythagoreans] also give this name generally (κοινῶς) to all the souls in general descending into genesis. For they thought that the souls sojourn in the water, which is divinely animated, as Numenius says; in support of this he cites the words of the prophet, "the spirit of God was borne upon the waters" [Genesis 1:2]; the Egyptians as well, he says in this connection, represent their divinities as standing not on solid ground but on a boat; this applies to the Sun and, in short, to all the deities. We must understand that these represent souls hovering over moisture, i.e. those souls descending to genesis. And he quotes Heraclitus as saying, "It is a delight, not death, for souls to become moist," meaning that the descent into genesis is a pleasure for them [DK 22 B 77]; and, in another place, "we live their death, they live our death [DK 22 B 62]." And he believes that this is the reason why Homer calls those in genesis "wet" [*Odyssey* VI 62], because they have their souls "moist." Blood and moist seed are dear to human souls just as the souls of plants are nourished by water.[88]

This account well illustrates how Numenius used a passage from Genesis, which he associated with Egyptian iconography on the basis of citations from Heraclitus to justify the name the Pythagoreans gave to the souls in the process of descending into the generation. This meant they descended into the sensible world, identified with humidity, an identification probably inspired by the like statement from *Politics* 273d–e. In order to bring out the figurative sense of "nymphs" and to go back to the true meaning of the word, a long work of interpretation involving several successive stages thus proves to be necessary.

Moreover, Numenius is thought to have written a work titled *On Plato's Secrets* (Περὶ τῶν παρὰ Πλατῶνι ἀπορρήτων). This title refers directly to an interpretation that identifies Plato with Pythagoras and holds that Plato bestowed his doctrine to only a small number of initiates. But why would Plato have refused to divulge his doctrine? Here is Numenius's answer, which evokes *Euthyphro:*

> If Plato had undertaken to write about the theology of the Athenians, and then in bitterness had accused it of containing mutual discords of the divinities, and their incests, and devouring of their own children, and of deeds of vengeance of fathers and brothers—if Plato had brought up all this in open and unreserved accusations, then according to my opinion he would have given them an occasion to commit another wrong, and to kill him, like Socrates.
>
> Now [Plato] did not indeed desire to retain life more than to tell the truth; but as he saw that he might live in security, and also tell the truth, so he represented the Athenians under the form of Euthyphro, a boastful and foolish man, who spoke about the divinities as badly as anybody else; but his own teachings he laid into the mouth of Socrates, whom he represented in his genuine form, as he was wont to confute every person with whom he associated.[89]

We can speculate that Numenius' work consisted of a series of commentaries on problematic passages from Plato. The practice of commentaries was the one preferred by the interpreters of Homer, who approached the *Iliad* and the *Odyssey* by attempting to answer a series of questions and problems.

If that was the case, the commentary on the myth of Er in the *Republic,* which would itself have served as framework of reference to the commentary on book XXIV of the *Odyssey,* would also have belonged to this particular work of Numenius. And we need to link to it the type of interpretation proposed by Numenius for the first part of the *Timaeus,* whereby the struggle of the ancient Athenians against the Atlantians represented the struggle between a superior group of souls associated with Athena and another group of souls concerned with generation.[90]

Basically, Numenius seems to have set out to show the agreement between Homer and Plato,[91] particularly on the fate of souls after death. To that aim, he attempted to understand both the myth of Er at the end of the *Republic* and the famous passage on the cave of the nymphs in the *Odyssey.*[92] The argument that winds its way from Plato through astrology (= the Magi), the mysteries, and Homer, ending up with Pythagoras, and the emphasis on the harmony of the doctrines, conforms to the general orientation of the fragment.

It is highly unlikely that Numenius proposed an exegesis of all of Homer's works. But he seems to have been the first to clearly express the following idea: a unique, absolute, immutable truth was revealed,[93] then transmitted in Greece by various figures—Homer, Pythagoras, Plato—and even elsewhere in Egypt, and among the Persians and the Jews. This truth that comes directly from the gods must thus be reserved to a small number by secrecy as it is in the mysteries.

Plotinus

The influence of Numenius and Cronius was decisive for Plotinus,[94] and his school as evidenced in Porphyry's *Life of Plotinus:* (1) Amelius, who was Plotinus's most dedicated disciple and, it seems, his assistant, had collected and recopied all of Numenius's writings as well as memorized most of them.[95] (2) The works of Numenius and Cronius were read by participants in the meetings held at the school.[96] Plotinus was even accused of plagiarizing Numenius.[97] (3) Amelius wrote a book in the defense of Plotinus titled *The Difference between the Doctrines of Plotinus and Numenius*[98] (4) As for Longinus, in his preface to his book *On the End,* he claims that Plotinus gave a clearer exposition of the principles of Pythagoras and Plato than his predecessors had done, including Numenius.[99] In this context, it would not have been surprising if the influence of Numenius and of Cronius on Plotinus also included the domain of myth interpretation.

Theory of Myth

We take for granted that there are realities existing outside of time and that time is consubstantial with the sensible world. This unavoidably brings up the following question. How can we express realities alien to time by means of an instrument belonging to the sensible world, that is, language made up of phonic or graphic traces succeeding each other in time? Poets, who had to talk about the gods whose origin and adventures lay outside of time, had to deal with a similar quandary. This is why Plotinus called upon the type of discourse emphasizing their specificity, that of preinterpreted myths.

Plotinus compiles a very lucid list of the advantages and disadvantages of myth as an inadequate yet necessary expression of the nontemporal truth it aims to invoke. As a narrative unfolding in time, myth describes as successive realities that are really simultaneous and only differ hierarchically: "Myths, if they are to serve their purpose, must necessarily import time distinctions into their subject and will often present as separate entities powers that exist in unity but differ in rank and faculty."[100] In other words, myth translates the synchrony of a system into the diachrony of a narrative. According to Plotinus, Plato gave an excellent example of this in *Timaeus*.[101]

Yet why should we have recourse to myth rather than be satisfied with a systematic exposition? Because myth is an instrument of teaching and analysis, for it separates in time those beings that exist simultaneously.

> But we have to think that if we conceive of this soul as entering a body and animating it, it is with the goal of teaching and to bring light to our thought (διδασκαλίας καὶ τοῦ σαφοῦς χάριν); because, at no time was this universe without a soul; at no time has its body existed in the absence of a soul; and there has never been matter deprived of order; but it is possible to conceive these terms, the soul and the body, matter and order, by separating one from the other in thought; it is possible to isolate the elements of all composites through thought and reflection (τῷ λόγῳ καὶ τῇ διανοίᾳ).[102]

And then one must also be able to reconstitute the unity that made it possible to analyze the myth in the first place.[103]

In short, Plotinus recognizes the analytical and didactic value of myth that makes it possible to express, in a narrative accessible to all, truths existing outside of time. This is because the philosopher experiences many difficulties in transmitting these truths through language, which is a means of transmission dependent on time. With this view, Plotinus remains faithful to Plato.

The Interpretation of Myths

But while Plato tended to reserve the use of myth to describe the nature of the soul and its peregrinations, Plotinus was to extend it to the exposition of the whole of his system.

The system as a whole. For Plotinus, the most important mythic theme in this domain is without doubt that of the three great gods of Hesiod's theogony: Ouranos, Kronos, and Zeus.[104] Plato rejects this myth with the following words:

> SOCRATES: There is, first of all, I said, the greatest lie about the most important of beings in telling most improperly how Ouranos did what Hesiod says he did to Kronos, and how Kronos in turn took his revenge, and then there are the doings and sufferings of Kronos at the hands of his son. Even if they were true I should not think that they ought to be lightly told, as is done, to persons deprived of reason, that is to children. It is best to bury them in silence (ἀλλὰ μάλιστα μὲν σιγᾶσθαι), or, if it is necessary to talk about them, only a very small audience should be admitted under pledge of secrecy (εἰ δὲ ἀνάγκη τις ἦν

λέγειν, δι' ἀπορρήτων ἀκούειν ὡς ὀλιγίστους), and after sacrificing, not a pig, but some huge and unprocurable victim, to the end that as few as possible would have heard these tales.

ADIMANTUS: Why, yes, . . . such stories are hard sayings.

SOCRATES: Yes, and they are not to be told, Adimantus, in our city, nor are they to be said in the hearing of a young man that in doing the utmost wrong he would do nothing to surprise anybody, nor again in punishing his father's wrongdoings to the limit, but would only be following the example of the first and greatest of the gods.[105]

It is hard to not interpret this passage as a total condemnation of the myths narrated by Hesiod as well as a matching radical refusal of all their allegorical interpretations. And yet it contains an allusion to the mysteries.[106] In spite of its definitely ironical and exaggerated tone, which could only express rejection, it was to be taken literally by a certain number of Platonists who wanted to include myth as part of philosophical initiation. This is probably what Numenius meant when he labeled his three gods respectively as "grandfather," "father," and "son."[107] Harpocration, a disciple of Atticus, claimed there were two demiurges and called the first "Ouranos and Kronos" and the second "Zeus and Zen." With Plotinus, this issue became quite clear. Plotinus saw in Ouranos, Kronos, and Zeus a mythical transposition of the three main hypostases of his system.[108] There is no doubt that Ouranos represents the One, but this correspondence was more assumed than explicitly developed.[109]

In contrast, the correspondence between Kronos and the intellect[110] is the object of several discussions in the fifth *Ennead.* The name of the god himself is given an etymological justification on the basis of the *Cratylus* (396b). Plotinus interprets the name of the god on the basis of the expression *koron nou,* in which the first word is taken not in the sense of "sharpness, clarity" but rather in that of "satiation."[111] This interpretation makes use of most of the details of the narrative. The fact that the intelligibles cannot be found outside of the intellect is illustrated by Kronos, fearing the prediction of Ouranos and Gaia, devouring his children as they are born. On this point, Plotinus assimilates myths with mysteries through the intermediary of the notion of "enigma:"

And [the Intellect] still remains pregnant with this offspring; for it has, so to speak, drawn all within itself again, holding them lest they fall away towards Matter to be brought up in the House of Rhea (in the realm of flux). This is the meaning hidden in the Mysteries, and in the Myths of the gods; Kronos, as the wisest of the gods before the birth of Zeus, absorbs his offspring and, full within himself, is the Intellectual-Principle in its plenty.[112]

Kronos is put in chains by Zeus because the Intellect cannot be dissociated from the Intelligible; thus Kronos mutilates his father Ouranos to show that the One remains in itself, separated from the intellect, to which it has transmitted its generating function.[113]

Thanks to Rhea's stratagem, Zeus, the last of the sons of Kronos, escapes from his father. This detail must be understood as follows: The intellect, satiated with the intelligibles, engenders the soul, which, like a last-born child, is charged with transmitting to the outside an image of his father and of those of his siblings remaining with their father.[114] As the soul hypostasis, Zeus can be assimilated to the demiurge who sets the universe in order and guides it.[115] By extension, however, he can be assimilated to the soul of the world,[116] and even to human souls.[117]

It is possible to descend further down the ladder of realities. Indeed the *Enneads* makes a brief reference to Dionysos's mirror:

> The souls of men, seeing their images in the mirror as Dionysus saw his, have entered into that realm in a leap downward from the Supreme: yet even they are not cut off from their origin, from their principle and the divine Intellect."[118]

We recognize here an allusion to the Orphic myth of the "passion" of Dionysos. As the son of Zeus, Dionysos received the kingship from his father. Hera, who could not stand this, tricked his guardians, the Kouretes, attracted the child with toys, including a mirror, and then had the Titans kill him. The Titans cut up the body in seven pieces, which they cooked and ate. But Dionysos's heart was saved by Athena, who brought it to Zeus, who managed to resuscitate his son. Plotinus interprets this myth on two levels: that of the soul of man and that of the soul of the world. As he himself specifies, myth pertains to the descent of human souls into generation, the mirror being an illustration of matter. Indeed, the situation is not very different for the universal soul, so that Plotinus's interpretation of the dismemberment of Dionysos was both metaphysical and anthropological, as it was to be in latter Neoplatonism. The soul of the world, cut up into seven pieces by the demiurge to make the circles on which the seven planets are traveling, is Dionysos, whose body is cut up in seven pieces, one for each of the Titans; and his heart is the intellect of the world soul, corresponding to the circle of the fixed stars.[119]

Finally, according to Plotinus, Cybele, the "Great Mother," as sterile as

the eunuchs of her entourage, personifies inert matter, while the ithyphallic Hermes represent intelligible reason, generator of the sensible world:

> This, I think, is what the doctors of old mean to say in enigmas as in the mys-
> teries and the initiations (μυστικῶς καὶ ἐν τελεταῖς αἰνιττόμενοι), by represent-
> ing a mature Hermes with the generative organ always in active posture. They
> want to convey that the generator of sensible things is intelligible reason; the
> sterility of matter, eternally unmoved, is indicated by the eunuchs surrounding
> the "Mother-of-all-things," a title they give her because they see this principle
> as the substrate but they give her this name so as to clearly show that she is not
> like a mother in all respects when the question is treated exactly rather than su-
> perficially. They indicate from afar, but as much as they could, that this "uni-
> versal Mother" was sterile and was not a woman in absolute terms. She is female
> in receptivity only, not in pregnancy. This is shown by the "universal Mother's"
> escort made up of beings that are neither female nor capable of engendering as
> they have lost through castration the power of engendering which belongs only
> to the being whose virility is intact.[120]

In the last chapter of the treatise *On the Impassivity of the Bodiless,* Plotinus,
relying on the passage in *Timaeus* (51a 4–5) where the receptacle is given the
name of "Mother," identifies matter with Cybele, whom he considers the
"Mother of the gods," and he introduces this exegesis by using the words
"mysteries" and "enigmas."

Cybele was the great goddess of Phrygia. She was often called "Mother
of the gods" or the "Great Mother." Her power encompassed the whole of
nature, and she personified the force of its vegetation. She was honored in
the mountains of Asia Minor, and from there her cult spread all over the
Greek world, then the Roman world when in 203 B.C. the Roman senate de-
cided to have the "black stone" that symbolized the goddess brought from
Pessinous and to build her a temple on the Palatine. The mythographer often looked upon Cybele as a simple incarnation, or even as a simple "appel-
lation" of Rhea,[121] the mother of Zeus and of the other gods, the sons of
Kronos. Nevertheless, Plotinus feels compelled to show that this name and
this interpretation in no way imply the fecundity of matter by evoking the
eunuchs surrounding the "Great Mother." The interpretation Plotinus proposed for the eunuchs who make up Cybele's retinue had no parallel;[122] it
was so original and fit so well with the thesis he wanted to illustrate that it
very well might have been his own ad hoc invention.

Fecundity is attributed to Hermes, depicted as mature and ithyphallic.
Porphyry and Cornutus give us information on the representation evoked

by Plotinus and on its meaning. Porphyry wrote: "The word, universal creator and interpreter (τοῦ λόγου τοῦ πάντων ποιητικοῦ τε καὶ ἑρμηνευτικοῦ), is represented by Hermes. Hermes in a state of erection (ὁ Ἑρμῆς παραστατικός) represents tension and also designates fecund rational power (σπερματικὸν λόγον) penetrating everything."[123] This last sentence is clarified by a passage from Cornutus: "The ancients represented Hermes bearded in his maturity and in a state of erection to show that, in older people, the mind is fecund and in a state of perfection."[124] Thanks to this double assimilation, Plotinus thus succeeds in expressing his metaphysical system with the help of various myths.

The domain of the soul. The domain where myths constantly play a role is that of the soul in general. And, as if by chance, the best example is the myth of the birth of Eros as told by Socrates in Plato's *Symposium.* Plotinus gave several different interpretations of this famous myth. At times he produced an exegesis akin to that provided by Plutarch.[125]

In the treatise *On Love* (Περὶ ἔρωτος), which is almost entirely devoted to the myth of the birth of Eros, Plotinus starts out by mentioning the differences in Plato regarding the genealogy of Eros. In the *Phaedrus* (242d–e), Plato makes him the son of Aphrodite; but in the *Symposium* (203c) he has him born of Poros and Penia. The reason for this duality is that there are two Aphrodites (*Symposium* 180d–e). One is Celestial Aphrodite, the daughter of Ouranos or of Kronos who stands for intelligence; she is thus the hypostasis soul, which, uniting with Kronos in uninterrupted contemplation, gives birth to Eros, that is, to the higher soul.[126] The other Aphrodite, born of Zeus and Dione, represents the soul of the sensible world; she engenders another Eros, who is her vision. Internal to the world, this Eros presides over marriages and helps those souls that are well disposed to remember the intelligibles.[127] Finally, as each individual soul, even that of animals, is an Aphrodite, it engenders its particular Eros, which corresponds to its nature and merit. Whence three types of Eros: a universal Eros, a cosmic Eros, and a plurality of individual Eroses. The first is a god, while the other two are daemons.[128]

Finally, in treatise VI 9 [9], Plotinus associates another myth to that of the birth of Eros: that of the love of Eros and Psyche. Psyche is of course the soul, and its intimacy with Eros is the sign that its nature partakes of the love of the One-Good.[129]

In contrast to the Stoics, Plotinus was not looking for a one-on-one correspondence between mythical characters and philosophical realities. He accepted the existence of a plurality of representations of the same mythical character, which led him to weave a complex network of relations between this character and the elements of his philosophical system. This stance could be explained by a radical change in philosophical perspective. While the Stoics wanted to find their own doctrine of the divinity of the sensible world in the poets they were citing, Plotinus considered poetry a different mode of exposition of a same truth, a mode belonging to a different world and a truth transmitted directly by the gods. Only philosophy could come close to it because philosophy refers to an intelligible reality that has its source in the One and of which sensible reality is only an image. In this perspective, the interpretation of myths is aimed not at confirming a system but at demonstrating the existence of a concordance between diachronic description (myth) and systematic exposition (the philosophical system) of one same reality, which is located outside of the time that itself rules over sensible reality.

On several other occasions Plotinus returned to myth, not through the intermediary of Plato as he did elsewhere, but directly from Homer and Hesiod.

Plotinus evoked the Fates when writing about the external determinants that can condition our freedom.[130] The One is represented by Apollo, whose name points to the absence of any multiplicity.[131] The vegetative soul of the earth is represented by Hestia and Demeter.[132] Plotinus takes liberties with tradition when he evokes the myth of Prometheus and Pandora. According to Plotinus, Pandora, who represents the arrival of the soul in the sensible world, is fashioned by Prometheus. The gifts given to Pandora by the gods are gifts that the soul receives from the intelligence it is leaving; but the soul must prefer the donor, intelligence, to the gifts themselves, and this indicated by Prometheus's refusal. Prometheus stands for Providence. He is put in chains by Zeus because Providence is linked to the work of Zeus by an external bond, which is severed[133] by the power of freedom personified by Heracles.[134] In the evocation of the dead described in book XI of the *Odyssey,* one of the shadows evoked by Odysseus is Heracles. Yet Homer takes care to specify that only an image of Heracles is in Hades, as his real person is with the gods (*Od.* XI 601–604). In this passage, Plotinus finds an expression of his own theory on the duality of the soul. We have two souls in us: one is divine and essential, having descended from the intelligence to our terrestrial body, and is capable of going back up to its source, while the other one is inferior and comes to us from the universe. In life they are united, but they separate at death.[135] The simple and essential soul is faultless; it is the composite of this soul with the other—the one subjected to the passions—that explains faults. In order to know the true soul, it must be isolated from this internal addition, just as the true figure of the sea god Glaucos[136] can be found only by getting rid of the shells that render him unrecognizable.

The human soul's destiny is represented by the wanderings of Odysseus as he tries to get back to his homeland. This journey is the way to avoid the fate of Narcissus,[137] whose contemplation of his own reflection led to his being pulled down into the water. Water thus stands for Hades, an identification that enables Plotinus to mention Heracles' ghost.[138]

> When he perceives those shapes of grace that show in the body, let him not pursue them: he must know them for images, traces and shadows, and he must hasten away towards the beauty of which they are but the images. For if anyone follows them as if they were real, he would be like the man who tried to grasp his beautiful reflection on the water as a myth is telling us, I believe, in the form of an enigma (ὡς πού τις μῦθος αἰνίττεται). This man sank into the depths of the current and was swept away to nothingness. So too, one that is held by material beauty and will not break free shall be precipitated, not in body but in soul, down to the dark depths nefarious to intelligence, where he will live only with shadows, there as here blind even in Hades.
>
> "Let us flee then to the beloved Fatherland": this is the soundest counsel. But what is this flight? How are we to gain the open sea? Like Odysseus, who escaped, it is said, from Circe, the sorceress, and from Calypso,[139] that is who refused to stay with them in spite of the pleasures of the eyes and all the sensible beauty he found there. Our Fatherland is the place whence we have come, and there is our Father.[140]

But it was Porphyry who was to be left with the task of elaborating, in the *Cave of the Nymphs,* a synthesis of the different mystical interpretations of the *Odyssey.*

Porphyry

Porphyry was first a disciple of Longinus at Athens before staying with Plotinus from A.D. 263 to 268. In the *Life of Plotinus,* which he wrote as a preface to his edition of the *Enneads,* Porphyry tells us:

> Once, during the celebration in honor of Plato, I read a poem, "The Sacred Marriage"; my piece, under the sway of inspiration, abounded in veiled words in the language of mysteries (διὰ τὸ μυστικῶς πολλὰ μετ᾽ ἐνθουσιασμοῦ ἐπικεκρυμμένως εἰρῆσθαι); someone exclaimed: "Porphyry has gone mad";

Plotinus said to me so that all might hear: "You have shown yourself at once poet, philosopher, and hierophant (καὶ τὸν ποιητὴν καὶ τὸν φιλόσοφον καὶ τὸν ἱεροφάντην)."[141]

This anecdote is pertinent in more than one way.

The allusion to the Eleusinian mysteries is evident. In its proper sense, as we have seen above,[142] the term *hierophantēs* designated a religious dignitary, belonging to the family of the Eumolpides, who, at Eleusis, "presented" the initiates with the sacred objects of the cult of mysteries.[143] During the Roman period his name could not be uttered: he was *hieronumos.* As interpreter of the unwritten laws that governed the unfolding of the celebrations, he could oppose the initiation of anyone he deemed unworthy.[144] Moreover, as Proclus noted, the reference to the "Sacred Marriage (τὸν ἱερὸν γάμον)" is an allusion, if not to the Eleusinian mysteries,[145] then at least to others.[146]

According to two other accounts,[147] in this passage Proclus was evoking the marriage of Zeus, identified with the demiurge, to Hera, identified with the world soul—a marriage from which nature issued. Was Porphyry aware of this interpretation? It is impossible to be certain. However, this account of Xenocrates does spring to mind:

> Xenocrates . . . holds that the divinity is at once monad and dyad. On the one hand it is a sort of male force, holding the place of the father and reigning in heaven; he then calls it Zeus, the supreme being, the intellect (*nous*), and it is he who is the first god. On the other hand, it is a sort of female force, a sort of mother of the gods, who reigns below heaven and who, according to him, is the soul of the universe (ψυχὴ τοῦ παντός). Heaven is also a god, and the heavenly fiery bodies are the Olympian gods, and the invisible daemons from below the moon are the other gods.[148]

Since the time of the old Academy, any union between two terms, one identified with a male principle and the other with a female principle, with the aim of producing a third term, was interpreted as a marriage. Hence, to speak of a "sacred marriage" was only a step away, and many were happy to take it.

There is thus no doubt that Porphyry saw myths and rites as the expression of the metaphysical system of his master in the form of enigmas and symbols, which he was to interpret in an increasingly original direction.[149]

This is just virtually all that has come down to us on the topic at hand. In contrast, concerning the destiny of the human soul, Porphyry's very important text *The Cave of the Nymphs* has survived.[150] In it, Porphyry acknowledged the joint patronage of Numenius and of Cronius,[151] though he didn't hesitate to criticize them, as we can see when rereading this passage from his work *On the Styx,* of which only fragments survive, in which he describes the methods he claims to use to read Homer.

> The poet's thought is not as easy to grasp as one might think. While the ancients expressed that which pertained to the gods and the daemons with the help of enigmas (δι᾽ αἰνιγμάτων ἐσήμαναν), Homer veiled (ἀπέκρυψε) his thinking on these matters much more deeply than the others: he does not speak of it directly, but uses what he is saying to present the rest [the deeper doctrine]. At any rate, among those who have sought to reveal the underlying meaning of what he said (ἀναπτύσσειν τὰ δι᾽ ὑπονοίας), it is the Pythagorean Cronius who seems to have performed this task in the most satisfying manner. In many cases, however, Cronius uses others [other sources than Homer] to make them accord (ἐφαρμόζει) with the proposed doctrines when he cannot adapt Homer's passage to them. Instead of adjusting his views to the poets' words, he seeks to pull the poet in the direction of his own thought.[152]

In this passage, we find yet again the themes and the words I have discussed throughout this chapter. Let us now see how Porphyry proceeded in practice by using the *Cave of the Nymphs* as example.

> At the head of the harbor there stands an olive tree with spreading leaves, and near it is a misty and pleasant cave sacred to the nymphs called naiads. In the cave are mixing bowls and amphoras made of stone, and in them bees store honey. There are high stone looms as well, at which the nymphs weave seapurple garments—a wonderful sight. Here spring waters flow forever. The cave has two entrances, the northern one for men to descend by, the southern one for gods. Men do not enter by the south at all; this is the way for immortals.[153]

Porphyry explains these lines by returning them to the context of a more general interpretation of the *Odyssey.* According to this view, the *Odyssey,* which tells of Odysseus's return to Ithaca,[154] is describing the history of the human soul. This soul, after its embodiment in the sensible world, a world identified with "the bottomless abyss of unlikeness"[155] and where all kinds of pleasures attempt to seduce it and prevent it from reaching its goal, turns back toward its point of departure, the intelligible world.

After citing these eleven lines (§ 1), Porphyry asks the question, does this cave exist? He quotes Cronius, who denied its reality and claimed that no narrative mentioned it (§ 2). Moreover, Cronius claimed that the description of this cave would be completely incredible if it were to be interpreted literally (§ 2), thus demonstrating the need for an allegorical interpretation (§ 3) of these verses by insisting on the unlikely nature of many of their details.

Porphyry stops quoting Cronius at this point. He claims that the cave of Ithaca really did exist, as evidenced by the account of Artemidorus of Ephesus (§ 4). But the reality of this cave should not lead us to forget that its layout is nonetheless symbolic, for the ancients did not consecrate sanctuaries "without mystical symbols (ἄνευ συμβόλων μυστικῶν)" (§ 4). However, before elucidating the meaning of the objects in the cave, its double entrance and the creatures that live in the cave, nymphs and bees, Porphyry explains that the cave itself represents the world (§§ 5–9). This is shown in his references to Aristotle, Plato, Empedocles, and the Pythagorean tradition. Furthermore, he argues, caves have at all times been linked to worship by both Greeks and Persians.

(a) *Interior arrangement.* The nymphs, or naiads, to whom the cave is sacred are water divinities and of the souls coming into generation by inhaling vapors (§§ 10–12). Moreover, the various "symbols" that the poet has placed in the cave pertain either to water divinities or to souls in general (§ 13). The stone mixing bowls and amphoras are appropriate both for the waters that spring from the stone and for the souls in the process of embodiment since they belong in the domain of matter, of which water and stone are the symbols (§ 14). The nymphs weaving purple garments on stone looms are the souls weaving their flesh bodies around bones (§ 14). The bees that hive in the stone mixing bowls and amphoras are souls too. Just as the work of the bees is honey, the image of sweetness and pleasure, the works of souls coming into generation is also pleasure, the pleasure they experience in becoming embodied and then in taking part in carnal unions, sources of other series of incarnations (§§ 15–16). Finally, bees can symbolize the best souls, those who have the desire to return definitively to their true fatherland (§§ 17–19).

(b) *The two entrances.* The cave has two entrances (§ 20); one open to the north, for human beings to come in; the other open to the south, for gods to come in. Since the cave is the image and the symbol of the world, everything has to be transposed to a cosmic scale. Following this principle, one of the entrances, with doors, is identified with the tropic of Cancer, while the other is identified with the tropic of Capricorn (§ 21). Indeed, Porphyry claims that the *Cave of the Nymphs* describes the destiny of the human soul. The souls coming into generation depart from the sphere of the fixed stars and descend to earth, but their descent must occur from a specific point: Cancer. The souls that fall from the heaven of the fixed stars are no longer pure souls: thus Homer was right to describe them as "men." After their death, the souls going back up take the opposite path: they reach the heaven of fixed stars through the constellation of Capricorn. And since these souls are freed from their bodies, they can be labeled "gods" (§§ 21–31). This linkage can be traced to the myth of Er the Pamphylian as told at the end of the *Republic.*

(c) *The olive tree.* An olive tree grows near the cave. It stands for Athena, or wisdom. Homer thereby signified that the universe is not the result of chance but is the work of a thinking being. At the foot of the olive tree, Odysseus discussing with the goddess the best way to get rid of the pretenders is the soul enlightened by wisdom, seeking to get rid of its enemies the passions (§§ 32–33).

So this is the general meaning of the Homeric poem. Odysseus symbolizes the soul descended from the heavens into generation, the soul that has become embodied but is called to return one day to its celestial homeland. Odysseus's long wanderings on the seas is an image of this exile of the soul in the land of matter, a theme known to Plato (§ 34; cf. *Statesman* 273d–e). The soul's journey out of matter was depicted by Numenius as the final ordeal imposed on Odysseus by Tiresias. The soul can be finally liberated only when it arrives in a world absolutely alien to the sea and thus to matter (§ 35).

And Porphyry ends with these words implying that his interpretation did encounter opposition even in the second half of the third century A.D.:

> It must not be thought that an interpretation of this sort is forced, that it is the type of thing dreamers of ingenious arguments know how to make plausible. When the wisdom of antiquity, all the intelligence of Homer, and his perfection in every virtue are taken into account, one should not reject the possibility that in the form of a fairy tale the poet was intimating images of higher things. For it would not have been possible for Homer to fashion the whole subject plausibly if he had not modeled his creation on certain truths. (§ 36)

The method of interpretation of myths practiced by Porphyry, a method going back much farther in time to Cronius and Numenius, can be very briefly characterized as follows.

Regardless of the genre to which they belong, texts pertaining to gods and daemons in the broad sense of the term, that is, to superior beings and even human souls, are ciphered, because they are covered by the seal of secrecy. Philosophers know this, particularly when their primary sense is problematic and cannot be interpreted literally. To grasp their truth, one must see that this surface meaning stands for a deep meaning, reserved for those who are capable and worthy of apprehending it; so these texts express through enigmas and symbols a certain number of truths on the gods and daemons. Hence myths are associated with mysteries.

Yet the correct key must be known in order to be able to decipher them. This key is found in a Pythagorean kind of Platonism and is based on three postulates: the distinction of the sensible from the intelligible; the existence of principles that give an account of the intelligible; and the destiny of the human soul played out in the cycles of alternating incarnations and separate existences. Pythagoras and Plato hold the key that makes it possible to understand the other texts because, on the one hand, they were initiated to the real mysteries and, on the other, they had gone to Egypt, the source of all civilization.

But how can it be proved that this deciphering is a serious, valid one?

SIX

The Neoplatonic School of Athens

In his preface to his *Platonic Theology,* in which he sought to realize the project of the Neoplatonic School of Athens, Proclus evoked the spiritual genealogy of the movement of which he was a part.

These exegetes of the Platonic *epopteia* (ἐποπτείας ἐξηγητάς)[1] who have unfolded to us sacred narrations of divine principles because they [the exegetes] were allotted a nature similar to their leader [Plato], I should determine to be the Egyptian Plotinus, and those who received the tradition of this doctrine from him, I mean Amelius and Porphyry, together with those in the third place who were their disciples and who attained such perfection that we could compare them to statues, viz.: Jamblichus and Theodorus of Asine, and any others, who after these, entered this divine choir to raise their own thoughts to the level of Dionysian ecstasy (ἀνεβάκχευσαν). From these, he who, after the gods, has been our guide to everything beautiful and good, receiving in an undefiled manner the most genuine and pure light of truth in the bosom of his soul, made us a partaker in all of Plato's philosophy, made us into his companions in the traditions he received in secret (ἐν ἀπορρήτοις) from those more ancient than he, and mostly made us a part of the choir of those singing the mystical truth (μυστικῆς ἀληθείας) of divine principles.[2]

This passage, permeated with the vocabulary of the mysteries, summarizes the history of the School of Athens and sets forth the essential part of its philosophical presuppositions.

According to Proclus, the stages were clearly marked. (1) First Plotinus; (2) then those to whom Plotinus transmitted the tradition of Neoplatonic doctrine, Amelius and Porphyry; (3) then their disciples, Iamblichus and Theodorus of Asine; (4) and finally Proclus's teacher, Syrianus. The "others" he refers to included particularly Priscus and Iamblichus II, who taught

Plutarch of Athens, who at the turn of the fourth century A.D. was the first scholarch to give to the School of Athens the philosophical orientation it was to keep until Damascius.[3]

The postulate on which the School of Athens was based was that Plato was a theologian. This postulate defined a two-sided task: to bring out the theology in Plato's work, and to show that it accords with all the other theologies, those of Pythagoras, the *Chaldean Oracles,* Orpheus, and Homer and Hesiod. The task of the interpreter, whether applied to philosophy or to poetry, came to be identified with that of the mystagogue, who, in the mysteries, guided the candidates toward initiation and the status of epopt.[4]

In terms of the relationship that philosophy has to maintain with myths, the School of Athens followed the path of Plotinus and Porphyry, who were inspired by Numenius and Cronius, among others. But the approach of the School of Athens was much more systematic in its treatments of both philosophy and mythology. Moreover, the *Chaldean Oracles* and the *Orphic Rhapsodies* were supplanting Homer's and Hesiod's poems as sources of myths, though these last two were not totally neglected.

PLATO AS THEOLOGIAN

The School of Athens considered Plato to be a "theologian" and looked upon his work as a "sacred text" revealing, though in a different mode, the same truth that was revealed in other "sacred writings," particularly those of Orpheus and the Chaldeans. How did the School come to this view?

Plato's doctrine could only be looked upon as a theological source on the basis of certain interpretations of the second part of the *Parmenides,* of which Proclus retraces the history in his *Commentary on the Parmenides.*[5]

The first step in this process involved the refusal to consider the second part of the *Parmenides* as a mere logical exercise with no real referent. It had been argued that Plato wrote it to refute Zeno on his own ground of logic,[6] or to provide an example of the appropriate method to overcome the difficulties posed by the doctrine of forms.[7] The rejection of these views implied that Plato's hypotheses, defined as a set of conclusions of equal value, should be assumed to make specific reference to reality. But what could this reality be? Proclus mentions three opinions on this: that the hypotheses have being as their object in the same sense as in Parmenides' poem;[8] that they have the different degrees of being proceeding from the One as their object;[9] or that they have the first beings that proceeded from the One as their object, that is, the gods, since the One is the first god.[10]

This view goes back to Plotinus, who interpreted the first three hypotheses in terms of his three "hypostases," but even more to Porphyry and Amelius, who applied the same exegetic method to all the hypotheses. The decisive step, however, was taken by Iamblichus,[11] who saw classes of gods as the realities dealt with by the first three hypotheses, and by the philosopher of Rhodes,[12] who held that the true meaning of the second part of *Parmenides* consisted in showing that the existence of any reality depends on the existence of the One, and that the hypotheses were divided into two corresponding groups. This interpretation was elaborated by Plutarch of Athens, systematized by Syrianus, and then adopted by Proclus.

According to Proclus, the first five hypotheses of the second part of the *Parmenides* posit the dependence of all realities on the existence of the One, whereas the last four hypotheses show, at the close of a *reductio ad absurdum* argument, that if the One does not exist, then nothing exists.[13] Moreover, each of the conclusions of these nine hypotheses pertain to a different order of reality, corresponding to a determinate divine order.[14] All of which invalidates the objection of those claiming that there is no systematic theological treatise in Plato but only a few theological fragments scattered in his writings.[15] Proclus, on the contrary, claims that the second part of the *Parmenides* contains the whole of the Platonic theological system, and the interpretation of all the other dialogues has to refer to this formal theological treatise.[16]

Plato dispenses his teaching on the gods in several ways: in a dialectical manner as in the *Parmenides* and the *Sophist;* in a symbolic manner as in the *Protagoras,* the *Gorgias,* and the *Symposium;* and in a manner that proceeds from images as in the *Timaeus* and the *Statesman.*[17] Proclus applies these same distinctions to the various "theologians": Orpheus, Pythagoras, the Chaldeans, and Plato. Orpheus reveals divine principles by means of symbols; Pythagoras uses images insofar as mathematical realities play the role of images in relation to divine principles; the Chaldeans express themselves under the effect of divine inspiration; and Plato is characterized by the scientific mode.[18] The table below summarizes these modes.[19]

The extensive use of this exegetical instrument enabled Proclus, on the

Exposition Modes	Plato's Works	Theologians
By using myths	*Protagoras, Gorgias, Symposium*	Orpheus
With divine inspiration	*Phaedrus*	Chaldeans
By using images	*Timaeus, Statesman*	Pythagoras
By using dialectic in a scientific manner	*Sophist, Parmenides*	Plato

one hand, to theologically interpret all of Plato's other dialogues in terms of the second part of the *Parmenides* and, on the other, to demonstrate the agreement of this Platonic theology with that of Pythagoras and those of the Chaldeans and of Orpheus.[20] It must be noted that, in the framework of this project, the interpretation of the works of Homer and of Hesiod was supplanted by that of the Orphic poems and of the *Chaldean Oracles,* which represented barbarian theology. Still, as we will see below, in spite of the magnitude of his project, Proclus overlooked neither Homer nor Hesiod.

THE AGREEMENT BETWEEN PLATO'S THEOLOGY AND OTHER THEOLOGIES

Proclus used words associated with the mysteries to write about Plato, Pythagoras, Orpheus, and the *Chaldean Oracles,* and he sought systematic agreement between them just as Philo of Alexandria, Numenius and Cronius, Plotinus and Porphyry did before him.[21] But to the extent that everything had become "theology," Proclus's practice extended it to a much broader field. He applied it to all exegetical projects, whether they pertained to philosophy or to poetry. Moreover, since Proclus practiced certain theurgic rites, this vocabulary could also be used to describe a philosophical experience that led to a mystical contemplation of union with the One. Through the intermediary of a theology indissociable from a theurgy, the distance between philosophy and mythology disappears upon perception of the unique truth that is at once veiled and revealed in the diversity of language. Language veils this truth only to reserve its revelation for those worthy of it. In this perspective, interpretation amounts to dissolving language so as to reach the state of contemplation.[22]

In order to gain an understanding of Proclus's stance, we need to place all this in a broader framework, that of the School of Athens and its program of studies, in which the interpretation of myths held a particularly important place.

In his *Life of Proclus,*[23] Marinus gives an account of the veneration his teacher had for both Orphic and Chaldean theologies and rites. Proclus regularly practiced Orphic and Chaldean purificatory rites.[24] During his final illness, he had hymns read to him, which seemed to ease his pain. He particularly appreciated Orphic hymns, of which he used to recite the middle and the end.[25] It was from the mouth of his teacher, Syrianus, that he learned the principles of Orphic and Chaldean theology. Marinus writes that Syrianus had proposed to Proclus and Domninus that they undertake the exegesis of either the *Chaldean Oracles* or of the Orphic poems. The disagreement between Proclus, who chose the *Chaldean Oracles,* and Domninus, who chose the Orphic poems, kept him from fulfilling his project. After his teacher's death, Proclus tried to better his knowledge of Orphism and of the *Chaldean Oracles.* So he studied Syrianus's commentaries on Orpheus, the many works by Porphyry and Iamblichus on the *Oracles,* and other related Chaldean writings. After this, he wrote a work consisting of seventy quaternions,[26] in which he mentioned the Chaldean doctrines and the most important of the commentaries on the *Oracles.*[27] The *Life of Proclus* ends with the words, "If they were under my control, of all the ancient books I would allow only the *Oracles* and *Timaeus* to be circulated," which makes his preference for the *Chaldean Oracles* quite clear.

This preference however, did not prevent Proclus from having a very strong interest in Orphism, as Marinus explains in chapter 27 of the *Life.*

> One day while reading with him [= Proclus] the Orphic poems, and hearing, in his exegesis, the interpretations not only of Jamblichus and Syrianus, but also many other things that had even more natural affinity with this theology, I begged the philosopher not to leave a poetry so divinely inspired without exegesis but to devote to it also [this is an allusion to his work on the *Chaldean Oracles*] a complete commentary. He answered me that he had often planned to undertake this, but that he had been explicitly hindered by certain dreams in which Syrianus discouraged him therefrom with threats. Thinking of no other expedient, I suggested that he at least write down his positions in his master's books. This man who was the most faithful image of Goodness agreed to write [his positions] in the margins of his commentaries. That is how we possess in the same set all the exegeses [on Orpheus's poems], and notes and commentaries on a substantial number of Orpheus's verses, even though he was not able to do the same for the ensemble of the myths pertaining to the gods and to the ensemble of the *Rhapsodies.*[28]

This anecdote helps explain the *Suda's*[29] confusing attribution of the same works on Orphism to both Syrianus and Proclus:

> —*On the Theology of Orpheus* (Εἰς τὴν Ὀρφεὼς θεολογίαν)
> —*On the Agreement between Orpheus, Pythagoras, Plato, and the Chaldean Oracles* (Συμφωνία Ὀρφεὼς, Πυθαγόρου, Πλάτωνος, πρὸς τὰ Λογία).

As K. Praechter[30] has well shown, these works should be attributed to Syrianus. Moreover, in the *Platonic Theology,*[31] Proclus, who seems to allude to the second of these works, attributes it to his teacher. Yet the length of Proclus's notes in the margins of Syrianus's commentaries on Orpheus probably led the readers of these works to think that both Proclus and Syrianus were their authors.

If this is the correct hypothesis, then the event that followed could be re-created thus: In Athens, under Syrianus's direction in A.D. 432, possibly in September, Proclus undertook the study of the authors who had to be pre-sented to the Academy: Aristotle, Plato, and the Theologians (chap. 13). But the disagreement between Proclus and Domninus, the former preferring the *Chaldean Oracles* and the latter the Orphic poems, along with Syrianus's death in 437, probably kept Syrianus from completing the project. In a se-ries of courses to which Proclus was probably referring in his *Commentary on Timaeus*,[32] when he wrote about *Orphic Discussions,* Syrianus only had time to discuss, along with the principles of the Chaldeans, those of Or-phism. Before or after these courses, Syrianus wrote commentaries on Or-pheus, most probably *On the Theology of Orpheus* and *On the Agreement be-tween Orpheus, Pythagoras, Plato, and the Chaldean Oracles,* commentaries that Proclus, shortly after his teacher's death, studied to better his knowl-edge of Orphism and in the margins of which, at Marinus's request, he wrote lengthy comments.

Proclus thus reproduced much of Syrianus's teaching. But Syrianus's in-terest in the *Chaldean Oracles,* Orpheus, and even Homer and Hesiod was shared by his other disciples and his colleagues too. Another disciple of Plutarch of Athens, Hierocles, devoted his book *On Providence* to showing that Orpheus and Homer had been Plato's precursors.[33] This way of think-ing, well established in Proclus's time, was to persist till the end of Neopla-tonism in Athens and Alexandria.

Proclus himself was to offer his disciples the same study program of which he had completed the first two stages under Syrianus's direction: Aristotle, Plato, and the Theologians. Isidore, Proclus's disciple who be-came the leader of the School after Marinus's death, lived in Alexandria, where he associated with Heraiscus and Asclepiades, two brothers who were both philosophers and deeply religious. Asclepiades, according to Damas-cius, planned to write on the general agreement between all the theologies.[34] Among Isidore's Alexandrian friends were also Sarapion and Asclepiodotus. Sarapion was an ascetic who had little interest in the subtleties of philos-ophy, and the few books he owned and read included the poems of Or-pheus.[35] And Asclepiodotus, who had been Proclus's disciple and served as pedagogue to Isidore, ranked philosophy below the study of nature and cer-tainly below religious observance.[36] Thus we should not be surprised at the importance of Orphism and the *Chaldean Oracles* to Damascius, the last head of the Academy, who was influenced by Isidore, Marinus, and Ammonius, the son of Hermias. Ammonius, like his father, aimed to demonstrate that Plato's theology agreed with all the other theologies, a predictable stance shared by other disciples such as Simplicius and Philoponus. This also held true for Olympiodorus.

In short, among the Neoplatonists of Athens and Alexandria, a consensus seems to have been established at the end of the fourth century on the necessity of uncovering the agreement between Plato's theology and all the other theologies, primarily those of the *Chaldean Oracles* and Orphism but also those of Homer and of Hesiod. Moreover, this practice fitted in a vast project of philosophical training; and it was probably this "institutionalization" that was to insure its permanency and its universality, two characteristics that were to explain the influence of this practice on the Byzantine world. But let us look at these things in detail.

The Chaldean Oracles

Theurgy was a movement of religious philosophy that is attributed to two "Chaldeans," magicians, both called Julian, who, it seems, lived together in Syria. To Julian the father, who is also referred to as the "Philosopher," a work *On the Daemons* is attributed; to Julian the son, who alone is referred to as a theurgist, three works in verse are attributed, the *Theourgica,* the *Telestica,* and the *Logia,* which probably were the *Chaldean Oracles.*[37] Julian the son lived during the reign of Marcus Aurelius (A.D. 161–180).

In *The Golden Chain,* Psellus gives us what seems to be some major information about these two Julians:

> The father of Julian the Theurgist, at the moment of engendering, asked of the god Assembler of the universe for an archangelic soul for his son. After his birth, he put his son in contact with all the gods and with Plato's soul, which was partaking of the existence of Apollo and of Hermes, and by means of hieratic art he lifted his son up to the epoptic state of Plato's soul so as to be able to ask of it what he wanted.[38]

Julian the father had prayed to the first transcendent god to give an archangelic soul to his son. The Chaldean hierarchy of the gods transmitted to us by Iamblichus goes as follows: gods, archangels, angels, good daemons, avenging daemons, bad daemons, archon, and souls.[39] It is clear that Julian requested a soul of the highest rank for his son, since it would rank immediately after the gods. Through the rites of the hieratic art, the father succeeded in putting his son into direct contact with the gods, including Plato himself, who was looked upon as a god, living in the company of Apollo and Hermes. The son even attained the epoptic state of a face-to-face vision of Plato, with whom he could converse freely and ask questions as directed by his father.

In short, the son was trained by his father to be the medium through which the father could question Plato in person and record, as if they were oracles, the words the philosopher was supposed to utter. By oracles, the Neoplatonists meant that Plato was reciting in verses the Platonic doctrine in the way Middle Platonism was interpreting it, a sort of transposition of the *Timaeus* into oracular hexameters.

Yet how can we explain the entry of the *Chaldean Oracles,* which may have occurred as early as Amelius[40] and certainly by the time of Porphyry, into the construction of Platonic theology? As we have seen, this theology had been developed since Plotinus according to the stages of the exegesis of the second part of the *Parmenides.* This happened basically for three reasons: the *Oracles'* Platonic content, their oracular form, and the need for the degraded human soul to have recourse to supernatural means. Since the *Chaldean Oracles* were supposed to report Plato's own words, a Neoplatonist could not find, except in the dialogues themselves, a more authoritative source of Platonism. And this Platonism was already interpreted in the manner that they were expecting. Moreover, the doctrine was presented in the form of an oracular revelation, which, from the second and third centuries on, filled a deep need, since philosophical doctrines, with the exception of that of Plotinus,[41] no longer provided the sole means of achieving the union of the soul with god. Thence it was necessary to have recourse to the hieratic art and to theurgy.

There has never been a truly satisfactory reconstruction of the theological "system" of the *Chaldean Oracles* owing to the elusive nature of the accounts dealing with them. This elusiveness can probably be explained by the great familiarity of the members of the School with the text. The doctrine of the *Oracles* is akin to that of Numenius. At the top is the intellect, also called Father, a transcendental god surrounded by silence but who sometimes resembles an immaterial fire, from which everything originated. Below him are the triads made up of the intelligible world, then the gods reigning beyond the celestial spheres (ἄζωνοι), and finally those presiding (ζωναῖοι) over these spheres. The Iynges, who are called "the transmitters of messages," are the thoughts of the Father, just as Ideas were in Middle Platonism. They form a triad with the assemblers and the teletarchs.

In addition, Proclus and Damascius established much more explicit relations between Platonic theology and that of the *Orphic Rhapsodies*. This can help us see how the elements of the *Chaldean Oracles* fit in them.

The Orphic Rhapsodies

We can reconstitute the narrative foundation of the *Orphic Rhapsodies* fairly well, for they seem to have been composed from a preexisting Orphic theogony and other writings attributed to Orpheus. But there is a problem that complicates everything: we don't know their length.[42] Their titles make these poems akin to the *Iliad* and the *Odyssey*, but is this plausible? Shouldn't we rather compare them to Hesiod's *Theogony*?

Most of the accounts of the Orphic theogony that have come down to us pertain to the version Damascius referred to as "current,"[43] that of the *Sacred Discourses in 24 Rhapsodies*.

In this version, the primordial principle is Kronos (= Time) (*OF* 66, 7ᴗ

From Kronos are born Ether and Khasma (= Chaos) (*OF* 66). Tᴗen in the Ether, Kronos makes a silver egg (*OF* 70), from which comes an extraordinary being with multiple names. It is a double being. He has two pairs of eyes (*OF* 76), two sexual organs (*OF* 81, 98) placed above the buttocks (*OF* 80). Moreover, he has wings on his back (*OF* 78) and several heads (*OF* 79), notably the heads of four animals: lion, ram, bull, and snake (*OF* 81). Just as he has multiple appearances, he also has many names. He is first called Phanes (the one who appears, the one who makes appear) because his radiance causes all things to appear when he is himself appearing. He is also called Eros. Sometimes that name is joined with Phanes as an epithet, sometimes it stands alone. Then there is Protogonos (the firstborn), as another of Phanes' names. He is also called Metis (practical intelligence). This because as a generator of all things, Phanes has to be providence, and so he must manifest practical intelligence in ruling the universe. Moreover, since he is to be swallowed up by Zeus, Phanes is linked to the Metis who, in Hesiod's *Theogony*, is swallowed by Zeus, thus making it possible to engender Athena. Finally, he is called Erikepaios, a name whose etymology is impossible to uncover.

Night has complex relations with this being of multiple appearances and names: indeed she is at once his mother (*OF* 106), his wife, and his daughter (*OF* 98). This tripling of the primordial female figure can be explained thus: being all things and possessing both genders, Phanes is actually in all possible kinds of relationships with his own feminine part. It is to Night, his daughter-wife who is also his mother, that Phanes hands down the scepter (*OF* 101) for the second reign.

The third "reign" belongs to Ouranos coupled with Gaia, who emerged from Night (*OF* 109).

Then comes the story of Kronos, coupled with Rhea, and who castrates his father Ouranos for the same reasons and the same manner as in Hesiod's *Theogony* (*OF* 127).

With Zeus, however, Orphic theogony diverges from that of Hesiod and takes a new path; it becomes a cosmogony. Zeus swallows Phanes. Having thus become the primordial principle, he reconstitutes the gods and creates the world (*OF* 167, 168). And since he thenceforth is identical to Phanes as a bisexual being (*OF* 168), he has the same relationships with Demeter (Zeus's mother) that Phanes had with Night. As Zeus's mother, Demeter is called Rhea, and as his wife-daughter she is called Kore.

Zeus and Kore engender Dionysos, to whom, when he is still only a child, Zeus transmits the kingship (*OF* 207, 208). Jealous, the Titans lure Dionysus with toys into a trap. They kill him, cut him into pieces, and after cooking him in a way that inverts the order of traditional sacrifice in ancient Greece, they eat him. When Zeus finds out, he becomes enraged and strikes them with lightning, which burns them. According to Olympiodorus, who is the only one to tell the following detail, human beings are born from the soot deposited by the vapor rising from the Titans. These humans are double beings since a part of their being comes from Dionysus and another part from the Titans who ate him (*OF* 210).[44]

Zeus entrusts the remains of Dionysus's body to Apollo, who buries them on Mount Parnassus (*OF* 209, 211). But Athena had succeeded in saving the heart, which was still beating; she puts it in a box and carries it to Zeus, who brings Dionysus back to life (*OF* 210). Thus Dionysus continues to share power with Zeus as he did previously.

And since Dionysos is also called Zeus, Erikepaios, Metis, Protogonos, Eros, and Phanes, everything can start again (*OF* 170).

A number of clues allow us to speculate that the *Rhapsodies* were composed from the old version of the *Theogony* and various poems attributed to Orpheus, around the end of the first or second century A.D. The main argument in favor of this dating is that there is no account of Khronos—the mythic figure who, preceding Night, makes it possible to distinguish the ancient version of the Orphic theogony from that of the *Rhapsodies*—dating earlier than the second half of the second century A.D.[45] According to specialists[46] on this issue, the introduction of this figure is the result of the influence on Orphism of Mithraism, which was introduced in the Roman empire at the beginning of the Christian era.

This dating makes it possible to explain why the *Rhapsodies* contain traces of Stoic allegories, and we can sense neo-Pythagorean influence (in the importance attached to numbers), and even Middle Platonic influence (double creation, divine triads). It is quite understandable then that the Neoplatonists had no trouble in finding a prefiguration of their system in this work.

It is not possible here to give even a summary of the essentials of the Neoplatonic system. What follows is merely an outline that systematically notes the correspondences between the elements of the system and the mythical figures in the *Orphic Rhapsodies* (referred to as *OR*) and in the *Chaldean Oracles* (*CO*).

1. the One
   OR: Kronos
   CO: the Ineffable
2. The Henads. Limiting–unlimited
   OR: Ether–Chaos
   CO: ?
3. Intelligible gods
3.1. Being: = limiting–unlimited–intelligible being
   OR: ?–?–primordial egg
   CO: the Father
3.2. Power: limiting–unlimited–intelligible life
   OR: ?–?–egg conceived and conceiving, Tunic, Cloud
   CO: Life
3.3. Action: limiting–unlimited–intelligible intellect
   OR: Metis–Erikepaios–Phanes
   CO: the Intellect
4. Intelligible–intellective gods
4.1. Being = Number in itself; one–otherness–being
   OR: Night$_1$–Night$_2$–Night$_3$
   CO: the three Iynges [Transmitters of the message]
4.2. Power = the maintaining class; one–multiple–all parts–limiting–unlimiting
   OR: the back of Ouranos–the depth of Ouranos–the canopy of Ouranos
   CO: the Maintainers
4.3. Action = "perfecting" power: ἔσχατα–τέλειον–σχῆμα
   OR: Hekatonkhires = Kottos–Briareus–Gyes
   CO: the Teletarchs
5. The intellective gods
5.1. Triads "of the parents": pure intellect–intellective life–demiurgic intellect

OR: Kronos–Rhea–Zeus

CO: First Intellect—Hekate—Second Intellect

5.2. Triad of the "immaculate gods," who maintain the preceding triad in transcendence

OR: Athena–Kore–Kouretes

CO: the three Implacables

5.3. "Separative" Monad, which maintains everything preceding separated from "cosmic" in all its forms

OR: castration of Ouranos by Kronos, and of Kronos by Zeus

CO: the Diaphragm

6. The hypercosmic gods, who appear at the level of the "impartible soul," that is the transcendent "soul of the world." This class is a dodecagon that decomposes into four triads.

6.1. Demiurgic triad corresponding to the three "young" gods, helpers of the demiurge in *Timaeus.*

OR: Zeus$_2$–Poseidon–Pluto

6.2. Vivifying triad

OR: Artemis–Persephone–(= Kore)–Athena

6.3. Converting triad

OR: Apollo: divinatory art–right hand–left hand

7. "Hypercosmic-endocosmic" gods, that is, the gods that are "detached from the world" are the ones reigning over "impartite nature." On the model of the class of the hypercosmic gods, this class can be divided into four triads of gods associated with the twelve gods in the *Phaedrus* (246e–247a). In the *CO,* these are Chief gods, Assimilators, Beltless (ἄζωνοι [who dwell beyond the celestial bodies whose circular motions are identified with belts]).

7.1. Paternal or demiurgic triad

OR: Zeus$_3$–Poseidon$_2$–Hephaistos

7.2. Triad standing guard

OR: Hestia–Athena–Ares

7.3. Vivifying triad

OR: Demeter$_2$–Hera$_2$–Artemis$_2$

7.4. Uplifting triad

OR: Hermes–Aphrodite$_2$–Apollo$_3$

8. "Encosmic" gods. These are the belted gods (ζωναῖοι) of the *Chaldean Oracles* [their circular revolutions are identified with belts]. The drama in which Dionysos is the protagonist in the *Rhapsodies* enables Proclus to interpret in Orphic terms what Plato writes about the soul of the world in the *Timaeus.* The intellect of the world soul, which corresponds to the circle of the world soul, is Dionysos's heart, which Athena brings back still beating to

Zeus. And the seven circles of the soul of the world are Dionysos's body cut into seven parts by the seven Titans. According to the *CO,* these are the belted gods because the circular motions of the celestial bodies are identified with belts.

8.1. the celestial gods. The seven planets are divinities that are divided into three groups:

1. Kronos–Zeus–Ares
2. Helios (= Sun)–Aphrodite–Hermes
3. Selene (= Moon)

OR: each celestial body can be looked upon as a divinity.

8.2. sublunar gods

OR: the gods mentioned by Plato in *Timaeus* 40e–41a: Ouranos$_2$, Gaia$_2$, Okeanos$_2$, Tethys$_2$, Kronos$_2$, Rheia$_2$, Phorkys$_3$, Zeus$_4$, Hera$_3$, and their descendants.

Under these cosmic gods are three classes of souls: universal souls, intelligible souls, and partial souls.

9.1. Universal souls.

In order to understand where this first class of universal souls is located, the class of divine souls must first be interpreted. The class of divine souls comprises three subclasses: that of the immanent soul of the world; that of the soul of the various cosmic divinities; and that of the universal souls, which, in contrast to the other two, constitutes a class of distinct entities.

The immanent soul of the world differs from the hypercosmic soul of the world in that it apprehends reality successively rather than simultaneously.[47] For Proclus the immanent world soul corresponds to Hipta, who picks up Dionysos (whom Proclus sees as the "cosmic intellect") right after his birth, places him on her head in a winnowing basket with a snake coiled around it, and carries him toward Mount Ida (*OF* 199), Crete being a substitute here for the intelligible.[48] In another passage, Proclus shows that there is agreement between the drama of which Dionysos is the protagonist in the *Rhapsodies* and Plato's doctrine in *Timaeus* on the constitution of the world soul and on the second creation (*OF* 210). It would be hard to be any more systematic than this.

The fixed stars also have souls, as do each of the seven planets.[49] The same holds for all the sublunar gods.[50]

Moreover, Proclus sets up between the class of souls of the encosmic gods and that of the superior beings an intermediary class, that of the universal souls corresponding partly to total time and partly to the parts of time: day, night, month, year.

10. Intelligible souls or superior beings: demons, angels, heroes.

Elements	Celestial Bodies		Subterranean Rivers
	Above the Sun	Above the Earth	
Earth	Sphere of fixed stars	Moon	Kokytos
Water	Kronos [winter]	Hermes [4 seasons]	Ocean
Air	Zeus [spring]	Aphrodite [fall]	Acheron
Fire	Ares [summer]	Sun	Pyriphlegethon

Under the universal souls are the intelligible souls that occupy an intermediary position between gods and human beings. Their class is subdivided into three subclasses—being, power, and actions—which makes it possible to establish a relation of analogy between it and the three members of the intelligible triad: the primordial egg, eternity, and Phanes.[51]

11. Partial souls.

In the last rank are the partial souls, the class to which human souls belong. They are subject to the cycle of reincarnations. In this context, Proclus interprets Prometheus's theft of the fire in Orphic terms.

12. Bodies.

In the cosmos, all the bodies are made up of the four same elements—fire, air, water, and earth—which, however, take on different states depending on the region of the universe they are in. Because of this hierarchic homogeneity, and based on the teachings "of the Orphics and the Pythagoreans," Proclus establishes through the intermediary of the four elements a series of relations between celestial bodies, seasons and the four rivers flowing under the ground, as indicated in the table above.

Thanks to this universal connection, that which is lowest in the sensible world is linked to that which is highest, thereby validating theurgy.

13. Matter

The last level of reality is "matter," the undetermined substrate of the four elements. Matter ultimately has its source in Chaos, which itself comes for the One.[52] Thus the circle is complete.

The Homeric Poems: The *Iliad* and the *Odyssey*

Proclus gave primary importance to the "barbarian" theology transmitted by the *Chaldean Oracles*. Furthermore, among the "Greek" theologies he assigned temporal and qualitative preeminence to the theology of the *Orphic Rhapsodies*. But he did not neglect Homer and Hesiod, whom he considered to have been "theologians."

From the outset, Proclus found himself in a difficult situation with regard to Homer and Hesiod. Indeed, in books III and X of the *Republic*,

Socrates heatedly attacks Hesiod and particularly Homer. Hence Proclus was faced with the dilemma of either banishing Hesiod and Homer or of admitting that Socrates, and thus Plato, was wrong. Yet Proclus refused to be locked into this dilemma. In the fifth and sixth essays of his *Commentary on the Republic,* he aimed to rescue Homer and Hesiod on the one hand, and Socrates and Plato on the other.

Proclus's task was made easier by the fact that there are several passages in Plato in which the philosopher praises Homer and Hesiod.[53] This led Proclus to think that Plato's attacks against poets in the *Republic* could be explained by specific historical circumstances[54] and could be bypassed when Hesiod and Homer were considered at a different level.

Human language exists only at the level of the rational and discursive soul (*psukhē*). But it is grounded in the unifying and generating power of the divinity, that is, at the level of the intellect (*nous*). But between the second hypostasis (*nous*) and matter are several levels of perception, each having a corresponding mode of discourse (*logos*). There are perceptions of sensation, of imagination, of opinion, and of science (*epistēmē*) that are rooted at a higher level. Beyond science, the *logoi* no longer constitute a language in the usual sense of the word; they are creative emanations of the Intellect (*nous*) that structure the universe.

This conception of language has two consequences. (1) The divinity cannot express himself directly in human language, as he does, for instance, in the Bible, even though the *Chaldean Oracles* can at times be considered as direct revelation. (2) Each level of the *logos* can be viewed in relation to the level below it, as a "metalanguage" capable of explaining it, of providing its meaning. Thence, each level of language must be interpreted with the help of the language level immediately above it.[55]

Proclus believes that Homer and Plato had perceived the highest truth. Since Homer expressed himself under the effect of inspiration, he could only have produced an account of great value. But his manner of expression is obscure because he had to adapt it to his audience. Proclus, in his commentaries on Homer, calls upon a metalanguage capable of resolving all the contradictions and dissolving all the scandalous elements of Homer's narrative so as to reach the higher truth.

Heir to the tradition described in the preceding chapters, Proclus sought to employ a kind of allegory that assimilated both myths and mysteries, regarding the myths transmitted by Homer and by Hesiod as "symbols" and "enigmas."[56]

This terminology is used to describe traditional mythic discourse, that is, poetic discourse, as a screen that hides the truth so as to keep mediocre people away from it by satisfying them and, at the same time, leads those who are worthy of it to uncover the underlying truth.

> If indeed, while myths have deliberately chosen the apparatus they put in the foreground rather than the truth that dwells in secrecy, and if they use visible screens to hide notions that are invisible and unknowable to common people— and this is where the most remarkable quality of myths resides, that is, not to reveal to the profane any of the true realities but only to present dim traces of the entire mystagogy to people naturally capable of being led by those traces to contemplation inaccessible to the common people—those critics who, instead of seeking the truth inherent in the myths, pay attention only to the visible aspect of mythic fictions and instead of purifying their intelligence remain stuck in the imaginary and the figurative, then there is no reason to make myths responsible for the disorderly conduct of these people, and we should rather put the blame for the fault they commit against myths to the people who misunderstand them.[57]

The metaphor developed in this passage is clear and coherent. Mythical discourse is identified with an object placed in front of another one to hide it. Proclus has no doubt as to the conscious and voluntary nature of this practice: the people responsible for it are the "fathers of mythology," or the "myth makers" as Plato puts it in the *Republic* when referring to Homer and Hesiod.

In this metaphor, the most concrete and interesting figure is the concept of a screen or, more precisely, that of a "curtain" (παραπέτασμα). This term is found in Plato's *Protagoras* (316e), where Protagoras explains that the Sophist, worried about his bad reputation, hides under the masks of poetry, initiations, gymnastic, and music. Proclus, however, attributes to the "myth makers" a different intention from that of the masters of sophistry evoked by Protagoras: it is not by an artifice of seduction that a myth leads to the truth, but by the shock triggered by its repulsive exterior:

> It seems to me that even that which is the most tragic, monstrous, against nature in the poets' fictions stimulates the audience to seek the truth in all sorts of ways; that there is something in this that draws people to secret knowledge, and does not allow us to be satisfied with the notions put forward as if they were plausible but forces us to go inside the myths and to scrutinize the meaning the mythographers have hidden in secrecy, to see what sort of natures, and what great power, they have introduced into the meaning of myths and directed them to posterity by means of this type of symbol.[58]

Poetic Modes

	Imitation Mode		Learned Mode	Inspired Mode
	μιμεῖσθαι, μιμητικός, μίμησις			
	Appearance	Reproduction		
Generic adjective	φανταστικός	εἰκαστικός	ἐπιστήμων	ἔνθεος
Associated terms	φαινόμενον ἐκφαντικόν ἐκφαντάζεσθαι φάντασμα	τύπος ἀποτυποῦσθαι	νοερός μέσος	σύμβολον σύνθημα μανία
Examples in Homer	"As the sun was rising from the fair sea" (*Od.* III 1)	Depiction of actions and characters	Description of the nature of the soul (*Od.* XI)	Zeus and Hera; Ares and Aphrodite, etc.
Singers	Thamyris (Il. II 595–599)	Clytemnestra's singer (*Od.* III 267–272)	Phemius (*Od.* I 337–338)	Demodocus (*Od.* VIII 478–498)

The scandalous nature of myth points to the need for interpretation. Such interpretation is based on the notion of double reference. Mythical discourse serves as a boundary between the world of appearances and that of true reality; on one side, it points to worldly beings, and on the other side to the reality of the world above.

The relations that both divide mythic discourse and reality and bring them closer together are of four types, corresponding to the four levels of poetic discourse distinguished by Proclus.[59] The result is a classificatory schema represented by the table above.[60]

This table appears highly coherent but the classification it lays out is far from firmly established in the texts. Let us then look at each of the levels of poetic discourse, by putting them in relation with the type of life to which they correspond.

Inspired Poetry

The highest and most perfect life carries the soul to the level of the gods. The soul then gives up its identity, transcends its individual intellect (*nous*), and succeeds in uniting with the One beyond all essences and lives.[61]

The fundamental characteristic of this poetry is that it proceeds through symbols. Symbols, however, are not imitations of the realities they symbol-ize.[62] Rather, they are the extremities of a divine succession descending from on high down to the lowest beings, passing through all the classes of beings existing in reality. This vertical classification makes it possible to use the lowest, most scandalous gesture, to rise up to the gods at the highest point in the series.[63] In this perspective, the myth of the adultery of Ares and Aph-rodite[64] becomes the symbol of concordance between dissimilar agents: while the universe needs the intervention of separation (Ares) because it is a factor of order and creation, it simultaneously needs unifying beauty (Aphro-dite).[65] Moreover, Proclus analyzes in detail the episode in the *Iliad*[66] of the seduction of Zeus by Hera: (a) the meaning of the union;[67] (b) Hera's dress;[68] (c) the place where they unite;[69] (d) the nature of Zeus's amorous desire;[70] (e) and finally, the meaning of Zeus's sleep.[71] It must be remembered that the union of Zeus and Hera, interpreted as a hierogamy, symbolizes the union of the limiting and the unlimited, the two supreme monads, a union prerequisite to the creation of everything else.[72]

Learned Poetry

The second life of the soul is that associated with the level of the intellect (*nous*). Here the soul turns back toward itself; "it merges thinking with that which is thought, and it reproduces the image of intellective life because it brings the nature of the intelligibles into a single unity."[73] The poetry that corresponds to this condition has knowledge of the essence of beings.

While inspired poetry corresponds to the higher discipline that the philosophers of antiquity called by different names—theology, "epopty," philosophy of the intelligibles—the domain of learned poetry is that of the two lower disciplines: physics and ethics. Indeed, learned poetry informs on the nature of corporeal objects (notably the four elements), incorporeal re-alities (notably the soul),[74] and moral duties.[75] By way of example, Proclus evokes two verses by Theognis cited by Plato in *Laws* (I 630a). Proclus does not see book XI of the *Odyssey* as a psychological treatise in verse but as a fic-tional narrative in which the relationship between Odysseus and his mother Anticleia is described in the mode of learned poetry.

Reproductive Poetry

The third life of the soul, the lowest, is borne along in the flow of powers of lesser value; it serves imagination and irrational sensations.[76] The poetry that corresponds to this condition is imitative poetry, of which there are two kinds: the poetry of reproduction and the poetry of appearance.

The notion of reproduction belongs to the mimetic genre, where it is opposed to the mode of appearance. Reproduction provides copies of reality, and Proclus looks upon them as castings, following Socrates' wish in the *Republic* (II 379a). What examples does Proclus give of this sort of poetry? The representative of Homeric singers is the anonymous singer whose songs temporarily maintain Clytemnestra on a straight path.[77] Homer provides another example of the poetry of reproduction in his depiction of the actions and characters of the heroes.[78]

Poetry of Appearance

This type of poetry produces appearances rather than reproductions.[79] According to Proclus, it is par excellence the poetry of the theater.[80] But Homer sometimes falls into this lower genre, for instance when he says, "As the sun was rising from the fair sea" (*Od.* III 1). Homer is wrong to imitate appearance; yet appearance does exist, which to some extent justifies him.

Even though Homer practiced these four types of poetry, inspired poetry is the only one that enabled him to raise his work to the level of genuine theology on a par with the *Chaldean Oracles* and the *Orphic Rhapsodies*. The inspired genre predominates in Homer.[81] The symbolic text is created by an inspired poet for an inspired exegete.[82] Moreover, the difference between the nature of a symbolic object and its uses in theurgical procedures becomes blurry. Dispossessed of its own nature, the inspired text becomes the universe itself.[83]

Hesiod's Poems: *Theogony* and *Works and Days*

In his commentaries on the *Timaeus* and the *Republic,* Proclus cites Hesiod far less frequently than Homer; though there exists a commentary on Hesiod's *Works and Days* that is attributed to Proclus.[84]

Proclus, who goes so far as to call Hesiod "the Theologian of the Greeks,"[85] mentions his name along with that of Orpheus, notably when he evokes the character and the adventures of Kronos, and when interpreting the myth of the races. Yet Proclus does recognize the divergences between the *Orphic Rhapsodies* and Hesiod's *Theogony.*[86] Besides, as far as Proclus is concerned, Plato made often use of Hesiod.[87]

In Proclus's view, therefore, Hesiod should be merged to a certain extent with Homer. They are the two Greek poets who, when inspired, could reach the heights represented by the *Orphic Rhapsodies* and the *Chaldean Oracles.*

The ambition of Proclus, Plato's *diadochus,* was to organize the life of his school, its curriculum, and the production of its works, so as to keep up the spiritual vitality of paganism and prepare for the future. Proclus attempted to reach this objective by seeking the harmony between Platonic theology and all the other Greek and Barbarian theologies. He knew of the growing power of Christianity only through imperial and ecclesiastic administrations, but he remained optimistic: he thought it wouldn't last. At his death, Proclus left a flourishing school and numerous active disciples. It was probably because the School of Athens was so lively and constituted a threat to his manner of governing that Justinian had it closed in 529.

SEVEN

Byzantium and the Pagan Myths

I n the thirteenth century, Nicephorus Blemmydes[1] was horrified when, visiting a church in Thessaly, near the Scamander river, he made out, among the figures represented on the frescoes, a young warrior identified as "the prophet Achilles."[2] And then Photius tells us that when Constantine IX (1042–1055) introduced his mistress Skleraina for the first time at court, a courtier murmured οὐ νέμεσις,[3] thus echoing the words the old men of Troy spoke when Helen walked in front of them.[4]

It is surprising how stubbornly faithful Byzantine society remained everywhere and at all levels to the culture of antiquity,[5] given that this society was so deeply Christian and looked upon religious matters, particularly theology, as extremely important. It was said that you couldn't buy fish at the market without entering into a discussion on the nature of the Trinity. We must remember, however, that this fondness for the culture of antiquity did suffer blows from the economic, social, and political crises affecting the Roman Empire, and it was not without danger for its most enthusiastic promoters. Pagan-oriented renaissances, such as that fostered by John Italos in the eleventh century and Gemistus Pletho in the fourteenth, were punished.[6]

Attachment to the culture of antiquity involved keeping a place for pagan works in education, and these were handed down under very favorable circumstances.

EDUCATION

The closure of the Neoplatonic School of Athens by Justinian in A.D. 529 was linked to the struggle of state Christianity against militant paganism, but this event did not mean that the Christian empire wanted to put advanced education, any more than primary or secondary education, into a religious mold.

The Lower Grades of Education

We have little knowledge of the lower grades of education,[7] but the classical tradition does seem to have survived in them. Several accounts indicate that Homer remained the main author studied. Michael of Ephesus (eleventh century), the disciple of Michael Psellus and friend of Anna Comnene, who was to become famous for his commentaries on Aristotle, tells us that boys had to learn Homer by heart in school. They had to memorize on average thirty lines per day, but the best students could memorize up to fifty.[8] Michael Psellus himself started to read Homer at the age of eight; one year later, he had read the whole of the *Iliad*.[9]

Advanced Education

We are a bit better informed on advanced education than on primary and secondary schooling.

At the height of the Roman Empire, the main schools in the Greek provinces were located in Athens, Ephesus, and Smyrna. There were much smaller ones in Pergamon and Byzantium.[10]

The situation had changed by the end of the fifth century. Athens was still a dominant center, but Ephesus, Pergamon, and Smyrna had lost all of their reputation. Antioch, Alexandria, and Gaza had become dominant, and there was a school of law in Beirut. To use the term "school" to designate this type of institution is problematic: teachers of rhetoric, law, or philosophy, sometimes supported and paid by the civil authorities, individually taught disciples they had attracted through their personal reputation. As the Empire declined, these schools gradually disappeared for all sorts of reasons until advanced education came to be available only in the capital.

The law school in Beirut did not seem to have recovered from the earthquake that devastated the city in 551. Antioch also suffered from earthquakes in 526 and in 528; and in 540 it was sacked by the Persians. We don't know the fate of the school of Gaza. In Athens, the teaching of philosophy was kept up during the sixth century; but, even though Justinian's edict of 529 had less effect that has been thought, there is no evidence that advanced education continued beyond the first half of the sixth century. In Alexandria, the tradition remained alive longer than elsewhere as we detect signs of activity up to the Arab conquest in 641.

It was only after the southeastern provinces fell into Arab hands that Constantinople acquired undisputed preeminence in the domain of education and culture.

In 330, Constantine had founded a "university," an *auditorium* in the parlance of the time, that of the Capitol. In February 425, an edict by Theodosius II enabled its extension. The emperor's edict[11] seems to have been limited to granting privileged status to a teaching establishment where teachers and disciples could undertake advanced studies. From 425 to 1453, this "university" remained a fruitful center of studies and the pillar of the classical tradition in the Byzantine world. Even though it underwent several transformations and experienced ups and downs in the course of the years, it remained faithful to the spirit that had presided over its creation. Its basic curriculum consisted in the liberal arts: geometry, arithmetic, music, and astronomy; while at the top were rhetoric, philosophy (which was represented by only a few authors), and law. Its role in society remained the same: to form an elite from which the Empire could recruit its civil servants. It shunned the teaching of ecclesiastical studies, as did the school created toward the middle of the ninth century by the basileus Theophilus in his Magnaura palace.[12]

The center for religious education that could match the profane education of the Imperial University was to be found in the very original institution of the Patriarchal School rather than in the monasteries which, even though they too had schools, kept these out of bounds for the worldly.

Monasticism had developed rapidly in the Eastern Church. Its prestige was such that the emperors and the patriarchs had to consider the monks' viewpoints regarding the great ecclesiastic and religious issues. Monastic asceticism, indissociable from a certain mysticism, maintained more or less close ties with the philosophical tradition, though it only allocated it an ancillary role.

Hence the import of the Patriarchal School, whose origins are still not very well known but are thought to date back to the sixth century. Even though the Patriarchate must have felt early on the need for an institution to train the members of the clergy, no reliable account on this school prior to the twelfth century has survived.[13] The main seat of this academy is thought to have been in Saint Sophia. Although the Patriarchal School was a genuine faculty of theology, it was widely open to the influence of profane culture and did not have, it seems, the puritanical asceticism of the cloisters.

THE TRANSMISSION OF TEXTS

The maintaining of the teaching of classical culture at every level was the engine for the transmission of the texts produced by this culture.[14] The schools needed these texts as instructional tools, which were used to train those who could read them, transmit them, and even shed light on them with critical notes and commentaries.

According to many historians, the reign of Heraclius (610–641) marked the end of the ancient world. In the course of his reign, Islam made its first major conquests. By closing off the Mediterranean to international trade, Islam undermined the economic basis of the Roman Empire. The structure of education remained, but culture suffered a definite decline. Yet we cannot ascertain to what extent the iconoclast controversy favored this decline. Its destructive role has probably been exaggerated insofar as it was not necessary to await the end of the controversy in 843 to observe the signs of renewed intellectual activity.

It must further be noted that in the course of those obscure centuries there were changes in the way texts were transmitted, changes that drastically transformed the situation: papyrus was replaced by paper, and the primarily uncial script (all capital letters with no space in between) was replaced by minuscule script (what we now call upper- and lowercase). These innovations lowered the cost of books and enabled an increase in their production. Yet the adoption of minuscule script required an effort of adaptation that also changed the nature of scribal errors.

Around the middle of the ninth century, a certain cultural thaw became noticeable with John Charax and George Choeroboscus. But the figure that dominated this period was that of Leo, a Platonist described as a *mathematikos* because he could teach courses in all branches of knowledge. He is considered to have been the leader of a new "school" created by the *basileus* Theophilus, the son of Michael II the Stammerer (820–829), in his palace of Magnaura. This school, whose aim was the education of future functionaries, had four chairs: in grammar, geometry, astronomy, and philosophy. Theodorus and Theodegius, about whom nothing else is known, respectively taught geometry and astronomy. Cometas, of whom some epigrams have survived in the *Greek Anthology* (*Anth. Pal.* XV 36–38), taught grammar while Leo taught philosophy. This Leo, it seems, also edited mathematical and philosophical texts.

A description of the renewal of cultural activity would be incomplete without mentioning an unknown scholar of the third quarter of the ninth century with Platonic tendencies. He was the owner of a library, from which dozens of manuscripts have survived.[15] The existence at Constantinople of such a collection is undeniable proof of the interest in Platonic tradition at the time.

This collection is all the more interesting in that, of the 280 chapters (or codices) of the curious monument of erudition making up the *Bibliotheca* of Photius (ca. 810–893), only three were devoted to philosophy: codices 214 and 251 dealing with the Neoplatonist Hierocles, and codex 212 dealing with the academician Aenesidemus. The rest of the collection includes as many references to theological works as to profane ones, with historical works predominating among the latter.

Among the following generation, the predominant figure is that of Arethas (ca. 850 to sometime after 932), who is generally thought to have been a disciple of Photius. Arethas owes his fame in modern times mainly to the fact that eight volumes of his library have come down to us, with margins annotated by his own hand.[16] The preserved volumes give us an idea of his interests, while the notes he wrote make it possible to assess his philosophical and literary culture. Several other manuscripts of this period have survived. They point to the existence of substantial works and demonstrate that Arethas was not the only erudite reader of his generation.

Around the end of the tenth century, the emperor himself, in the person of Constantine Porphyrogenius (912–959), was involved as the initiator and one of the authors of an enormous encyclopedic work that was never to be completed. The *Suda*,[17] less ambitious than the emperor's project though it was a major undertaking, was probably completed at the beginning of the eleventh century and enables us to assess the quantity and quality of knowledge in a multitude of domains at that time.

The intellectual history of the eleventh century was dominated by Michael Psellus[18] and his friends and disciples.

Born at the end of the very long reign of Basil II (976–1025), Psellus was the student of John Mauropus, who, in an epigram, prays Jesus to spare Plato and Plutarch from his threats since both, by their thinking and their souls, were close to the Law that he himself preached.[19] Throughout his life, Psellus tried to combine philosophy and rhetoric by establishing their agreement with each other. He looked at them not as ends in themselves but, with the addition of politics, as means of forming a complete man. It was in this spirit that he reformed the "university." Beginners were first taught grammar, rhetoric, and dialectic. They then progressed to the advanced curriculum: arithmetic, geometry, music, and astronomy. From there they started on philosophy, beginning with Aristotle's logic.

In the eulogy he gave for his friend and collaborator Nicetas,[20] who held the chair of grammar and rhetoric, Psellus explains that Nicetas did not limit himself to giving literal explanations for the texts he was studying but proposed interpretations based primarily on allegory. Thus prepared by Nicetas, the students then went on to Psellus's course, in which Psellus, as we will see below regarding a specific point, would develop his allegorical exegesis inspired by Neoplatonism.

Having mentioned Psellus's teacher and main colleague,[21] we must now move on to his most eminent disciple, John Italus. John Italus succeeded Psellus at the university after the latter had been the object of several attacks, which he was able to resist. John Italus did not fare as well and was condemned for heresy.

During the last five centuries of the Byzantine Empire, an antiecclesiastical trend strove for the independence of philosophical thought, which in fact amounted to a rebirth of Proclus's Neoplatonism. It is obvious that Italos was brought before the holy synod and condemned as a representative of this trend. He was forbidden to engage in any public or private teaching and was exiled to a monastery. His students were arrested as well, but in the end almost all were acquitted.

The situation that followed this condemnation would be clearer if the complete works of Theodore of Smyrna, Italus's successor at the university, had been published. But we can see evidence of caution in the work of Isaac Sebastocrator, a member of the family of the emperor Alexis Comnene, who wrote three essays inspired by minor works of Proclus, on evil, on providence, and on freedom.[22] Besides this, the emperor's daughter, Anna Comnene, for whom her mother Irene had great ambitions and who was forced to go to a convent after being accused of fomenting a plot against her brother, wrote the history of her father's reign, and favored Aristotelian studies, a project on which Michael of Ephesus, Stephan (of Sylitzes?), and Eustratius of Nicea collaborated.

Gregory of Corinth was the first of the twelfth-century figures, but not the most notable one. He was followed in time by the Tzetzes brothers, who were much more important. The eldest, Isaac, died young in 1138. The youngest, John, lived much longer, and in spite of a catastrophic start to his career, produced a substantial body of works. He was a prolific author and claimed to have written over sixty books. Most of his works derived directly or indirectly from his teaching and were devoted to Homer, whom he interpreted allegorically. But Eustathius is probably the best known among Byzantine scholars, and his major works have survived. Born around 1115, he convinced the Normans to respect religious tolerance when Thessalonika fell to them in 1185. He died around 1195–1199. Famous mostly for his commentaries on the *Iliad* and the *Odyssey*,[23] Eustathius was not very original, but he made use of a considerable number of works, whence the interest of his account.

The fall of Constantinople to the Venetians and their allies in 1204, and the withdrawal of the court from Byzantium to Nicea until 1261, marked a pause in the cultural development of the Byzantine Empire. The emperor

John Doucas Vatatzes (1225–1254) established a school of philosophy at Nicea. Its leader, Nicephorus Blemmydes, was sent to buy and, if need be, copy precious manuscripts from a number of locations, notably Thrace, Macedonia, Mount Athos, and Thessalia. After Constantinople was retaken by the Byzantine forces, the university was reestablished.

Under the reign of Andronicus II Palaeologus (1282–1328), signs of incurable economic and political weakness became evident, even while, paradoxically, cultural life reached unprecedented heights. Among the first scholars of the Palaeologos dynasty we have to mention Maximos Planoudes (ca. 1255–1305). His interests extended to all the branches of the trivium and the quadrivium. Moreover, and this was exceptional for the time, his knowledge of Latin enabled him to translate several texts produced in the West. Among Maximos Planoudes' less important contemporaries, we must cite Georgius Pachymeres, Manuel Moschopoulos, Demetrius Triclinus, and Theodorus Metochites.

While Asia Minor was gradually being occupied by the Turks, Mount Athos became the most important center of monastic life in Byzantium. The monk Gregory of Sinai settled there. Gregory set out to teach hesychastic practices, that is, contemplation, to monks who had previously been oriented exclusively to cultic practice. In 1340, the monk Barlaam, a Calabrian from Seminara (1290–1348) triggered the hesychastic controversy in Thessalonika in which a number of important figures participated. The debate brought a certain number of philosophical doctrines to the fore, notably those of the Stoics. The hesychast quarrel ended up with Barlaam's defeat and his condemnation by the synod in 1341. But the consequences of the preference for mysticism over rationalism continued to have an impact for a long time.

In the fifteenth century a burning nostalgia for the culture of antiquity and the love of Plato reached its highest expression in Pletho. This astonishing personage changed his original name of George Gemistus to Pletho, which means almost the same thing but more closely resembles Plato's own name. The Plato that Pletho was familiar with was the one in the tradition of Psellus inspired by Neoplatonism. Pletho was increasingly drawn to mysticism, and in the middle of the fifteenth century he contemplated renewing the attempts of Porphyry, Iamblichus, and Proclus to found a new universal religion on the ruins of Christianity.

Pletho's presence at Ferrara, then at Florence during the council for the union of the Churches (1438–1439), can be looked upon as the most interesting episode of his life along with that of the rebirth of Platonic philosophy in the West. Under Pletho's influence, Cosimo de Medici conceived the project of a Platonic Academy, a project that Marsilio Ficino was to realize in 1459 in Florence.

The Byzantine world was concerned to the very end with preserving the Greek culture it had inherited. Even though another religion, Christianity, predominated, the myths that embodied pagan religions continued to be passed down, provided they were submitted to an interpretation making them acceptable to an audience belonging to an entirely different culture from that which had enabled their advent.

THE INTERPRETATION OF MYTHS

Regardless of the context in which a myth is communicated, its receiver is seeking less a textual or literary critique than an interpretation, which, as I mentioned earlier, makes it possible to adapt the myth to the context of its performance—whence the enduring success of "allegory" through the centuries. The problem the myths of antiquity raised for the Byzantines was more complex than those they had raised for pagan philosophers. To make myth acceptable to the most orthodox Byzantine thinking, pagan allegory had to be combined with Christian allegory. This issue was akin to the one the church fathers had had to face.[24]

The Byzantines were to call upon all known types of interpretation, including interpretation of the moral, physical, and historical types of Stoic inspiration by grammarians such as Eustathius and Tzetzes, and Neoplatonic inspired mysterical interpretation by a philosopher such as Psellus.

In most of these cases, we will use as a guiding thread[25] the interpretation of the famous passage on the "golden chain" in the *Iliad*.[26] Zeus has assembled the gods on the highest summit of Olympus. He forbids them to help the Trojans and the Danaans and threatens those who would dare disobey him. He ends with these words:

> Then he will see how far I am the strongest of all the immortals.
> Come, you gods, make this endeavour, that you all may learn this.
> Let down out of the sky a cord of gold; lay hold of it
> all of you who are gods and all who are goddesses, yet not
> even so can you drag down Zeus from the sky to the ground, not
> Zeus the high lord of counsel, though you try until you grow weary.
> Yet whenever I might strongly be minded to pull you,
> I could drag you up, earth and sea and all with you,
> then fetch the golden rope about the horn of Olympos

and make it fast, so that all once more should dangle in mid air.
So much stronger am I than the gods, and stronger than mortals.[27]

Let us see how Eustathius, Tzetzes, and Psellus comment on this passage.

Eustathius

Eustathius (ca. 1115–1197) had been professor of rhetoric at the Patriarchal School of Constantinople before becoming archbishop of Thessalonika (ca. 1174–1177). His Παρεκβολαί on the *Iliad* and the *Odyssey* have survived; these were probably manuscripts written by his own hand and, in all probability, were the texts for the courses he taught at the Patriarchal School before his departure for Thessalonika. To achieve this enormous work, Eustathius had at his disposal not only exegetic commentaries on the *Iliad* and the *Odyssey* produced by the Byzantines, but also a version of the ninth- and tenth-century compilation of Homeric textual criticism that was richer than the one that has come down to us in the manuscript *Venetus A*.[28] This is why he was able to reproduce the physical, moral, and historical interpretation of so many of the passages in the *Iliad* and the *Odyssey*.

The first allegorical interpretation that Eustathius proposed identified the Homeric golden chain with the links between the four constitutive elements of the cosmos:

> Some say that the golden chain is chain-like relations of the four elements, according to the qualities within them; it is said to be made of gold because it is of a precious nature and the sun gives it a golden shine. It is said that one day, these relations will be completely unsettled and from them will be born a universe transformed either by a flood through a great storm come from on high, from Zeus, or by a great heat in a general conflagration.[29]

The allusion to the sun is reminiscent of the interpretation given by Plato (*Theaetetus* 153c–d). Moreover, the mention of the flood and the general conflagration is reminiscent of *Timaeus* (22c–23d). But the use of the term ἐκπύρωσις makes the allusion to Stoicism transparent.

A second allegorical interpretation identifies the golden chain with the chain of days:

> The others think that the golden chain is the days of duration that are blended with gold through the splendor of the sun and are suspended one from another like a chain; they form our lives with their links, they too will end one day and

bring back their elements to the whole, while Zeus remains impassible, he whom the ancients proclaim to be the soul of the All.[30]

The allusion to the "impassibility" (ἀπάθεια) of Zeus, identified elsewhere with the soul of the world,[31] brings to light the Stoic inspiration of this interpretation going back as well to the *Theaetetus,* in which Socrates asks:

> Need I . . . to complete the argument, press into its service that "golden rope" in Homer, proving that he means by it nothing more nor less than the sun, and signifies that so long as the heavens and the sun continue to move round, all things in heaven and earth are kept going, whereas if they were bound down and brought to a stand, all things would be destroyed and the world, as they say, turned upside down?[32]

Indeed, Eustathius continues to elaborate: "Plato says that the golden chain is the sun itself; for he attaches the All to the sun."[33]

Eustathius also mentions another interpretation of the golden chain as an allegory for the planets: "Others believe that the golden chain is the circles of the planets, the highest one being Kronos (= Saturn) and the one closest to the earth being that of the moon. In these circles, the various conjunctions of the planets produce multiple changes of the All."[34] Again this brings Stoicism to mind,[35] but a Stoicism on which we sense the influence of Chaldean astrology. Immediately afterwards, Eustathius incriminates the Stoics by name:

> The Stoics allegorically explain Zeus' threat solely by the general conflagration. Indeed, Zeus is the Ether; the golden chain, they say, is the sun, in which, rising from below, will flow and spread as into a heart the exhalation of the moist elements, when, in the future, drawn up, it seems, by exhalation, the sea will dry out. Then the fire desiring nourishment, will draw up the moist elements from the depths of the earth and will dissolve the earth itself; and Zeus will not be drawn down below but the things from below will rise through the triumph of the fire.[36]

The point of departure is the same as in Plato (golden chain = sun), but Homer's image is turned toward a different direction: the total subversion with which Zeus threatened the gods is conceived here as the normal end of the evolution of the universe subjected to the mechanism of exhalation and is identified with the universal conflagration, the consequence of the triumph of fire.

Finally, Eustathius mentions a strange interpretation: "There are some who are hesitant to speak, claiming that this threat is an enigma of the monarchy and that everything depends on a single one and is submitted to a single power: indeed, as in the things below, the government by several is not good, and this holds even the more so for the things from above."[37] This political interpretation becomes less strange than it might appear at first when we replace it in a more general context, that of the Indo-European "binding" gods.[38]

Tzetzes

John Tzetzes also interpreted Homer allegorically. However, in contrast to Eustathius, he boasted of his innovations. He was a flamboyant individual who wrote on every topic and had several patrons. He was one of the first in the European world to live from his pen. Three of his works dealing with an allegorical interpretation of Homer have come down to us.[39]

The first is a commentary on the *Iliad* written around 1140, when John Tzetzes was no older than thirty. Allegory was Tzetzes' favorite subject, but he buried it in a series of more or less pertinent concerns that he drew from the scholia extant in a more complete version of the *Venetus A* than the one we have today. The version he used was also the one known to Eustathius.[40] This collection of commentaries has partially survived and was only published recently.[41]

Tzetzes' two other works, his *Allegories of Homer,* were addressed to a very different public, and their full text has only recently become available.[42] They are two long poems dedicated to the empress Irene, wife of Manuel I. Born Bertha von Sulzback, the empress, sister-in-law of the Hohenstaufen emperor Konrad III, had been introduced while still a young girl to the Constantinople court. This is why she requested an easy introduction to the greatest poet of her adoptive country. Tzetzes accepted this task.

Tzetzes also discusses allegory in the first and only surviving 527 lines of his *Chronicle.*[43] In his very first lines, after tracing the origin of allegory to Egypt, Tzetzes describes its causes and mechanisms:

Allegory is a discovery of the Egyptians,[44] and the offspring of the Hellas also practiced it for they learned it from Kadmos, who borrowed it from the Egyptians. Indeed, of all human beings, the Egyptians were the first to submit to allegory the narratives pertaining to the gods, thus showing a sane judgment of the mind. They hid these narratives from profane ears after enclosing them in an envelope of writing. Having thus consigned many other things in writing by means of symbols that are not symbols,[45] they transmitted them through an unclear discourse.[46]

Then, after classifying myths into three groups, those needing allegory, those not needing it, and those needing it in part, he evokes the three methods of allegorical interpretation.

These, in fact, are the three known methods of physical, psychological, and historical allegory. After applying these methods generally to the gods as a whole, Tzetzes applied them to specific ones. Let us take Kronos as an example. According to the historical interpretation, Kronos is the infanticide king. According to the physical interpretation, Kronos is the fog that was spread over everything at the origin; in other words, it is matter; and Kronos is also time. Finally, according to the psychological interpretation, Kronos is the ignorance of the intellect which, immersed in the fog, moves from opinion toward science. Then Tzetzes applies the same treatment to several other themes and mythological figures.

One of Tzetzes' contemporaries went even farther. Isaac Porphyrogenetus—who has been identified with Isaac Comnene,[47] the son of Alexis I, brother of Anna Comnene, and the father of Andronicus I—wrote a short work in prose[48] in which the main characters involved in the war of Troy are described as they would be in police files. Agamemnon is tall, pale of complexion, with an aquiline nose, a thick beard, black hair, and large eyes; he is intrepid and wellborn. And then we learn that when Paris was a young man, he studied rhetoric and wrote a cosmogonic poem. How did this belief come into being? The unedifying narrative of the judgment of Paris seems to have been the object of an allegorical interpretation during Hellenistic times, according to which Paris had written a treatise or a poem showing that love is more powerful than wisdom and truth. We find traces of this allegorical interpretation in the treatise by Saloustios, *On the Gods and the World*.[49] Even at that time the interpretation was thought to be questionable. Love, as any philosopher knew, is the principle that enables the cohesion of the elements with each other so as to form the universe. Thus Paris is represented as spending his free time on Mount Ida writing philosophical poems on the origin of the universe.

Psellus

Psellus was the only thinker to achieve a double synthesis: on the one hand, between all the pagan theologies, Greek and barbarian, and, on the other, between these pagan theologies and Christian theology.

Psellus's education, which was the same as the one he himself helped to impose on the imperial school, explains his attempts at synthesis. In his praise of his teacher Nicetas, Psellus confesses, "Before giving myself over to philosophy, I was in love with rhetoric."[50] He had carefully and assiduously read Demosthenes, Plato, Plutarch, and Lysias in order to develop his own style. He confided in a letter, "I am combining philosophy with rhetoric, and I seek to be in accord with all things with their help."[51]

The aim of the philosophy course that Psellus conducted at the Imperial University was to impart the foundations of philosophical thought through Aristotelian logic and physics. But philosophy was only a preparatory stage for metaphysics. And in this domain everything came from Plato rather than from Aristotle, though a Plato interpreted by Plotinus and Proclus. So we see how philosophy could be identified with theology. As in Proclus's work, the history of philosophy was not limited to Greek thought but also included "barbarian" wisdom (Egypt, Chaldean, Palestine).

Psellus provides us with precious information on the *Chaldean Oracles*, thanks to the thoroughness of his writing. He devoted several works to the *Chaldean Oracles*. The three most important ones are (1) *Commentary on the Chaldean Oracles*, (2) *Exposition of Chaldean Beliefs*, and (3) *Sketch of the Beliefs of the Chaldeans*.

Besides these major texts, we occasionally come across some short essays in which Psellus summarizes the Chaldean system. The determining influence of the *Oracles* on Psellus was not the end point in their survival: still in the sixteenth century, Nicephore Gregoras, commenting on Synesius's *Treatise on Dreams*, cited them abundantly,[52] and we owe the first edition of the *Chaldean Oracles* to Pletho.[53]

As Proclus had proposed, Psellus wanted to harmonize Plato's and Pythagoras's theologies with those of the *Orphic Rhapsodies* and the *Chaldean Oracles*. Unlike Proclus, however, he also attempted to harmonize these theologies with Christian theology. He achieved his aim thanks to the theory of plagiarism, according to which the Greeks had borrowed everything from Moses. But his interest in the *Chaldean Oracles*, among other things, compelled him to express his opposition to theurgy, divination, and the cult of daemons. This did not protect him from being accused of pagan tendencies by Xiphilinus of Trabzon.

Psellus's allegorical treatises can be classified into two categories, those that drew their inspiration from Stoicism, as Eustathius and Tzetzes did after him, and those that were inspired by Neoplatonism.[54]

Stoic Inspiration

In the first category are the commentaries on the myth of Tantalus,[55] evoked by Euripides:

Tantalos, whom everyone called
the happiest of men, the son, they say,
of Zeus himself . . . ,
now shoots through the sky, terrified
by the huge rock looming over his head.
This is the price he pays, and why?
So they say, when he sat
with the gods at the same table, a mere man
banqueting with them as an equal,
sick with insolence, shamefully
he let his tongue run away with him. (*Orestes* lines 5–10)[56]

After listing three interpretations of the figure of Zeus, Psellus reduces the myth of Tantalus to physical considerations.

Tantalus is the personification of the ether. Euripides describes him as suspended in midair in order to show that fire is lighter than air. The rock that hangs over Tantalus's head is the *sphairos* of Empedocles, which Psellus identifies with the sphere of the fixed stars. Like a flat stone it planes over the upper surface of the ether. The whole of this interpretation reproduces the disposition of the universe according to the Stoics, who placed air above water, the spheres of ether above air, and finally, containing the whole, the sphere of the fixed stars.

Why is Tantalus seized by terror when he sees the rock hovering over his head? Through its perpetual and rapid rotation, the sphere of the fixed stars exerts a strong pressure over the ether, which makes it impossible for any space to exist between the elements submitted to violent agitation. This is why fire appears to shiver.

As for the doubt expressed by Euripides in the lines cited above, it indicates that the poet is not convinced by the Stoic identification of the originating god with universal fire.

Finally, why does Tantalus, a mere mortal, share the table of gods? The answer to this question calls on the notion of "sympathy": the artist's fire is the principle of all things that are born, and that communicate with one another.

One could associate the myth of Kronos[57] with that of Tantalus. Kronos is identified with the notion of time (χρόνος). He devours his offspring because everything is contained in time and nothing escapes the law of time. Time should have flowed away and disappeared, but by tying it with solid bonds, Zeus stops it from draining away. The myth adds that Kronos almost devoured Zeus but failed; Kronos can make his offspring disappear as individual creatures, but he can do nothing against Zeus, who is the source of all creatures.

After evoking Stoic cosmology, Psellus goes on to psychology. Zeus is the symbol of reason. Everything corporeal succumbs to the power of time. Only reason escapes it. That is why, of all Kronos's children, Zeus is the only one to not be devoured by him. Moreover, the stone covered by swaddling clothes, which Rhea gives to Kronos to swallow, stands for expressible reason, the simulacrum of Zeus or of fiery reason. The rest of the treatise describes the various stages of the progress of reason according to the Stoics.

Neoplatonic Inspiration

With the treatise on the *Golden Chain*[58] we move on to Neoplatonic interpretation. In accordance with Neoplatonic metaphysics, Kronos, coming after Ouranos, who is identified with the One, is considered the pure intellect that gives birth to the world soul and to which the whole of demiurgic creation is linked.

After determining the rank occupied by Zeus in the system, Psellus goes on to the etymology of his name. This god is sometimes called "Zeus" and at other times "Dis." These two names, united into one, express his function and his power. As such, Zeus gives birth to all the gods, all the angels, all the heroes, and their female equivalents. These beings are classified into couples because male divinities pertain to the intellect and female ones to the souls.

According to Psellus, the golden chain is the symbol of the linkage of all things. It links inferior beings to the first cause. Even though linked to Zeus, the inferior beings are incapable of making him descend, while Zeus can make them rise, in the context of the dual movement of "procession" and "conversion."

The treatise ends on an interpretation of the motive of the golden chain in the spirit of Christianity, but this is only a matter of vocabulary. Psellus is content merely to replace the names of Zeus and of pagan divinities by those of the Christian god and the celestial spirits. This enables him to explain how the golden chain is the link uniting angels and men to this god, who is placed at the superior end of the chain.

The tendency to make Greek myths serve Christian religion is also at play in the interpretation of the figure of Circe.[59] The fatherland dear to Odysseus's companions, whom Circe has transformed into pigs, is none other that the celestial Jerusalem, the region from which we came down into this passion-filled world. The tendency is even more striking in the allegorical interpretation evoked at the beginning of book IV of the *Iliad*:

Now the gods at the side of Zeus were sitting in council
over the golden floor, and among them the goddess Hebe
poured them nectar as wine, while they in the golden drinking-cups
drank to each other, gazing down on the city of the Trojans.[60]

Psellus sees the God of Christianity in Zeus. The divinities assembled in Zeus's palace stand for the first beings of the descending procession: cherubim, virtues, principalities, liturgical powers or spirits. The gods seated at the feast stand for all those who turn their spirit toward the supreme being and partake of his beatitude. Hebe pouring the nectar to the divinities of Olympus stands for the vital power of the gods, who remain eternally young. This idea links up with that of Proclus, according to whom the intellect undergoes no change, grows no older or younger, because it needs no cause.

Nectar, the drink of the gods, is the image of the intelligible world. Elsewhere, Psellus identifies the nectar with the Christian communion. As to the city of Troy, which the gods look upon as they are holding golden goblets, it signifies the sensible world.

Psellus also explains that, in the allegory of the Sphinx,[61] man is composed of similar parts. In this he adheres to the Neoplatonic doctrine, whereby every animal contains an inferior part mixed with the body and a superior part that is the true human being. Moreover, between divine life and animal life, there is an intermediary life. In the *Chaldean Oracles* it is described as something half shining and half dark. To Psellus, it represents human life.

In Psellus, the riddle the Sphinx puts to Oedipus is the object of an explanation based on the harmony of numbers. As a square number, the number four is divine because it resembles unity, but as an even number it is imperfect because it is divisible. Thus, in the riddle the number four corresponds to man as a child when he is closely tied to animal nature. The number two expresses the equivocal tendencies of a boy coming into his manhood. The number three, whose excellence and sacredness had been recognized by Hesiod and the Pythagoreans, corresponds to the man who, in the evening of his life, receives from on high the pure intelligence that allows him to embrace the essence of beings and things.

Here we find an echo of the mathematical speculations of the Neoplatonists as the author returns to the concerns expressed by Iamblichus in his *Theology of Arithmetic*,[62] for which Psellus remains a primary witness.

Finally, Psellus was not satisfied with bringing the hidden sense of myths to light and elucidating the symbols referred to by numbers. He also reinterpreted proverbs allegorically, arguing that the language they used was ordinary rather than erudite, which showed that it too was appropriate for offering an image of divine matters.

Pletho

Pletho was to take up Psellus's theses and push them to the limit, for Pletho's Platonism led him to negate Christianity. Pletho's universe is made up of an ensemble of divine and nondivine beings. The divine ones are pure intelligences residing above the sky, while the nondivine ones reside in it and consist of a soul and a body, or simply a body. This entire universe emanated in a downward motion from the thought of Zeus, the great god, and the first principle; the universe is co-eternal with Zeus because it proceeds from him as a cause, and not in time.

Realities are classified according to the order of their generation. Poseidon, Zeus's oldest son (according to Pletho), presides over creation as a whole, his brothers preside over the elements, Hera presides over numbers and the multiplication of beings, and the inferior gods preside over the laws of being. As one ascends in the hierarchy, attributes gradually become less general, because, according to the Platonic theory of forms, the general encompasses the particular. After the sphere of the gods come the genies, daemons, and disembodied souls, which are immortal like the gods but fallible, and finally human beings, made up of a soul and a body, who must to strive to be like the gods.[63]

I. *Abstract categories = superhuman or divine world = Zeus and the children of Zeus*

    A. *Atemporal = legitimate children of Zeus*

        1. Being = Zeus (God)

        2. Action = Poseidon (*Nous*)

        3. Power = Hera

        4. Identity = Apollo

        5. Otherness = Artemis

        6. Rest = Hephaistos

        7. Motion

           (a) spontaneous = Dionysus

           (b) communicated = Athena

        8. Astral nature = Atlas

           (a) of the wandering stars = Tithonus

           (b) of the fixed stars = Dione

        9. Daemonic nature = Hermes

        10. The human spirit = Pluto

      11. Corporeal nature = Rhea

      12. Ether and Heat = Leto

      13. Air and cold = Hecate

      14. Water and Fluidity = Thetis

      15. Earth and solidity = Hestia

   B. *Temporal = illegitimate children of Zeus*

      16. Time = Kronos

      17. Reproduction = Aphrodite

      18. Human corporeal life = Kore

      19. Animal life = Pan

      20. Vegetative life = Demeter

II. *Concrete categories: the children of Poseidon*

   A. *Immortals = Poseidon's legitimate children*

      21–27. The sun, the moon and the other wandering stars or planets = Helios, Selene, Eosphoros, Stilbon, Phainion, Phaethon, Pyroeis

      28. Fixed stars and other fixed celestial bodies = other nameless astral gods

      29. Daemons

   B. *Mortals = Poseidon's illegitimate children*

      30. Human beings

      31. Animals

      32. Plants

      33. Inorganic substances

In Pletho's view, being and its laws—the essence, origin, resemblance, and differentiation of beings—are all at play beneath the names he attributes to the gods of Olympus. In short, Pletho's gods are akin to intelligible forms, but intelligible forms that are persons.

According to Pletho, philosophy is theology, it is a national theology insofar as it is rooted in Greek tradition: "Men have very diverse opinions on the divinity (. . .). We ourselves remain attached to the doctrine we know to be the best, that of Zoroaster [to whom Pletho attributed the *Chaldean Oracles*], also advocated by Pythagoras and Plato; it stands above all the rest by its exactness, and, moreover, for us it is a national one."[64] Pletho had founded at Mistra, very near ancient Sparta, in the Peloponnese, a kind of secret society, where he taught Neoplatonism. We find in him an acute form of the nostalgia that had long been pushing Greek thinkers to reappropriate the whole of their traditions, including myths.

Pletho died on May 26, 1452. In 1460, Scholarius, then a patriarch going by the name of Gennadius, burned the manuscript of the *Treatise on the Laws* in Constantinople because he found the work anti-Christian and filled with impiety. In contrast, Italian scholars' veneration for Pletho was so great that his remains were exhumed from his tomb and carried in 1475 to Rimini, where they were deposited in the church of Saint Francis on the orders of Sigismond Pandolpho Malatesta de Rimini, who had succeeded in taking Mistra from the Turks. The remains of the Mistra Platonist, like his disciples and his ideas, thus rested in an Italy that henceforth alone could make a Renaissance possible.

EIGHT

The Western Middle Ages

In the Campanile in Florence we can see an image of Jupiter wearing a monk's robe, holding a chalice in one hand and a cross in the other. How did this happen? According to the astrological system that spread during the Middle Ages, each region of the earth is dependent on a specific planet. Jupiter is sovereign over Western nations,[1] so he is the patron of Christians. It follows that he has to have the image of a Christian; and, following the principles of sympathetic magic, those who ask his help have to dress like him. To pray to Jupiter, the *Ghaya* advocates the use of the following words:[2] "Be humble and modest, dress like monks and Christians, because he is their patron; do what the Christians do and wear their dress: a yellow coat, a belt, and a cross" (III 7, 204). This is an admirable example of the alterations that the figures of the best-known pagan gods underwent during the Middle Ages under the influence of various interpretations and currents of thought that made their survival possible.

THE SURVIVAL OF MYTHOLOGY

In the course of the Middle Ages,[3] Greco-Roman mythology survived on several levels, particularly that of folklore, art, and classical culture.

Folklore

Mythology endured first in folklore. The advent of Christianity did not mean the annihilation of the ancient cults and beliefs, which survived particularly in rural areas. The capitularies of the councils provide us with the best evidence, for they continued to denounce superstitious practices up to Carolingian times. Yet the councils' anathemas remained powerless. Pope Gregory the Great (who held papal office 590–640) already recognized the inertia "of hard minds." The only means of fighting this superstition consisted in covering it with the mantle of Christian orthodoxy by building churches on ancient temples, placing crosses on monuments, and so forth. Although we now have to exercise a great deal of prudence when attempting to make out pagan mythological figures superimposed onto certain figures valued by Christian tradition, it is nonetheless clear that strange identifications linked some saints to gods. For instance, Saint Christopher became heir to Mercury and even to Anubis, probably on account of their relation with all forms of communication.

But the gods were replaced mostly by daemons. These amalgams and avatars were also forms of survival. The pagan origins of the Sabbath were denounced by the Council of Aix-la-Chapelle, which had uncovered Diana, *paganorum dea,* among the women of ill repute riding animals in the company of Satan.

Art

Mythology endured in the domain of art also, as antiquity fostered inspiration. Originally, the remains of pagan sanctuaries and shrines were incorporated into new Christian constructions. Sarcophagi were transformed into altars, their fragments into stoups and baptismal fonts, while diptychs and ivory chests were used as reliquaries.

Sculptors who copied these pagan relics first looked to them for decorative forms and formulas as well as technical and stylistic lessons; but spontaneously profane themes got mixed in with sacred representations. Sculptors from Arles decorated the cover of sarcophagi in Christian tombs with mythological motives such as Castor and Pollux or Eros and Psyche. Romanesque art associated allegories of earth, ocean, and even the moon and the sun mounted on their chariots with Christ's crucifixion and his glorious apparition. At Vézelay, the education of Achilles by Chiron was represented. At Chartres, besides Achilles' education by Chiron, we recognize the abduction of Deianira by Nessus. The end of the twelfth century presents one of the most unexpected examples of a pagan monument within a cloister: the famous fountain of Saint Denis, whose damaged basin is now exposed in the courtyard of the Ecole des Beaux-Arts in Paris. Its edges are decorated with medallions—perhaps copies of cameos—in which approximately thirty heads are sculpted in relief, among which we can make out those of Jupiter, Neptune, Thetis, Ceres, Bacchus, and various rustic divinities.

Gothic art abandoned antique forms, retaining only the Sibyl. However, in one of the foundation blocks of the Auxerre cathedral portal we recognize a sleeping Eros.

Classical Culture

Mythology cannot be reduced to a rustic superstition. It was an integral part of classical culture, which the church had adopted in the course of its first centuries of existence. The church fathers were permeated with it and conscious of the difficulty as well as the danger of maintaining a literature and an art indissolubly linked to polytheism as a part of schooling. Yet they agreed to let youths be educated in schools of the Greco-Roman type, where allegory provided the ideal instrument for tempering the nefarious effects of mythology. The last generation to receive this type of education was that of Ausonius (ca. 310–394), a Latin poet and teacher.[4]

Invasions destroyed classical schooling, which disappeared till the seventh century. In the sixth century, school life was maintained in Rome and in Africa until the collapse of culture and the decadence of letters.[5] Yet the sources of antiquity did not dry up. Two rebirths occurred, accompanied by rises in paganism: the Carolingian renaissance, with which Alcuin's name was associated; and the twelfth-century renaissance, when Chartres and Orléans became great centers of classical studies. Also during the twelfth century, Ovid became extremely popular again (*aetas ovidiana*). His *Metamorphoses* were looked upon as a treasure trove of truths, and monks' correspondence was filled with mythological allusions.

INTERPRETATION AS THE CONDITION OF THIS SURVIVAL

Throughout the Middle Ages, the gods of antiquity survived in classical culture and the fine arts by virtue of interpretations of their origin, names, and nature that had been developed during the classical age itself.

Myth interpretation practiced during the Middle Ages can be grouped into three forms of Stoic inspiration: Euhemerism, physical interpretation, and moral interpretation.[6] The influence of Neoplatonism was to become predominant only during the Renaissance with the rediscovery of the Greek texts. In the Middle Ages, the Latin authors that were studied had largely been influenced by Stoicism. Neoplatonism was mainly represented by Greek authors, who remained inaccessible to the medieval interpreters who only knew Latin.

Literary Tradition

The Middle Ages had the merit of borrowing its knowledge of the pagan gods from contemporaries of paganism such as Minucius Felix,[7] Saint Cyprian,[8] Tertullian,[9] Arnobius,[10] Commodius,[11] Lactantius,[12] and, to a lesser extent, Firmicus Maternus,[13] while the church fathers and those for whom paganism was already a bygone religion were used only rarely. Most of the authors used perceived the pagan gods through the prism of the various currents of Stoic interpretation.

Historical Interpretation and Euhemerism

The first current of interpretation was represented by Euhemerism,[14] popularized by Ennius. As we have seen,[15] according to this interpretation, gods were men whom their contemporaries turned into gods on account of their services in a variety of domains to their fellow human beings. Christian apologists and the church fathers had gladly adopted this interpretation to use as a weapon against paganism. But it was a two-edged sword, because, while lowering gods to the level of mortals, it confirmed their existence and enabled them to enter into history.

The theologian and historian Paul Orosius (after 414) attempted to take account of the whole of the past, including mythology.

Saint Augustine's *City of God* soared so high over its subject matter that Augustine asked a Spanish priest, who had taken refuge in Africa to flee persecution by the Goths, to write the history of all the scourges experienced in the past by pagan peoples. Paul Orosius accepted this task and proceeded to demonstrate that "all the strangers to the city of God," that is, those called *gentiles* or *pagani* because they lived in villages (*pagi*), had suffered ills the more cruel in that they themselves were far away from the true religion.

Although he wrote against the pagans,[16] Paul Orosius attempted to unravel the past, including the mythical past, by way of Euhemerism. In the seventh century, we find the most interesting use of Euhemerism in Isidore of Seville's *Etymologies* (or *Origins*).[17] The author divides the history of the world into six periods: (1) from the Creation to the Deluge; (2) from the Deluge to Abraham; (3) from Abraham to David; (4) from David to the captivity in Babylon; (5) from the captivity in Babylon to the birth of Christ; and (6) from the birth of Christ to Isidore's time. Isidore positioned groups and dynasties of mythological figures into this scheme, which he had reconstructed by drawing from Lactantius, Varro, and even Ennius.

Chapter 11 (*De diis gentium*) of book VIII of the *Etymologies* opens with a statement of principle:

> Tradition tells that those whom the pagans thought to be gods used to be men, and that among the pagans they came to be worshiped after their death on account of their lives and merits: thus Isis in Egypt, Zeus in Crete, Juba among the Moors, Faunus among the Latins, and Quirinus among the Romans. Likewise, Minerva in Athens, Juno in Samos, Venus in Paphos, Vulcan at Lemnos,

Liber at Naxos, Apollo in Delos. Poets participated in praising them, and by composing songs in their honor, they transported them to heaven.

In these primitive times, Isidore found civilizing heroes, slayers of monsters, founders of cities, and inventors of the arts. In the process, he restores to mythical figures their dignity and their independence. They are remembered for good reasons, since they are the benefactors of humankind. Furthermore, they should not be subordinated to the figures of sacred history, for they can be placed at least in the same rank, if not in the same lineage, as patriarchs, judges, and prophets.

After Isidore of Seville, no chronicler or writer of universal history neglected inserting the humanized gods into their lists of kings and heroes of antiquity.

Among the numerous successors of Isidore, the most important was Ado of Vienna, whose *Chronicle* of the six ages of the world was inspired by Isidore's *Etymologies*. After writing about Moses and the Exodus, Ado evokes events taking place among the pagans during that period.

Prometheus, who is thought to have made human beings with mud, is said to have lived at that time; during the same epoch, his brother Atlas was considered to be a great astrologer; the grand son of Atlas, Mercury, was a scholar learned in several arts: for this reason, after his death, his contemporaries' aberration placed him among the gods.[18]

Henceforth, nothing was to stop this movement.

Around 1160, Peter Comestor (the Eater), dean of the church of Notre-Dame in Troyes and the future chancellor of Notre-Dame in Paris, wrote a *Historia scholastica,* a history of the people of God, which in Guyart des Moulins' translation (*Bible historiale,* 1294) was distributed all over Europe. In this work we can sense the Euhemerist interpretation that had been codified since Isidore of Seville. In an appendix, Peter Comestor condensed the mythological material handed down from Isidore and his predecessors Orosius and Saint Jerome. This appendix took the form of a series of short chapters in which pagan and sacred history were placed on the same plane. In both cases, Peter Comestor recognized the existence of great geniuses. Zoroaster invented magic and inscribed the seven arts on four columns; Isis taught the alphabet and writing to the Egyptians; Minerva taught several arts, including weaving; Prometheus, who was renowned for his wisdom, created human beings. All those powerful minds, he argued, deserve as much respect as the patriarchs, for earlier they were the guides and teachers of humankind.

For the remainder of the Middle Ages after Peter Comestor, nothing came to counterbalance the success of this type of mythological exegesis. Vincent of Beauvais followed in Peter's footsteps with his *Speculum historiale* (written around 1244), in which he dealt with the origin of idolatry. Vincent repeated verbatim the short chapter of the *Historia scholastica* on the foundation of the worship of the gods by Ninus, and he even cited Isidore of Seville's statement of principle.[19]

This mythical past then became something nations wanted to appropriate for themselves. In order to justify their claims, clerics sought witnesses and ancestors in antiquity. One of these "fables" gained particular renown. It claimed the French descended from the Trojan Francus, just as the Romans descended from the Trojan Aenaeias, a theme that was to be taken up and developed in the sixteenth century by Ronsard in his *Franciade.*

Physical Interpretation

Until the twelfth century, the only sources of cosmology for western thinkers were the commentaries of Macrobius *On Scipio's Dream,* those of Firmicus Maternus, the commentaries on the *Timaeus,* and the works of Isidore and Bede. The thinkers they inspired had also inherited the theory of the macrocosm and the microcosm handed down from Boethius and developed by Bernard of Tours. Through this handful of authors, to whom we should add Martianus Capella, it was possible for the influence of Neoplatonism on myth interpretation to be felt in the Middle Ages.[20] The synthesis of all these traditions made it possible to link all the physical beings to the planets by means of these fundamental qualities.

The identification of gods with stars was complete by the end of the pagan era. For constellations as for planets, the process of mythologization was gradual and irregular. Two influences favored this process: Stoic allegory and the growing influence of eastern religion, particularly the Persian worship of the sun and the Babylonian worship of planets.

The absorption of the gods by celestial bodies ensured their survival. Dethroned from the earth, they remained masters of the celestial spheres. That was why human beings continued to fear and invoke them. Astrology soon came to be mingled with natural science, to the point that not only astrology but also mineralogy, botany, zoology, physiology, and medicine came under its jurisdiction. Whence the compilation of correspondences of the type depicted in the table opposite,[21] which features the system of a second-century A.D. astrologer, Antiochus of Athens.

In spite of the threat these studies might represent, the church fathers included them in Christian education for two reasons: the concern that Christians not be inferior to other peoples, and the necessity for a good understanding of their own religion. In order to read the Bible and to acquire the science of divine things, it was necessary to know natural history and astronomy.

This tradition was continued and developed, notably by the Chartres masters Bernard of Chartres, Gilbert de la Porrée, and Thierry of Chartres.

Bernard of Tours was also linked to these Chartres masters. He dedicated to Thierry of Chartres his *De mundi universitate sive Megacosmus et Microcosmus.* In the *Macrocosmus,* Nature complains and laments to divine Providence about the confusion of primary matter, and begs Providence to set the world into a more beautiful order. Providence gladly consents. In the *Microcosmus,* Providence puts the world in order and creates human beings. This scenario is filled with the evolutions of allegorical figures and with a whole mythology featuring Physis, Urania, and the old demiurge Pantomorphos.

From the twelfth century on, the influence of Arab science gave a new viability to astrology. The *Ghaya,* a manual of practical magic made up of eastern and Hellenistic materials, was translated into Spanish at the court of Alphonso X.[22] We know of about twenty manuscripts of this work, which circulated under the title *Picatrix.* This manual taught how to conjure up celestial powers and to make them favorable; it taught prayer formulas and invocations and prescribed the instruments to be used: images of Jupiter, Venus, Mars, and Saturn, which, when engraved on stones, could capture the influence of the corresponding divinities.

Moral Interpretation

The third type of interpretation consisted in uncovering spiritual meaning in the figures of the gods and moral meaning in their adventures. This type of allegory, which had been used by the first critics of Homer, was systematized by Stoics such as Cornutus.[23]

Having applied this method to the scriptures themselves, the apologists and the church fathers in turn were led to moralize mythology. In the sixth century, the biblical allegories of the *Moralia*[24] of Gregory the Great were paralleled by the profane allegories of Fulgentius's *Mythologies.*[25]

In Carolingian times, a poem by Theodulf,[26] bishop of Orléans, explained how wise men can turn poets' lies into truth, this beginning with Ovid. He first stated the following principle:

Signs of the Zodiac	Seasons	Ages of Life	Elements	Winds	Basic Qualities	States of the Body	Humors	Temperaments
Ram Bull Gemini	Spring	Childhood	Air	South	Moist heat	Liquid	Blood	Sanguine
Cancer Lyon Virgo	Summer	Youth	Fire	East	Dry heat	Subtle (gaseous)	Bile	Bilious
Libra Scorpio Sagittarius	Fall	Middle age	Earth	North	Dry cold	Dense	Black bile	Melancholic
Capricorn Aquarius Pisces	Winter	Old age	Water	West	Damp cold	Solid	Lymph	Phlegmatic

The stylus transmits the falsehood of poets and the truths of the wise.
But often the wise have to transform the poets' falsehoods into truths.

Thus he interpreted Proteus as truth, Hercules as virtue, Cacus as the rascal. And he commented on the attributes of Cupid:

Your depraved mind is symbolized by the quiver, your trickery by the bow.
Your arrows, child, are your poison; your torch your ardor, O Love.

The whole of mythology tended to become *philosophia moralis.* This was even the title of a work attributed to Hildebert of Lavardin,[27] bishop of Tours, who drew as many examples from pagan poets as he did from the Bible. In this context, pagan myths were seen as prefigurations of the Christian truth.

From the twelfth century on, this type of exegesis was surprisingly wide in scope. John of Salisbury,[28] the disciple of Bernard of Chartres, was interested in pagan mythology, "not out of respect for its false gods, but because they disguise secret teaching not accessible to ordinary people."[29] During this same period, Ovid was referred to as *ethicus* and as *theologus,* and collective explanations became increasingly numerous. Arnolph of Orléans[30] and John of Garland come to mind.[31]

A *Moralized Ovid*[32] was published during the first years of the fourteenth century. It expressed the allegorical principle that "everything for the benefit of our learning" can be found in the *Metamorphoses.* Indeed, the anonymous author found in the *Metamorphoses* all of Christian morality and the Bible itself: the peacock is the arrogant, self-glorifying person; Diana is the Trinity; Actaeon is Jesus Christ; Phaeton represents Lucifer and his revolt against God; Ceres searching for Proserpina is the church seeking to bring back lost souls to the fold, and so on.

Conventional allegories and moralization can also be found in Dante's work, in which they hold a surprising large place.[33]

The most extravagant and systematic work was the *Fulgentius metaforalis,*[34] written by the Franciscan John Ridewall in the mid-fifteenth century. As its title indicates, it was a revised version of one of Fulgentius's treatises in which all possible sources had been made use of. In it, the order of the chapters is structured by the identification of gods with virtues. Saturn is prudence, and, since the elements of prudence are memory, intelligence, and foresight, Ridewall then deals with Saturn's children, Juno-Memory, Neptune-Intelligence, Pluto-Providence, and Jupiter-Benevolence, himself the synthesis of prudence, wisdom and intelligence. To Pluto are subordinated

Cerberus-Cupiditas and Proserpina-Beatitudo. Likewise Apollo is truth, Danae modesty, Perseus courage, and so forth. We see here the extraordinary ingenuity of this commentary, in which each interpretation is based on an authority: Cicero, Saint Augustine, or Bernard of Chartres.

Synthesis

In the end, the gods survived, thanks to these three systems of interpretation. The systems were not exclusive, as all three were frequently applied to the same figure and the same myth.

In his cosmography,[35] Peter of Ailly (1350–1420), a distant disciple of Isidore, regarded the gods sometimes as celestial bodies and sometimes as sovereigns. Alexander Neckham (1157–1227), in his *De natura rerum*,[36] codified the relations between the planets and the virtues that had already been established during the ninth century. Dante, in his *Convivio*, relates these same planets, "based on their properties," to the liberal arts: grammar corresponds to the moon, dialectic to Mercury, rhetoric to Venus, geometry to Jupiter, and so on. As to the sphere of the fixed stars, it shows "manifest" resemblances to physics, metaphysics, ethics, and theology.

Illustration

These relationships were often represented graphically, with intertwining circles forming symmetrical compartments.

Representations of mythological figures underwent profound transformations during the Middle Ages, to the point of eventually becoming unrecognizable. These representations can be divided into two groups, according to whether their model was visual or simply a descriptive text.

Visual tradition was made up of several subgroups. The first went back to the manuscripts of the *Aratea,* the *Phaenomena,* in which Aratus described the constellations as a mythographer rather than as an astrologer. Carolingian copies of the *Aratea* still render the classical model with striking faithfulness. Yet strange new types appeared at the close of the Middle Ages. They came from the East and are found either in Arab manuscripts or in the illustrations of a treatise by Michael Scot, astrologer to Frederick II, written in Sicily around 1250.[37]

Outside of astronomical manuscripts, examples of the visual tradition are found almost exclusively in Byzantine art.[38]

The types that originated from a descriptive text in a "literary" source make up a distinct group. This family of gods usually appears in allegorical treatises. Such treatises contained two parts, the first descriptive and the second moral. The elements of the description were usually drawn from mythographers and commentators of late antiquity such as Macrobius, Servius, Lactantius Placidus, Martianus Capella, and Fulgentius. A manuscript of the *Commentary* by Rémi of Auxerre on Martianus Capella depicts a series of gods: Cybele, Apollo, Saturn, Mercury, and so on. But they are difficult to identify because the miniaturist had only a text to guide him, and this text, when followed faithfully, yielded only barbarian images. The same holds true for the *Fulgentius metaforalis*.

The *Liber imaginum deorum* by Albricus[39] was to have a lasting influence on iconography. This work was popular as an aid for reading profane poets. Two centuries later, the *Libellus de deorum imaginibus*[40] became an aid for artists.

In short, by the close of the Middle Ages, the two traditions, the visual and the literary, led to a profound alteration of the classical forms of the gods. Poor copies, substitutions, disguises, and naive reconstitutions: we don't know which of these procedures mistreated them the most, not to mention reading and translation errors that aggravated the corruption and probably stemmed from the texts' wanderings from east to west and north to south. Stripped of their classical forms, the gods became pure concepts, clothed in the most surprising attires.

The Renaissance was to give them back their classical forms, but within the framework of its own very particular intellectual context.

NINE

The Renaissance

T he Renaissance[1] received and developed the various interpretations of the gods proposed during the Middle Ages. This was a domain in which the Renaissance was largely beholden to the Middle Ages, a continuity that has often been overlooked because the forms of the ancient gods had become degraded, even unrecognizable.[2]

The gods of antiquity became once again what they used to be through the work of scholars who edited, translated, and commented on Greek texts that had not been available in the Middle Ages, and who published and explained the numerous visual representations that they had uncovered. By means of this constant interaction between the works of scholars, historians, and philosophers on the one hand, and the works of artists of all kinds—sculptors, painters, engravers, and the like—on the other, allegory ventured outside the limits of language and established itself in the domain of visual representations.

This originality, however, was embedded in the framework of a remarkable continuity in interpretations. The historical interpretation inspired by Euhemerism was to become very fashionable. Alchemical interpretation drew upon the relations established in classical antiquity between the divinities of the Greco-Roman pantheon and the constitutive elements of the sensible world. The moral and metaphysical interpretations took up the main lines of the grandiose Neoplatonic system Christianized by Byzantium and brought it to new extremes of subtlety.

The increasingly widespread use of printing was to give to published works on allegory a diffusion hitherto unknown.[3]

THE PERSISTENCE OF THE MIDDLE AGES

During the Renaissance, the gods thus gradually recovered their true forms. Yet certain factors slowed down this process. Paradoxically, the most important factors were the influence of printing[4] and the prestige of the illustrated book.

Besides Cicero's *De natura deorum*,[5] the first mythographic works published in print were those that had nourished the Middle Ages, along with the medieval compilations themselves, beginning with the *Liber* of Albricus.[6] Boccaccio's *Genealogia deorum*, heir to this tradition, was to remain the great mythological repertoire of the first half of the fifteenth century. It was published eight times between 1473 and 1532, whereas Apollodoros's *Bibliotheca*, which had been used by the Byzantines, was published only in 1555. Starting in 1549, various treatises were published, some ancient and others more recent, juxtaposing mythological, allegorical, and astronomical texts of very unequal quality. At the same time, Italy and the rest of Europe were inundated with editions of the *Metamorphoses*, but these were the "moralized Ovids."[7] In short, the principal authors used during the first part of the sixteenth century to perpetuate the knowledge of the gods of antiquity were those who were read during the Middle Ages and medieval authors themselves.

In addition, illustrated books played a vital role in the dissemination of an entirely medieval iconographic tradition. The great mythological incunabula, such as Boccaccio's *De casibus virorum et feminarum illustrium*,[8] contributed to this trend. At the same time, in Antwerp and Paris, three major works appeared: the *Recueil des histoires de Troye;* the *Faits et proësses du chevalier Jason;* and the *Destruction de Troye la Grant*, a work by Jacques Millet that went into nine editions between 1484 and 1526. The tradition perpetuated by these works was that of the *Libellus*,[9] of Nordic rather than classical inspiration, and their woodcuts could have just as well illustrated knightly romances.

While the archaeological discovery of antiquity had been going on for a long time, and the direct access to Greek texts had become an incontestable fact, what we find at the end of the fifteenth century are representations inherited from the Middle Ages.

THE ORIGINALITY OF THE RENAISSANCE

Direct contact with antiquity, primarily through Greek texts but also through various types of visual representations, helped Renaissance scholars restore to the pagan gods their true images. Interestingly, fake texts and images strongly contributed to the impetus of this movement of renewal.

The Texts and Their Editors, Translators, and Commentators

Knowledge of Greek enabled the publication and translation of texts that had remained practically unknown during the Middle Ages. Yet the Renaissance reader, like the medieval one, read a text solely for its teaching, particularly moral teaching. Hence the enormous effort the Renaissance put into this domain. The project consisted in helping to adapt myths so that they could fulfill the expectations of the public they were aimed at, a process no longer automatic, as it had been in a civilization in which communication was exclusively oral.[10] Knowledge of Greek made available to the educated European public, whether directly or indirectly (through translations), the most important and useful texts for learning about the Greek pantheon, beginning of course with the *Iliad* and the *Odyssey.*

Homer

During the Middle Ages,[11] the heroes of the Trojan war were considered to be dukes, counts, and knights, and their adventures and personalities were known not through Homer but by way of Ovid, Virgil,[12] Statius,[13] Dictys,[14] Dares,[15] Benoît,[16] and Guido.[17] The medieval *Iliad* was reduced to a *Pindarus Thebanus de bello Trojano,* a summary of the epic poem in 1,200 mediocre Latin hexameters.[18]

The translation of Homer into prose that Boccaccio had requested and Pilato[19] had accomplished filled Petrarch with pleasure; but he probably read it for its moral teaching just as he had read the *Aeneid.* Pilato's attempt was not to remain a solitary one. However, Homer was not truly read in the West before Angelo Poliziano set out to complete the translation of the *Iliad* started by Carlo Marsuppini, though he did not get beyond book V.[20] Like Petrarch,[21] Poliziano read Homer in quest of moral teaching.

The same concern was manifest among the first publishers of Homer, Chalcondyles, and Acciaiuoli, who, in the Florence edition of 1488, included a speech on Homer by Dion Chrysostomus, as well as a biography of Homer attributed to Herodotus and *Homer's Life and Poetry* attributed to Plutarch. The later editions and translations of Homer[22] became enriched with increasingly numerous allegorical commentaries. The movement culminated with a number of publications, including Porphyry's *Homeric Questions* and *The Cave of the Nymphs* in 1531, Eustathius's commentaries on the *Iliad* and the *Odyssey,* Proclus's Homeric commentaries (treatises V and VI of the *Commentary on the Republic*) in 1542, the *Home-*

ric Allegories attributed to Heraclitus[23] in 1544, and an anonymous work titled *Moral Interpretation of Odysseus's Travels*.[24] Jean de Sponde was the only one who resisted this movement, which entailed the inclusion of the means for moral interpretation of the text along with the text itself. In 1583, he published in Basel a text devoid of moralizing explanations.

Other scholars dealt with Homer, no longer from a more or less moralized literary perspective but rather from a historical viewpoint by using arguments drawn from Euhemerism. In his *Antenor* (Padua 1625), Lorenzo Pignoria attempted to show that Antenor[25] was the true founder of Padua. Reiner Reineck described[26] Odysseus's travels through most of the countries of Europe. Samuel Bochart,[27] a disciple of the British theologian Julius Cameron, set out to prove that Odysseus's adventures took place along the coasts of the Latium and Campania. Francesco Bianchini developed[28] a theory according to which Zeus had been king of Ethiopia; Juno, queen of Syria; Neptune, prince of Caria; and Apollo, prince of Assyria. Finally, Hermann von der Hardt[29] went so far as to claim that Odysseus should be identified with Thesprotus of Pandrosia, who had fortified Mount Hypatus, represented by the Trojan horse, from which he emerged to found colonies in various places.

A third group of scholars established all sorts of parallels between Homer on the one hand and the Old and New Testaments on the other. Some even found traces of Christian doctrines in Homer, a discovery they also made in Plato, Seneca, Orpheus, Virgil, and other Greek and Roman authors. Thus J. B. Persona,[30] Nicolas Bergmann[31] and Johannes Roth[32] succeeded in turning Homer, if not into a Christian theologian, at least into a Christian philosopher. As for Jacques Hugues[33] he was convinced that the fall of Troy must be interpreted as the synthesis of the taking of Jerusalem by the Babylonians on the one hand and by the Romans on the other; hence the lack of compunction with which he identified Helen with the "incarnate god," blind Tiresias with Abraham; Cassandra who predicted the fall of Troy, with Jeremiah; and so forth. Zachary Bogan[34] offered an enormous compilation of passages in Homer that he believed paralleled the Bible.

Finally, James Duport[35] thought that the moral doctrines propounded by Homer came to him from the studies of the Old Testament he had done in Egypt. He thus wanted to show the superiority of Christ over Apollo, of David over Pindar, of Paul over Seneca, and of Solomon over Homer, and he exhorted his readers to be Christians first and admirers of Homer, Aristotle, and Cicero second. Moreover, explained Duport, when Homer described the gardens of Alcinoos, he had a vague memory of the Garden of Eden, and likewise the narrative of the attack of the Giants and the Titans against Olympus came from the memory of the building of the tower of Babel. The numerous traces of Hebrew wisdom dispersed in Homer's epics are what explains Plato's aversion for him, for Plato was not capable of understanding this profound poetry with its abundant mysteries.

The Egyptians

Homer had acquired all the knowledge he hid in the *Iliad* and the *Odyssey* during his years of study in Egypt. This was a widespread opinion, even among the Greeks, who credited several other personalities, including Solon, Thales, Plato, Eudoxus, and Pythagoras, with journeys to Egypt, the source of all civilization. To the Christians, however, Moses was more important and more ancient than Homer; therefore, according to the various authorities, either the poet had taught the lawgiver or the lawgiver had taught the poet.

This is the context of the discovery of the *Hieroglyphica*[36] in 1419 by Christoforo de Buondelmonti, an associate of the antiquarian Niccolo Niccoli. This work was supposed to have been written in the Egyptian language by a priest called Horapollo[37] and translated into Greek by a certain Philip. On the basis of 189 examples, the *Hieroglyphica* bring out the similarities between pagan and Christian interpretations of animals: the pig symbolizes a harmful man, the weasel a weak man, the swan an elderly musician, and so on. After its publication in Greek in 1505, this odd dictionary of symbols was republished at least thirty times in Latin, French, Italian, and German translations.

The fashion for Egypt that this work generated was intensified by awareness of the existence of a bronze table decorated with hieroglyphs and silver figurines which was actually a fake owned by Cardinal Bembo.[38] While still in the museum of the Duke of Mantua, the relic known as the Bembine Table was copied and engraved by Vico of Parma, who published the first engravings of it in Venice in 1600. At the request of Marcus Velser, Pignoria reprinted Vico's engravings and added explicative texts to them.[39] Even though Pignoria was not able to dissociate the gods and goddesses of Egypt from the hieroglyphs accompanying their representations, he attempted to identify them, recounted their history, gave an idea of their cult, and established their relations with their emblematic animals along with the signs that identified them. In the third volume of his *Oedipus Aegypticus,* Athanasius Kircher, putting his imagination to the service of his immense erudition, undertook a much less sober interpretation of the *Mensa Isiaca,* the name he gave to the Bembine Table, which by then had disappeared.[40] He divided the *Mensa Isiaca* into series of triads that all originated in the three central figures of Egyptian theosophy: father, power, and spirit; or faith, truth, and love. Each square centimeter of the Bembine Table was used to describe the detail of the descending chain leading from the Ideas of God to matter.

Despite their lack of authenticity, the *Hieroglyphica* and the Bembine Table rekindled the Renaissance's interest in allegory and symbols.

The immense popularity of the *Hieroglyphica* led to the production of dictionaries offering a compilation of symbols. The first dictionary of this genre was that of Piero Valeriano Bolzani.[41] In his inscription dedicating the book to Cosimo de Medici, Valeriano Bolzani evoked his conversations with Cardinal Bembo about the obelisks in Rome and Roman monuments that were as worthy of preservation as Michelangelo's statues in the Saint Laurence basilica. In 1576, the *Hieroglyphica* by Celio Agostino Curio, Bembo's publisher and the historian of the Saracens, was published as an appendix to an edition of Valeriano's work. Two major names stand out among Valeriano's successors: Nicolas Caussin and Athanasius Kircher.

In Paris in 1618, Father Nicolas Caussin had published an *Electorum symbolorum et parabolorum historicarum syntagmata*, which included Horapollo's *Hieroglyphica*, a summary of Valeriano's work, and a number of texts on hieroglyphs.

In 1630, Pietro della Valle bought the manuscript of a Coptic-Arab dictionary on which Athanasius Kircher based his book *Prodromus coptus*, published in 1636. It was a Coptic grammar and vocabulary, preceded by a preface that was five times as long as the body of the work. Though far from perfect, this manual still remains the basic work for Coptic studies. In 1664, Kircher had published in Rome a *Lingua aegyptiaca restituta*, which corresponded to Pietro della Valle's dictionary and included in an appendix ten essays on subjects pertaining to Egypt. In 1650 the *Obeliscus pamphilius* was published in Rome; it dealt more precisely with the interpretation of symbols. Two years later *Oedipus aegyptiacus; hoc est universalis hieroglyphicae veterum doctrinae temporum iniurai abolitae instauratio* was published in four folios, the whole consisting of more than two thousand pages, in which Kircher describes the religion, culture, and politics of Egypt. Here, Adam was born of parents whose origin went back to the moon, and he himself was a priest of the moon. Adam beseeched human beings to worship this heavenly body, until Seth taught him the true path. Human beings, however, did not renounce the worship of heavenly bodies, and even at that time Adam, Eve, the serpent, Cain, and Seth were looked upon as divinities in the context of a theology that Shem had carried into Egypt and that became more and more degraded, thus making possible the apparition of the Egyptian pantheon. Moreover, all languages derive from Hebrew, the language that was taught to Adam by revelation at the same time as the other sciences. But the first human beings to make use of the symbol defined as "the sign signifying a hidden mystery" were the Egyptians. The Greeks learned from them.

Virgil's *Aeneid*

In the Middle Ages, when people barely knew Homer's name and the content of the *Iliad* and the *Odyssey*, they were at least aware that these works had been at the origin of Virgil's *Aeneid*.[42] Miracles were attributed to the great Roman poet, and it was taken for granted that he had hidden in his texts a wisdom that had been lost. The medieval interest in the *Aeneid* explains why this work was transmitted to the Renaissance with allegorical commentaries as pious as those accompanying the scriptures. Virgil's works were reprinted during the Renaissance along with the grammatical commentaries by Junius Philargyrius and Valerius Probus, and comments by Maurus Servius Honoratus and Tiberius (or Aelius) Donatus.[43] Fulgentius's *De expositione Virgilianae continentia*,[44] published for the first time in 1589, was subsequently included in editions of the *Aeneid*. The commentary by Bernard Sylvester,[45] however, was published only during the Renaissance.[46]

Virgil's most important and influential interpreter during the Renaissance was Cristoforo Landino, a member of the Platonic Academy of Florence, directed by Marsilio Ficino under the patronage of Lorenzo de Medici. In 1487–1488, Landino had an edition of the works of Virgil published. At the end of his introduction to the *Aeneid*, he refers to the *Quaestiones Camaldulenses*,[47] which may have appeared for the first time in 1480 and were supposed to reveal "the internal meaning of the poem." In 1577 and in 1596 the *Quaestiones* were printed as an appendix to the Basel edition of the *Aeneid* and by then had been retitled *Allegoria platonica in XII libros*. The title is misleading because Landino, like most commentators, did not go beyond book VI. But the two discussions of Virgil's allegory that serve as a conclusion to the *Quaestiones* well illustrate the philosophical postulates basic to Landino's allegorical practice. This practice was rooted in the Christian Platonism of the Florence Academy; it was thus an allegory of the moral and metaphysical type. These ideas were not totally original, for in January of 1427, F. Filelfo had claimed in a letter to Cyriacus of Ancona that Virgil had written the *Aeneid* in order to educate magistrates, thereby imitating Homer's *Odyssey*.

By dedicating his book on Virgil[48] to Pope Clement II, Girolamo Balbi wanted to persuade the spiritual and temporal leaders of Christendom to crush the Turks and free the republics of Europe from the danger threatening them. Balbi developed this idea by quoting numerous passages from ancient authors and particularly Virgil, from whose work he extracted moral and psychological lessons. Sebastiano Regoli, who commented only on the first book of the *Aeneid*,[49] adopted a similar approach.

Gradually, however, allegorical interpretation was replaced by more technical studies before reappearing in commentaries in the vernacular. One such commentary, on a very lengthy scholium on the *Aeneid* by Giovanni Fabrini,[50] offered the following interpretation of Cerberus, the dog guarding the entrance of the underworld:

> In my opinion, Cerberus is thought to have three heads so as to show the natural and necessary needs without which one cannot live or accomplish anything. These are hunger, thirst, and sleepiness, which are found in the body and hound reason, never letting it alone until it has satisfied them. This is the truth, for when it is hungry, thirsty, or sleepy, the body cannot do anything and has to satisfy those needs. Consequently, when Aeneas, who has just entered the underworld, that is, a state of contemplation, is troubled by natural and necessary needs, he has to satisfy them before entering this state of contemplation. The Sybil who advises him gives a bone to Cerberus to make him sleep. Virgil uses this means to teach that there is no wrong in satisfying natural needs, up to a certain point. Anyone who refuses to satisfy the needs of nature ends up discovering that he was wrong and that he must obey. Because of all this, it is an act of virtue to fulfill virtuously and voluntarily the needs of existence with the aim of pleasing God, to be charitable and to make penance. And to show that nature is satisfied with little, a simple bone was enough to make Cerberus fall asleep, because when its nature is hungry, it demands nothing more than bread, and when it is thirsty, it is satisfied with water, and when it is sleepy, a small hut is sufficient. Epicurus, who locates the supreme good in pleasure, does not seek any other flavoring than hunger and thirst, because hunger makes all food pleasing, and thirst make drinks sweet.

In this passage, Fabrini, who had been shown the path by Landino, adds to the exegesis of his illustrious predecessor by ending with rather unexpected praise of Epicurus.

Ovid's *Metamorphoses*

Ovid's *Metamorphoses* were known to the Renaissance in the company of several medieval commentaries.[51] The Middle Ages might be said to have "invented" the idea that Ovid's *Metamorphoses* could be interpreted allegorically.[52]

After the edition of *De vetula* in 1470, Ovid's complete works were published almost every year. Editions included commentaries by Giorgio Merula, Paoli Marso, and Raffaello Regio among others. These commentaries were mostly explicative, though their authors seem to have been aware of allegory. In the first half of the sixteenth century, a certain Petrus Lavinius[53] proposed "allegorical and tropological" commentaries on some myths.

The *Fabularum Ovidii interpretatio tradita in Academia Regiomontana* was published in 1555 at Wittenberg. Its author was Georg Schuler (= Sabinus), a disciple of Melanchthon and a friend of Bembo and Aleandro. In this work, Schuler practiced all the types of allegorical interpretation. For instance, in his astrological interpretation, Hermaphrodites was the son of Venus and Mercury, for when Mercury is ascendant, it modifies the male or female nature of the other planets. In Schuler's Euhemerist interpretation, Prometheus was an astronomer who came to the Caucasus to study the sign of the Eagle (Aquila). In his physical interpretation, Semele is the rich and humid earth, which allows grapes to grow, and Jupiter is warmth and hot air, which allow fruits to grow and their juices to ferment. This is why Jupiter and Semele are said to be the parents of Bacchus, identified with wine. In Schuler's psychological interpretation, envy becomes personified. And in his favored type of interpretation, the moral one, the myth of Cadmus sowing the dragon's teeth has its origin in the true history of the spread of revolt among the disinherited sons of King Dracon, who organized a military plot against their father.

Other names can be associated with that of Schuler. They include an unknown author with the initials T. H.;[54] Giuseppe Horologgio, who wrote moral annotations to the edition of the *Metamorphoses* published in Venice in 1571; Ercole Ciofani;[55] Jacob Spannmueller;[56] and Johann Ludwig Gottfried.[57]

In a commentary devoted to the first four hundred lines of the *Metamorphoses*,[58] Abraham Fraunce made the nature of his project explicit. Poetry and painting transmit the most deeply hidden secrets of ancient philosophy. Pythagoras; Plato in the *Phaedrus,* the *Timaeus,* and the *Symposium;* the Indians, the Ethiopians, the Egyptians, and the Greeks: all of these camouflaged their secrets in this manner. The same goes for the *Song of Songs* of King Solomon. George Sandy drew on this source of inspiration in his well-known translation and adaptation with commentaries of Ovid's work (five-volume edition, 1621; complete edition, 1625; standard edition, 1632), which followed the rather dull translation by Arthur Golding published in 1567.

In France,[59] before the publication of Sandy's work, Nicolas Renouard published a translation of the *Metamorphoses* in Paris in 1614.[60] Even while maintaining a moralizing orientation, Renouard attempted to rediscover in Ovid's *Metamorphoses* the great principles of philosophy: Plato's forms, Pythagoras's harmony, Heraclitus's fire, Hermes Trismegistus's stars, Chrysippus's numbers, and Aristotle's entelechy. Renouard perceived the influence of Moses behind the philosophical doctrines evoked in book I: Prometheus represented Providence and could be regarded as an astronomer; the myth of the four "races of metal" (gold, silver, bronze, iron) was inspired by one of Daniel's prophecies; the Giants built the tower of Babel; Lycaon gave a lesson in piety and hospitality; Deucalion should be identified with Noah; and so forth. Renouard was more original in his interpretation of the other books. The story of Pyramus and Thisbe is a warning not only to children against the temptation to disobey their parents, but also to parents against their tendency to oppose their children's love affairs. Medusa represents the French Protestants, and Perseus is obviously identified with Henry of Navarre. The myth of Icarus is really the story of an arrogant astrologer adhering to false doctrines, whose reputation is consequently destroyed. In 1660, Renouard's translation yielded to that of Pierre du Ryer.[61] This translation in turn was supplanted by that of Banier,[62] who offered a Euhemerist interpretation.

Mythographers and Antiquarians

The editors, translators, and commentators of the poetic texts carrying the myths of Greek and Roman antiquity were helped by new types of professionals who made their appearance during the Renaissance: mythographers, who undertook the compilation of myths; and antiquarians, who could be called the forebears of archaeologists. Mythographers depended on the interpretations that necessarily accompanied the myths they were collecting. Antiquarians had to refer to the texts of antiquity to interpret their finds. There was a consequent back-and-forth among specialists as they kept on broadening the circle of knowledge and interpretation of the myths of antiquity.

The Mythographers

The professional mythographers who studied the myths of the ancients and sought to explain them were, in a sense, a creation of the Renaissance. The manuals they wrote were carefully consulted by artists, by writers, and by the educated in general. In completing their compilations, mythographers made use of medieval literary texts, the first commentaries on those texts, medieval mythologies, and recently discovered classic interpreters.[63] Except perhaps for Giraldi, tradition proved to be the determining factor as authors produced Euhemerist, ethical, moral, and symbolic interpretations. The common thread was a genuine fascination for hidden meaning.

In 1336, Petrarch's good friend Boccaccio, through the good offices of Donnino of Parma, was asked to provide for the king of Cyprus, Hugo IV, "a genealogy of the pagan gods" and "an explanation of the meanings that illustrious men have found beneath the surface of myths." The compilation of his *Genealogia deorum gentilium* was to occupy the rest of Boccaccio's life.[64]

According to Boccaccio, who was later imitated by Georg Pictor,[65] myths have several meanings. Thus, the myth of Perseus cutting off the Gorgon's head and lifting himself off the ground on winged sandals can be taken either literally as the narrative of an actual event, ethically as the symbol of the victory of a wise man rising toward virtue after having crushed sin, or allegorically as the symbol of Christ triumphant over the prince of this world and returning to his father in heaven. But Boccaccio went further and became a genealogist, wondering who created the Greek gods. He claimed it was Demogorgon, a frightening divinity who kept company with Eternity and Chaos in a cavern at the center of the earth. The whole of the lineage of the gods, heroes, and human beings descended from Ether, son of Erebus, who issued from Demogorgon. This genealogy takes on an even more "fabulous" character when Demogorgon turns out to be a *lapsus calami,* a catastrophic error, made by a certain Theodontius, a person we know nothing about but who miscopied and misunderstood one of Lactantius Placidus's glosses on Statius's *Thebaid* (IV 516): "*Dicit* (Statius) *autem deum demiourgon, cuius scire non licet.*" The common ancestor of the gods, daemons, and humans is thus reduced to very little!

Between 1548 and 1568, three manuals, important for their scope and success, appeared in rapid succession in Italy.[66] Appearances to the contrary, none of these works made decisive progress in relation to previous treatises, for none brought anything essentially new. Overall, they relied on the methods and the images of the past.

The immense success not only of Giraldi but more notably of Conti and Cartari made useless the publication of other works in the same genre,[67] though the works of Cartari and other mythographers did lead to the publication of illustrated mythologies.[68]

Like most commentators, the majority of the mythographers indulged without any compunction in a nonliteral reading of poetic texts. The reaction to their approach was a rather strident questioning of its value. François Rabelais showed little tolerance for allegory in his prologue to *Gargantua*.

> But do you faithfully believe that Homer, in writing his *Iliad* and *Odyssey*, ever had in mind the allegories squeezed out of him by Plutarch, Heraclides Ponticus, Eustathius, and Phornutus, and which Politian afterwards stole from them in his turn? If you do, you are not within a hand's or a foot's length of my opinion. For I believe them to have been as little dreamed of by Homer as the Gospel mysteries were by Ovid in his *Metamorphoses;* a case which a certain Friar Lubin,[69] a true bacon-picker, has actually tried to prove, in the hope that he may meet others as crazy as himself and—as the proverb says—a lid to fit his kettle.[70]

This statement didn't keep Rabelais from relying on his copy of Horapollo's *Hierogolyphica* to explain the white and blue colors of Gargantua's coat of arms (chapter 9 of *Gargantua*).

Luther denounced allegory, though he occasionally made use of it. In his commentary on Genesis 30: 9–11, written toward the end of his life, he reminded his readers that the Turks interpreted the Koran allegorically, and went on to say:

> Indeed, allegory is like a beautiful whore offering caresses so that she can't help but be loved, particularly by lazy, inexperienced people. People of this kind think they are in the midst of Paradise and in God's bosom each time they give themselves over to this sort of speculation. At first, allegory originated with stupid, lazy monks; and finally it became so widespread that many people interpreted the *Metamorphoses* allegorically. They made a laurel tree Mary, and Apollo they made Christ. Although this is an absurd practice, it is nonetheless true that when it is offered to adolescents lacking in experience but loving and studying literature, it pleases them so much at this point of their learning that they are totally taken by such interpretations. This is why I hate allegory; but if someone wants to use it, let us show him how to use it sensibly.[71]

Luther's associate Melanchthon largely shared his views, but that did not prevent his practicing allegory of the rhetorical type he called "mythologian," which corresponded to a form of Euhemerism. This enabled him to present the Cyclops as a kind of primitive people using a shield with a hole in the middle. His position, firm but moderate, was shared by Calvin, who wrote:

Whatever the case may be, we should keep the simplicity of the text because to play with the Holy Scriptures by transforming them into allegory is a bad thing; and allegories should only be taken from the natural meaning: as we see Saint Paul do in the *Epistle to the Galatians* and other passages.[72]

Erasmus[73] gave a genuine explanation of "allegory" and adopted a conciliatory though cautious attitude toward it: allegory could be used to explain the Bible, but any attempt at transforming all the myths told by the poets into Christian allegories ought to be resisted (*Adage* 2878). British reformers like Myles Coverdale and, to a lesser extent, William Tyndale agreed with Erasmus. But at the beginning of the seventeenth century the Protestants, though retaining a certain respect for analogy, became increasingly distrustful of meaning that was nonliteral.

This distrust can be seen even in Francis Bacon, the best interpreter of mythology according to the rules of allegory.[74] In *The Advancement of Learning* (1605) he attacks Paracelsus along with all those who, like him, sought "all natural philosophy" in the Bible. Thus he states in book II:

In many the like encounters, I do rather think that the fable was first, and the exposition devised, than that the moral was first, and thereupon the fable framed. For I find it was an ancient vanity in Chrysippus, that troubled himself with great contention to fasten the assertions of the Stoics upon the fictions of the ancient poets; but yet that all the fables and fictions of the poets were but pleasure and not figure, I interpose no opinion. Surely of those poets which are now extant, even Homer himself (notwithstanding he was made a kind of scripture by the later schools of the Grecians), yet I should without any difficulty pronounce that his fables had no such inwardness in his own meaning.[75]

Still, Bacon agrees that one can have some doubts on the mystical meaning that the myths might contain, although he admits that such meaning does exist. The preface of *De sapientia veterum* (1609) takes up again and makes more precise the doctrine expressed in *The Advancement of Learning*.

The Antiquarians

Scholars who undertook the systematic study of monuments and art objects may be said to have favored this movement of mistrust toward the kind of allegorical interpretation that had allowed Christian morality and physical science to be found in Homer, Virgil, Ovid, and Egyptian hieroglyphs. Still, objects discovered under the ground had to be interpreted, and in order to do so, the antiquarians had to go back to the texts or consult the mythographers' work.

Nostalgia for historical places goes back at least as far as Alexander, who, when visiting the ruins of Troy, had libations offered on the heroes' tombs, notably on that of Achilles.[76] But the birth of the antiquarian movement came about in the fifteenth century with names such as that of Poggio Bracciolini, Antonio Lusco, and Cyriacus of Ancona. The profession of antiquarian came into its own when Pomponio Leto founded the Academy of Antiquarians, which was eventually to be closed by Pope Paul II. During the whole of the fifteenth century, scholars cooperatively attempted to date and to explain the antiquities of Greece and Rome. In the course of the sixteenth and, particularly, the seventeenth century the profession became a true discipline. This movement culminated with the publication in 1719 by the abbé Bernard de Montfaucon of the fifteen volumes in-folio of *L'Antiquité expliquée et représentée en figures,* which was completed in 1724. A number of specialists can be distinguished among the antiquarians.

(1) *The numismatists.* The first numismatist to publish the reverse sides of medallions was Aeneas Vico, a student of Raphael and the first engraver of the Bembine Table,[77] who, from 1548 to 1557, published three works[78] in which he sought to interpret the symbolism on the heads of coins. Guillaume du Choul[79] was the first to use reverse sides of coins as documents with illustrative value. His disciple was Gabriele Simeoni.[80] But the first true professionals were Sebastiano Erizzo,[81] Costanzo Landi,[82] and Hubrecht Goltz.[83] They were acknowledged by their successors, Antoine le Pois,[84] Antonio Agustin, Bishop of Tarragona,[85] Charles Patin,[86] Abraham de Goorle,[87] Jacques de Bie,[88] and Ezekiel Spanheim.[89]

It should be noted that antique medallions and Egyptian hieroglyphs found on obelisks, on the Bembine Table, and in Horapollo's work were to be the sources of a long tradition of illustrated books titled *Emblems,* that is, books of cryptograms. The first book of *Emblems* was by Alciati.[90] It was published in 1531 and was to reappear more than fifty times in all the languages spoken in Europe. Mythology holds an important place in this type of work, in which the figures and attributes of the gods are interpreted as signs concealing truths and moral maxims. Mythographers therefore derived much inspiration from them. A byproduct of these cryptograms was the strange deviations they introduced in the visual renderings of mythology, deviations that paradoxically favored the reconciliation of paganism and Christianity.

(2) *Iconographers.* The symbolist explanation of the numismatists was also attractive to specialists in iconography, who published images of statues, fig-

urines, mosaics, and murals and sought in Greek and Roman texts material that would help explain the visual representations they were pondering. For the sixteenth century we may mention Andrea Fulvio;[91] for the seventeenth, Lorenzo Pignoria,[92] François de Jon,[93] Lucas Holstenius,[94] Joachim von Sandrart,[95] and, notably, *Le pitture antiche del' sepolchro de Nasonii*.[96]

(3) *Experts on sculpture and engraving.* Those who focused on sculptures and engravings met with the same problems as the iconographers. Oftentimes experts in one field were also expert in another. The first to try to interpret the historical signification of a column was Alphonse Chacon.[97] Giovanni Pietro Bellori and Pietro Sante Bartoli[98] followed his example, as did Raffaelo Fabretti.[99] F. Andrea Palladio[100] was the first to draw the ruins of Rome. Palladio's drawings were reproduced in Andrea Fulvio's guide, published in 1588 by Girolamo Ferruci,[101] who added commentaries that occasionally applied allegorical interpretations to the drawings. A telling example in this regard is the interpretation of a bas-relief representing Mithra stabbing an ox with a dagger, and surrounded by several other figures and symbols pertaining to this sacrificial scene. As Ferruci was ignorant of the scene and the cult evoked by it and unable to understand the meaning of the inscriptions, he interpreted the bas-relief as an allegory of agriculture. The wise peasant, observing the phases of the moon and the course of the sun, works his land night and day and is helped in his work by virtues such as strength, prudent providing, and persistence. The ox represents the earth, which is pierced by the dagger of work, and the blood that flows can be interpreted as the fruit of this labor. The dog licking the blood represents love and faith; the serpent coiled around the oxen is prudence; the lion represent energy and strength; and the scorpion stinging the testicles of the bull represents generation. In this view, Mithra is thus the figure of the good peasant. As to Girolamo Aleandro, he offered a symbolic commentary on the *Tabula Heliaci*.[102]

(4) *Experts on epigraphs.* While the specialists in sculptures and engravings were mostly interested by the historical localization of the events represented on columns and on the friezes of triumphal arches, scholars such as Jan Gruytere,[103] Thomas Reinesius,[104] Rafaello Fabretti,[105] and Antonio Bosio[106] took pride in interpreting the symbolism of funerary monuments.

(5) *Gemologists.* The interpretation of the intaglios on gems, which preoccupied people like Leonardo Agostini[107] and Jean Tristan de Saint-Amant,[108] became increasingly oriented to symbolism, and Fortunio Liceti[109] was no exception. Liceti indulged in symbolic interpretation encompassing occultism, literary tradition, and even philosophy. Here, for instance, is the way he interpreted a gem depicting a Cupid who, with a stick, is trying to make a bird perched on a tree enter a cage hanging on a branch.

He included each element in the image in his analysis. After reminding his readers of the hidden meaning of Homer's *molu*[110] and of the tree of good and evil, Liceti explains that this is the tree of human wisdom. It must thus be a laurel tree, the emblem of the knowledge that is not given to humans by God but is acquired through hard labor. The tree is not covered with flowers because humanity's goal is truth, not pleasure. But this tree bears fruits that we cannot see because they are the imaginary fruits of symbol, allegory, and metaphor. The bird that the Cupid is trying to catch is the "world," because Homer says that the world is "winged" and "resembles a bird." This bird must be a nightingale, the symbol of the person who, thirsting for knowledge, attains eminence in the domain of letters. The bird's song teaches Cupid. Finally, the cage, a prison for the bird, represents the book in which human wisdom is locked up.

INTERPRETATIONS

Editors, translators of Greek and Latin texts and their commentators, along with mythographers and even antiquarians offered interpretations of the ancient myths they were studying, whether in texts or in visual representations, their interpretations depended on projects that were historical, alchemical, or philosophical in nature. Indeed, the Renaissance attempted with all possible means to integrate mythology into sacred history and Christian theology.

Those who proposed an allegorical interpretation of Homer, Virgil, Ovid, and Egyptian hieroglyphs; those who offered symbolic interpretations of objects from antiquity; and the compilers of mythographical and symbolic works—all were haunted by the same feeling of divine mystery that had led their associates to search for traces of Christian doctrines and holy history, traces they assumed had been largely forgotten or diabolically corrupted in the remains of paganism. Few people living in the Renaissance era were able to step back from their work and ask themselves whether they had found the interpretations they defended in the texts and objects of antiquity or in their own imaginations.

Historical Interpretation: Euhemerism

At the beginning of the sixteenth century, Euhemerist interpretation was known through the use its pagan supporters and the church fathers had made of it. Giovanni Nannio of Viterbo[111] claimed to have discovered some very ancient historians. His claim was all the more interesting to those who were intent on proving that Greek mythology taken as a whole could ultimately be explained as a distortion of history stolen from Moses. Among the dozens of authors "rediscovered" by Nannio was a *History of the Chaldeans,* supposedly written by Berosus of Babylon. In spite of the doubts expressed by some skeptics, this fake was widely used until the eighteenth century, and its chronology was systematically referred to.

The motive behind this massive effort was to demonstrate, with the help of etymological research and comparative biographies, that the Old and New Testaments underlay the doctrines, cults, and history of the other religions.

The first to propose a coherent Euhemerist interpretation was Jean Lemaire de Belges,[112] whose work was published in the first decade of the sixteenth century and reprinted a number of times. A fascinating book was written in English by Richard Lynche,[113] who undertook to endow Britain with Trojan origins. Johann Bertels wrote a *Historia Luxemburgensis,*[114] so as to provide his compatriots with ancient origins.

Walter Raleigh, for his part, wrote a *Historie of the World,*[115] in which he claimed that Moses could draw not only from an oral tradition but also from manuscripts written by Enoch. This enabled Raleigh to systematically link the Bible to Greek mythology. He identified Adam with Saturn. Cain, who married his own sister, was known under the name of Jupiter. Eve became Rhea, and so forth. This same approach was taken by Hugh Sanford,[116] who, however, laid great emphasis on the phonetic origin of names. Sanford's postulate was that the Jews transmitted their knowledge to the Egyptians and the Phoenicians, who then transmitted theirs to the Greeks. The oral transmission of this tradition unavoidably entailed a distortion in the names. This postulate led Sanford to discover that Isis was really Moses's mother and that Moses was also known as Mises and Meso. The philological manipulations in which Sanford took such delight drew on the speculations of those who, like Ficino, Steuco, and Pansa, had wanted to establish agreements between biblical figures and the pagan gods, an obsession that was to persist throughout the Renaissance and ended only with the Enlightenment.

This obsession, however, did raise an important question: how could human beings, filled with divine light and science, sink into darkness and ignorance? This issue stemmed from the puzzle of the pagan origin of certain Christian rites. Several authors with very different interests were to seek an answer to this question during the seventeenth century: Giovanni Casalio,[117] Noël Alexandre,[118] D. Mayer,[119] S. Jones,[120] Abraham Darcie,[121] Antonius van Dale,[122] Gerard Johann Vossius,[123] and Samuel Bochart.[124]

The debate, broadened in scope, revisited the question of origins with John Owen,[125] Edward Stillingfleet,[126] and Theophilus Gale.[127]

Things evolved during the last part of the seventeenth century. Studies on religions other than Christianity multiplied, and they tended to show that most religions had many things in common and that all originated in certain primitive fears and hopes. Christianity still held the first place, but already the apologetic project was yielding to other preoccupations, as we sense when reading Edward Herbert.[128] The movement was maintained and accelerated with Antonius van Dale,[129] Pierre Bayle,[130] Bernard de Fontenelle,[131] Arthur Young,[132] and, above all, Pierre-Daniel Huet.[133]

In discovering that most of the beliefs, rites, and moral convictions of Christianity were found in various nations throughout the world, Huet was on the verge of making important discoveries in anthropology. But his Christian convictions blinded him, and he returned to Ficino's and Steuco's ideas on the agreement between religions.

Physical Interpretation: Alchemy

Alchemy[134] was transmitted by Byzantium[135] and by the Arab and western Middle Ages.[136] It always remained associated with mythology and experienced a resurgence during the Renaissance. At that time, alchemy found a new justification in Egyptian wisdom, of which the basic works had just been "discovered."

The first historical accounts of the relationship between alchemy and mythology that were cited during the Renaissance belonged to the Byzantine and the medieval worlds. These included the *Suda;*[137] Albert the Great's *De mineralibus,* which explained the origin of rocks by the myth of Pyrrha and Deucalion and also by that of the Gorgon; and the *Pretiosa margarita novella*[138] of Peter Lombard (Petrus Bonus Lombardus), written around 1330, which drew much from the *Bucolics,* the *Georgics,* the *Aeneid,* and the *Metamorphoses,* as well as from Proteus, Phaethon, Medea's Labyrinth, Jason sowing the dragon's teeth, and Pyramus and Thisbe. Philippe Eléphant's name also belongs in this group.[139]

Giovanni Aurelio Augurelli seems to have been the first Renaissance poet to sing of alchemy under the veil of myth.[140] He is thought to have been imitated by Pico della Mirandola, if we are to judge by the poems inserted in the *De auro libri.* Lilio Gregorio Giraldi tells us that when he had taken refuge in the castle of the Mirandola after the sack of Rome, he brought away with him one of Psellus's manuscripts[141] on royal art. Giraldi and his friend read the *Argonauts*[142] with "chemical eyes,"[143] for the golden fleece evoked the transmutation of all things into gold.

Around the same time, a number of manuscripts were circulating in France bearing the title *Le grand Olimpe, ou Philosophie poétique attribuée au très renommé Ovide,* traduit de latin en langue françoise par Pierre Vicot, prestre, serviteur domestique de Nicolas Grosparmy, gentilhomme normand et Nicolas le Vallois.[144] Giovanni Bracesco da Ioarca Novi, for his part, gave an alchemical meaning to the main myths in *La espositione di Geber,*[145] the most important Renaissance work in the domain of alchemy. Most of the symbols known in that century were listed in the two folios published in 1591 by Antonio Ricciardi,[146] a friend of Pietro Bongo.[147] To these interpretations, Jacques Gohory added those of medieval romances.[148] With Gohory's name we can associate those of Blaise de Vigenère,[149] Clovis Hesteau de Nuysement,[150] Caelius Firmianus Symphonius[151] and even Claude Barthélémy Morisot (who used the pseudonym Alitophilus).[152]

The most famous work in this field was that of Michel Maier,[153] and its main substance was restated later by Antoine-Joseph Pernety.[154] Maier's work was original in that he offered an interpretation not only of the gods but also of celebrations, ceremonies, customs, and the like. At the beginning, according to him, those in charge of preserving esoteric knowledge were probably threatened with death should they reveal it. That is why they wrote it in symbols that only a few could understand. Other authors we can cite here are Salomon Trismosin[155] and Jacob Tollius.[156]

Moral and Metaphysical Interpretation: Philosophy

Of all the intellectual influences exerted in Italy and even beyond in the course of the Renaissance, that of Ficino was doubtless the most important and lasting. Born in 1433, Marsilio Ficino[157] began to learn Greek in 1456, after studying grammar, medicine, and theology. In 1462, Cosimo de Medici put the villa Goreggi at his disposal so that he could establish a kind of Platonic academy in it.

Marsilio Ficino translated into Latin the *Poimandres,* a revelation of Hermes Trismegistus (1463);[158] Plato's *Dialogues* (translation carried out between 1460 and 1475 but only published in Florence in 1484); Plotinus's *Enneads;* several Neoplatonic treatises (1484–1492); and the *Mystical Theology* and *Divine Names* by pseudo-Dionysius (1492). In addition to important commentaries, he wrote the treatises *On Pleasure* (1457) and *On the Christian Religion* (finished in 1474); a psycho-medical study, *The Triple Life* (1489); and, most important, *Platonic Theology: On the Immortality of the Soul* (henceforth abbreviated *PT*),[159] written between 1469 and 1474 but published only in 1482. The *Commentary on Plato's Symposium,*[160] of which there is a manuscript in Ficino's hand, dated July 1469, may be considered its preface.

While professors in Padua were teaching Aristotle as interpreted by Averroes, Ficino criticized the latent pantheism of this doctrine and claimed that, as Augustine wrote, "with just a few changes, the Platonists would be Christians."[161]

In his *Platonic Theology*, Marsilio Ficino starts out with the hypothesis that a Platonic theology coming from Zoroaster and relayed by Hermes Trismegistus, Orpheus, Pythagoras, Plato, and even Aristotle travels the same path as Christian theology and can help to describe it (*PT* VI 1).

In his amazing theological system, Marsilio Ficino claims the existence of five levels: body, qualities, souls, angels, and God. Whether going up or down, one can see that the soul is located on an intermediary level, in the third position.

Rational souls themselves are divided into three levels: the first, that of the soul of the world; the second, that of the souls of the spheres; and the third, that of the souls of the living creatures contained within each of the spheres.

According to the Magi, that is, according to Zoroaster (*PT* IV 1), the universe has three chief rulers: Oromasis, Mitrim, and Arimanim—that is, God, intelligence, and soul. God's particular attribute is unity, that of intelligence is order, and that of the soul is movement. Ficino finds this tripartite scheme again in the *Letter II* attributed to Plato. Gods created intelligence, which created the soul. The world has a soul, and so does each of the celestial spheres as well as each of the spheres of the elements.

According to Orpheus, continues Marsilio Ficino, the souls of the spheres possess dual powers, one consisting in knowledge and the other in the animation and the direction of the bodies of the sphere. The table below synthesizes all this information.

Sphere	Knowledge	Animation + Direction
Earth	Pluto	Proserpina
Water	Oceanus	Thetis
Air	Jupiter	Juno
Fire	Phanes	Aurora
Moon	Bacchus Licnites	Thalia
Mercury	Bacchus Silenus	Euterpe
Venus	Bacchus Lysinus	Erato
Sun	Bacchus Trietericus	Melpomene
Mars	Bacchus Bassareus	Clio
Jupiter	Bacchus Sabasius	Terpsichore
Saturn	Bacchus Amphietes	Polymnia
The fixed stars	Bacchus Pericionius	Urania
Soul of the world	Bacchus Eribromus	Calliope

And Marsilio Ficino concludes:

Accordingly, in Orpheus's scheme a particular Bacchus rules over the individual Muses, and the powers of the Muses, drunken by the nectar of knowledge divine, are signified by his name. Thus the nine Muses along with the nine Bacchuses together celebrate their ecstatic rites around the single figure of Apollo, that is, around the splendor of the invisible Sun. (TP IV 1)[162]

This last sentence should be understood as a reference to Pythagoras.

According to Ficino, the One itself is the universal Apollo, to the extent that his name, as was already indicated in the *Cratylus,* comes from ἁπλοῦν, meaning "simple," or from ἀπολύς, meaning "apart from multiplicity." The intelligence, which is One, Ficino also calls the Good. This First One and the First Good are situated immediately above the prime intelligence. The prime intelligence in turn is located above the multiple intelligences. First of all, perhaps, it is above the twelve principal intelligences and the twelve dozen that are beneath them, then above the multitude of souls, and finally above the soul of the universe, which is one. The one soul of the universe is above the twelve souls of the twelve spheres. The souls of the twelve spheres are above the dozens of souls; that is, the soul of each sphere is above the most noble souls of that sphere. Finally, the twelve dozens of souls preside over the innumerable souls, because in each sphere these first twelve souls guide all the other souls of this sphere. Hence the following scheme:

One-Good
Intelligence	12 × 12
Soul	12 × 12

And Ficino concludes: "This choir of Muses sings and dances perpetually, as Orpheus says,[163] in musical measures to the command of Apollo himself."[164]

But why does each soul in each sphere contain twelve souls? The answer: to imitate the soul of the first and last spheres.

In the first sphere, that is, in the sphere of the fixed stars, is the band of the Zodiac, divided into twelve parts to which are assigned twelve divinities:

Heart of the Sign	Divinity
Aries	Pallas
Taurus	Venus
Gemini	Phoebus
Cancer	Mercury

Leo	Jupiter
Virgo	Ceres
Libra	Vulcan
Scorpio	Mars
Capricorn	Vesta
Sagittarius	Diana
Aquarius	Juno
Pisces	Neptune

In addition, in the last sphere, that of earth, are twelve kinds of human life, based on whether human beings live more or less according to each of the parts of their souls:

	Reason	Irascibility	Desire
1	more	less	not at all
2	more	as little as possible	less
3	less	more	not at all
4	not at all	more	less
5	little	very little	much
6	little	fairly little	much
7	dominant	dominated	
8	dominated	dominant	
9		dominant	dominated
10		dominated	dominant
11	dominant		dominated
12	dominated		dominant

Like the first and the last spheres, the ten other spheres also contain twelve souls. The kinds of souls rise as far as the intelligences, and the intelligences rise as far as the One.

We could pursue this further and give even more details. It seems clear that Ficino takes up the doctrines of the Neoplatonic School of Athens (discussed in chapter 6 above) and systematizes them by trying as much as possible to show how they are in agreement with Christian doctrine. In fact, Marsilio Ficino's *Platonic Theology* was merely the first work attempting to gather onto a single monument the parts of a primitive theology, that is, the dialogues of divinity with the beginnings of humankind.

In the Platonic Academy of Florence, the quest for a deep meaning hidden under the superficial meaning came close to being an orthodoxy. Each group among these scholars depended on the discoveries of others, and each owed a debt to the long tradition of Christian exegesis. But the editors, translators, and interpreters of Plato did not all agree with this notion of a double theological tradition. Jean de Serres, for instance, who translated the text edited by Robert Estienne (Geneva 1578) into Latin, remained faithful to another apologetic tradition, according to which "Plato drew these symbols from Jewish doctrine." But what Ficino and his young associate, Pico della Mirandola, had uncovered in the Platonists led to a genuine passion, driving other thinkers to seek the divine totality in an infinity of parts, some of which could hardly be seen as divine.

After the members of the Florence Academy, one of the first philosophers who sought to harmonize the writings of pagan philosophers and poets with the Scriptures inspired by the Holy Ghost may have been Agostino Steuco de Gubbio, bishop of Kisamos.[165] Steuco elaborated the following hypothesis: Before the fall, Adam, who conversed with God and the angels, learned the "perfect theology," which he transmitted to his descendants. But throughout the nine centuries that separated Adam's death from the Flood, the doctrine that had come directly from heaven deteriorated. After the Flood, and as a result of the chaos and barbarism that followed, the theology that had originated in paradise disappeared. A group of Noah's descendants, the Chaldeans—among whom were Abraham and Noah's daughter-in-law, the Cumaean Sybil—preserved Adam's message more faithfully than others did. At that time, all wisdom was transmitted orally—Steuco did not know exactly when writing was invented—and the primitive theology became obscure and corrupt.

The Hebrews were the best guardians of Adam's legacy. Therefore the nations whose languages derive from Hebrew—Chaldeans, Babylonians, Assyrians, Egyptians, and Phoenicians—preserved that legacy better than non-Semitic nations. The Greeks, a people of surprisingly recent formation, looked upon these more ancient and more civilized peoples as barbarians, yet they drew their mythology, philosophy, and theology from them. Unable to adopt a critical attitude regarding their origin, the Greeks bragged about their ancientness without being able to produce the monuments on which their claim was based. The Greeks could only name Orpheus, Linus, and Musaeus before Homer and Hesiod, the poets who codified their philosophy and theology. Regardless of the authenticity of the works attributed to some of these theologian-poets, it was evident to Steuco that Homer and Hesiod had teachers whose works had disappeared. Hermes Trismegistus, for instance, was known to have written more than a hundred thousand books, only a handful of which survived. If these lost books could be found, they would give access to the pure truth contained in primitive theology.

Fortunately, the message of Hermes Trismegistus, irreparably corrupted after the Flood, was revised by Moses and restored by the new Christian revelation. Despite this stroke of luck, Steuco thought it would be useful to search for the traces of "this perfect theology" in the universal library, because he was convinced that much of what could be discovered in it would help to establish the sole truth of Christianity.

This is why he managed to find in Plato, Aristotle, Hermes Trismegistus, Proclus, Porphyry, Plotinus, the Magi, and the Sybils, among others, the concept of a divine intellect, which reproduced itself through a series of hypostases; even the Arabs and the Delphic Apollo shared this belief. Empedocles, Parmenides, Zeno, and Melissos believed in a doctrine of creation akin to that in Genesis. Moreover, the doctrine of the eternity of the world traditionally attributed to Aristotle actually resulted from a mistaken interpretation. Propelled by his own rhythm, Steuco had no difficulty in rediscovering all sorts of Christian notions in mythology, such as angels, daemons, and immortality. In 1621, in Venice, the Dominican Raimondo Breganio published an abridged version of Steuco's work in his *Theologiae gentium de cognitione divina enarrationes*.

Steuco's huge undertaking quickly found continuation in the work of Stefano Convenzio.[166] With the help of Plato, the Neoplatonists, and Aristotle, this mystical philosopher described the descent of the preexisting soul into the "cave" of the body. However, he did not seek agreement between Platonism and Christianity.

In 1577, Francesco de Vieri, professor of philosophy in Florence, compiled in his *Compendio della dottrina di Platone in quello che ella é conforme con la fede nostra* an inventory of resemblances, each more far-fetched than the other, between Christian doctrine and that of Hermes Trismegistus, Pythagoras, Aristotle, Plato, and Socrates.

Ficino, Steuco, Convenzio, and de Vieri made a place for Aristotle in their project of synthesis. That was not true of the Platonist Francesco Patrizzi, however, a professor in Padua who energetically defended Plato's Christianity by heatedly attacking Aristotle in his *Discussio peripateticorum* (Basel, 1571) and in *Nova de universis philosophia* (Ferrara, 1591).

The increasingly strong praise of Plato turned into acerbic criticism when, in 1594, Giovanni Battista Crispo, a poet and a friend of Tasso and Caron, published in Rome the first installment of a five-volume work.[167] In this work, which dealt with the soul and its immortality, Crispo sought to demonstrate that only the Catholic Church was correct, and those who read Plato and Aristotle risked being led into heresy.

Less than a decade later, Muzio Pansa[168] revived the polemic by endorsing the theories of Ficino, Steuco, and Patrizzi and by adding new names to the list of authorities his predecessors drew from. Pansa was followed by the theologian Georges Pacard, who devoted almost six hundred pages of his *Théologie naturelle*[169] to reconstituting the knowledge that pagans might have had of God, Providence, and so forth. In his view, only Aristotle's material realism should be condemned.

This thesis was taken up again by Livio Galanti[170] and Pierre Halloix.[171] Halloix subscribed to the idea that Moses was Plato's teacher, and he showed how Socrates' last works in *Phaedo* announced Christ's coming. Galanti, for his part, discovered in *Phaedo* the garden of Eden along with the serpent, although he advised caution when reading Plato.

This was the state of mind that inspired the Cambridge Platonists,[172] Henry More and Ralph Cudworth, whose doctrine was more akin to that of Plotinus than that of Plato. Nevertheless, John Spencer and John Marsham were the first to raise doubts about the idea that Moses was inspired by the Egyptians in his laws and his writings, and their position caused a lively reaction among most of the eminent theologians of the time. This did not prevent Spencer and Marsham from adopting and even further elaborating the most traditional convictions, particularly the one according to which all human beings had received the same revealed truths, a notion underlying all allegorical interpretations of myths.

However, the great geographic discoveries, particularly that of America, led to a drastic modification of the problem by establishing a comparison between classical mythology and that of the "savages." The acknowledged convergence between the mythology of Greece, the mother of "reason," with that of the "savages" provoked a scandal by pointing to the existence of an irreducible irrationality at the very heart of Greek culture, a culture that sought to translate everything into rational terms. This scandal became the point of departure for all later mythological studies, which systematically turned away from allegory.

Allegorical interpretation turned out to be a gigantic project for cultural integration. Yet its death warrant was not signed by the predominance of any philosophical system, ideological orientation, or even religion. Rather, its end came with the historical event of the great voyages of discovery.

Conclusion

Allegorical interpretation, which continued to be practiced in one form or another during Greco-Roman antiquity, in Byzantium, and during the western Middle Ages and the Renaissance, enabled myths to survive. It thus ensured that there would be constant adaptation between myth and the public, whose cultural and moral needs kept changing, though the adaptation was not automatic as it had been in an oral civilization.

In a civilization in which communication occurred solely by word of mouth, as had been the case in Greece before the eighth century B.C., the transmission of the memorable took a narrative form that, since Plato, we have come to call "myths." This sort of narrative was created by poets who were the privileged intermediaries between a community and the systems of explication and values to which it adhered. Yet oral transmission of messages whose content was apt to model the behavior of their audience was also affected by a sort of censorship involving the ongoing adaptation of the message to the expectations of the public that poets or their interpreters addressed. In such a context, poets were required to render to the public an image which, in the main, responded to its expectations. This requirement was all the more basic in face-to-face communication, since there could be no communication, not even the making of a message, in the absence of an audience.

From the eighth century B.C. on, the widespread use in Greece of a new means of communication, a system of writing that could easily be deciphered, had a major impact on the content of the communicated message.

The use of a new means of communication that put transmitted messages into a fixed form gradually prevented the constant, virtually automatic adaptation of a message by the expectation of its recipients, thus modifying the mental habits of a growing number of individuals. These transformations brought about the appearance of a discourse that used prose rather than poetry, that replaced narrative with description and particularly with argumentation, that gave priority to visual testimony over oral tradition as a "criterion of truth," that was able to manipulate abstract entities, and that favored critical thinking.

These changes and transformations made possible the appearance in ancient Greece of other types of discourse, notably that of the "historian" and that of the "philosopher." These new discourses, by way of feedback, encouraged a radical questioning of poetic discourse. Until then, only the positive aspect of poetic activity had been taken into account; but from the moment poets no longer fulfilled their public's expectations, the negative aspect of their activity came into focus and became the target of criticism. Poets were no longer credited with making myths appear vividly to the public, but were regarded as conjurers of misleading and immoral appearances.

The attitude of the "historian" and particularly that of the "philosopher" toward myth was always ambivalent. No other philosopher adopted an attitude of rejection as radical as that of Plato, who condemned myth without reservation by rejecting any sort of allegorical interpretation, at least in theory. Instead, most philosophers and historians were inclined to save myths by attempting to look beneath literal meanings that were morally shocking or scientifically absurd and to find deep meanings conforming to the most recent doctrines in the domain of ethics, psychology, and even physics. Allegory was among the various forms taken by this type of exegesis in the course of the centuries. For entirely practical considerations, allegory was retained whenever precision was not a major requirement.

Having arisen during the sixth century B.C., myth interpretation, widely practiced during Plato's and Aristotle's time, came into its full flowering with the Stoics. Now, to the three existing types of interpretation—moral, in which divinities became virtues; psychological, in which divinities become faculties; and physical, in which divinities become natural elements or phenomena—the Stoics added historical interpretation, inspired by Euhemerus, who maintained that divinities and heroes were human beings raised to the rank of gods on account of the important services they had rendered to humankind.

The Stoics' attitude towards myths was contested by the Epicureans and the members of the New Academy, who mocked the practice of reducing gods to common and trivial material realities or simple human beings, and criticized the tendency to turn ancient poets into historians or unwitting philosophers.

Beginning with the first century B.C., however, a new exegetic trend developed, responding to these objections by assimilating myths to mysteries. Proponents of this trend argued that myths and mysteries are two complementary means used by the divinity to reveal truth to religious souls. Myths present this revelation in a wrapping of legendary writings, while mysteries present it in the form of tableaux vivants. In this view, one that links religion, philosophy, and poetry, poets must be regarded as initiates to whom a truth has been revealed, which they transmit in such a way as to reserve its access to only a small number of people who are worthy of it. Hence the use of a ciphered code, a discourse with double meaning in line with the trend toward secrecy, in which everything is expressed through enigmas and symbols as in the mysteries. In this context, poets are no longer philosophers in spite of themselves but theologians responsible for carefully transmitting a truth to which philosophy has given them direct access.

This view was to be shared by the Neoplatonists of the fifth and sixth centuries A.D., who undertook the formidable project of establishing agreement between the Platonic doctrine they considered a "theology" with all the other Greek and barbarian theologies. The circle was closing once again with these Neoplatonists, who held that myth, like philosophy in general and Plato's philosophy in particular, was the vehicle to a unique truth that they had to uncover in Plato, Homer, Orpheus, the *Chaldean Oracles,* and similar sources.

The problem became more complicated with the appearance and, more important, the dominance of the new state religion, Christianity. Not only did myths have to harmonize with history and philosophy, but they absolutely couldn't clash directly with church dogma. Hence new efforts at adaptation, and thus at interpretation, were undertaken first by the church fathers, and then during the Middle Ages in both the Eastern and Roman churches, and again during the Renaissance.

Indeed, it is somewhat surprising that Byzantine society, so deeply Christian and attaching so much importance to religious matters, particularly to theology, remained obstinately loyal to the culture of antiquity. This attachment, however, was not found everywhere and not always at the same depth. It was affected by the economic, social, and political crises that were shaking the Byzantine Empire, and its more enthusiastic adherents faced danger as somewhat paganistic revivals, such as those favored by John Italos in the eleventh century and Gemistus Pletho in the fifteenth, were repressed.

In the medieval western world, there were no longer any means of referring directly to Greek sources. So "visual" and "literary" traditions led to the deep alteration of the "classical forms" of the gods, who were rendered unrecognizable through unfaithful copies, substitutions, disguises, and naive reconstitutions, such corruption aggravated by mistakes and misunderstandings. The Renaissance was to give the gods back their classical forms, but in its own very particular intellectual context.

During the Renaissance, the gods of antiquity were to become again what they used to be, thanks to the work of scholars. Some of these scholars edited, translated, and commented on Greek texts that had not been available during the Middle Ages. In so doing, they were renewing links with the Neoplatonic school of Athens by way of Byzantine civilization. Others published and explained the numerous visual representations that had been discovered. The increasingly widespread use of the printing press permitted all these works the sort of diffusion that had not been possible up to that time.

From Bacon and Vico up to the present, myth, emancipated from the tutelage of allegorical interpretation, has come to be looked upon as testimony to a stage of development of the human mind, its discursive organization, and even its logic.

Chapter One

1. Luc Brisson, *Platon, les mots et les mythes* (Paris: Maspero, 1994), appendix 2. [*Plato the Myth Maker,* trans. and ed. Gerard Naddaf (Chicago: University of Chicago Press, 1998).] In the following pages I will take up again some of the results I arrived at in that work. I also would like to acknowledge my debt to Jean-Pierre Vernant, "Naissance d'images" [1975] in *Religions, histoires, raison* (Paris: Maspero, 1979), 137.

2. See Brisson, *Les mots et les mythes,* 120–125.

3. Walter Burkert, *Greek Religion: Archaic and Classical* [1977], trans. John Raffan (Orford: Blackwell, 1985), 54–55.

4. Luc Brisson, "Du bon usage du dérèglement," in *Divination et rationalité* (Paris: Le Seuil, 1974), 220–248.

5. *Republic* II 376e–379e; X 598b–601b. Plato is quoted here in English from *The Collected Dialogues of Plato,* ed. Edith Hamilton and Huntington Cairns (Princeton: Princeton University Press, 1971).— *Trans.*

6. This was evident in the programs of the great Panathenaia and the urban Dionysia festivals, where the narration of myths held an important place and presented all of these dimensions: aesthetic, political, ethical, and religious. On this topic, see Brisson, *Plato the Myth Maker,* chap. 4.

7. Walter Burkert, *Greek Religion,* 95–98.

8. On this new system of writing and its consequences, see Eric A. Havelock's works *Aux origines de la civilisation écrite en Occident* [1976], trans. E. Escobar Moreno (Paris: Maspero, 1981) [*Origins of Western Literacy: Four Lectures Delivered at the Ontario Institute for Studies in Education, Toronto, March 25, 26, 28, 1974* (Toronto: Ontario Institute for Studies in Education, 1976)]; *Preface to Plato* (Cambridge, MA: Harvard University Press, 1963); *The Literate Revolution in Greece and Its Cultural Consequences* (Princeton: Princeton University Press, 1982); *The Greek Concept of Justice: From Its Shadow in Homer to Its Substance in Plato* (Cambridge, MA: Harvard University Press, 1978).

9. There are only two articles on reading in ancient Greece: Pierre Chantraine, "Les verbes signifiant 'lire' (ἀναγιγνώσκω, ἐπιλέγομαι, ἐντυγχάνω, ἀναλέγομαι)," in ΠΑΓΚΑΡΠΕΙΑ *Mélanges Henri Grégoire,* Annuaire de l'Institut de Philologie et d'Histoire Orientales et Slaves [Université libre de Bruxelles] 10 (1950) 2:115–126; Bernard M. W. Knox, "Silent reading in Antiquity," *Greek, Roman and Byzantine Studies* 9 (1968): 421–435. On writing and reading in ancient Greece, see the bibliography compiled by Giorgio Camassa and Stella Georgoudi,

"Tracés bibliographiques," in *Les Savoirs de l'écriture en Grèce ancienne,* ed. Marcel Detienne, Cahiers de philologie 14, Série Apparat critique (Lille: PUL, 1988), 525–538. See also Jesper Svenbro, *Phrasikleia: Anthropologie de la lecture en Grece ancienne* (Paris: La Découverte, 1988).

10. This example is mentioned by Havelock in *The Greek Concept of Justice.*

11. On this topic see the work of Jack Goody, a part of which was published as *La Raison graphique: La domestication de la pensée sauvage,* trans. and ed. Jean Bazin and Alban Bensa (Paris: Minuit, 1978), esp. chap. 3. [*The Domestication of the Savage Mind* (Cambridge: Cambridge University Press, 1977).]

12. DK21B14. [English translation drawn from G. S. Kirk, J. E. Raven, and M. Schofield, *The Presocratic Philosophers,* 2d ed. (Cambridge: Cambridge University Press, 1983), 168–169.]

13. DK 21B16.

14. DK 21B15.

15. DK 21B11.

16. For an overall view of the issue, cf. Jean Pépin, *Mythe et allégorie: Les origines grecques et les contestations judéo-chrétiennes* (Paris: Les Etudes Augustinennes, 1976).

17. Cf. Jean-Pierre Vernant, "Le moment historique de la tragédie en Grèce: Quelques conditions sociales et psychologiques" [1968], in *Mythe et tragédie en Grèce ancienne,* ed. Jean-Pierre Vernant and Pierre Vidal-Naquet (Paris: Maspero, 1972), 1:13–17. [*Myth and Tragedy in Ancient Greece,* trans. Janet Lloyd (New York: Zone Books, 1988).]

18. André Rivier, "Remarques sur les fragments 34 et 35 de Xénophane," *Revue de Philologie, de Littérature et d'Histoire anciennes* 30 (1956): 37–61.

19. DK 59B21a = Sextus Empiricus, *Adv. Math.* VII 140.

20. Léonce Paquet, *Platon: La médiation du regard* (Leiden: Brill, 1973).

21. Anne-Marie Malingrey, *Philosophia: Etude d'un groupe de mots dans la littérature grecque, des Présocratiques au IVe siècle après J.-C.* (Paris: Klincksieck, 1961).

22. Here is their inventory:

I. For *philosophos:* (1) Heraclitus (DK 22 B 35 = Clement of Alexandria, *Stromate* V 140, 6). Jean Bollack and Heinz Wismann (*Héraclite ou la séparation,* Paris: Minuit, 1972, 143–144) are right to stress that in Heraclitus this term can have the meaning of "philosopher." T. M. Robinson, in his commentary on this fragment (Heraclitus, *Fragments,* Toronto: University of Toronto Press, 1987, 104), notes that some commentators have thought that the term was added by Clement of Alexandria. (2) According to the *Suda* (s.v. Ζήνων, vol. II, p. 506.26 Adler = DK 29A2), Zeno is supposed to have written a work titled Πρὸς τοὺς φιλοσόφους. But Plato (*Parm.* 127b–d, 128a–d) and Simplicius (*Arist. Phys.* 139.5 Diels) seem to have been aware of only one work by Zeno (on this topic, see Maurice Caveing, *Zénon d'Eléee,* Paris: Vrin, 1982, 134–135). (3). In his Περὶ ὁμονοίας (DK 87B44a = Philostratus, *Vit. Soph.* I 15, 4), Antiphanes writes of γνωμολογίαι τε λαμπραὶ καὶ φιλόσοφοι. It does seem that φιλόσοφοι designates here a quality of language equivalent to λαμπραί. Similarly, in his *Encomium on Helen* (DK 82B11, § 13), Gorgias uses the expression φιλοσόφων λόγων to indicate the quality of speech expressing thought adequately.

II. For *philosophia:* (1) Only one instance found (in *The Treatise on Ancient Medicine,* § 20). This instance would present major interest if, as A.-J. Festugière thought, one could prove that the work was written around 420 B.C. But most scholars recently estimate the work was written after 380 B.C. (cf. Charles Lichtenthaeler, *Chronologische und gedankliche Bezugssysteme in und um "Über die alte Medizin"* [Geneva: Droz, 1980] 27n42.).

III. For *philosophein:* (1) Herodotus (I 30) used this verb in a very broad sense to designate the acquiring of knowledge in general. (2) Thucydides (II 40, 1) has Pericles state the following concerning the Athenians as he was giving the eulogy for 431/0 B.C.: "We cultivate beauty in simplicity and the things of the mind without lacking in firmness (φιλοσοφοῦμεν ἄνευ μαλακίας)." The activity designated by the verb *philosophein* could only be the acquisition of knowledge in general.

23. Based on Robert Joly's translation in "Platon ou Pythagore? Héraclide Pontique, fr. 87–88 Wehrli," in *Hommage à Marie Delcourt,* Collection Latomus 114 (Brussels: Latomus, 1970), 136–148.

24. See ibid.

25. Walter Burkert, "Platon oder Pythagoras: Zum Ursprung des Wortes 'Philosophie,'" *Hermes* 88 (1960): 159–177.

26. Werner Jaeger, "Über Ursprung und Kreislauf des philosophischen Lebensideals," *Sitzungsberichte des Preussichen Akademie der Wissenschaften,* Philosophisch-historische Klasse (1928): 390–421. An English translation of this article can be found as appendix 2 of Richard Robinson's translation of Werner Jaeger's *Aristotle.*

27. *Symposium* 204 a.

28. *Phaedrus* 278 d.

29. Monique Dixsaut, *Le Naturel philosophe: Essai sur les dialogues de Platon* (Paris: Les Belles Lettres / Vrin, 1985), 45–51.

30. Frag. 8 Ross = Philoponus, *Commentary on Nicomachus of Gerasa's* Eisagoge, ed. Hoche (Teubner) 1.8–2.42. This text has been translated into French and annotated by A.-J. Festugière, in *La Révélation d'Hermès Trismégiste,* vol. 2, *Le dieu cosmique* (Paris: Gabalda, 1949), 221–229, particularly 222–223.

31. Cf. Anne-Marie Malingrey, *Philosophia,* 1961, 42–46.

32. *Phaedrus* 247d–e.

33. As early as the *Phaedo* 80e et seq.

34. Cf. A.-J. Festugière, *Contemplation et vie contemplative selon Platon* [1936] (Paris: Vrin, 1975).

Chapter Two

1. The themes discussed in this chapter follow those developed in *Plato the Myth Maker* (see chap. 1, n. 1).

2. *Dire* and *parole* in French.—*Trans.*

3. *Timaeus* 21e–23d.

4. *Timaeus* 22b3–4, 23d4–5. Luc Brisson, "L'Egypte de Platon," *Les Etudes Philosophiques,* 1987: 152–167, esp. 155–162.

5. The French text has *contre-rôle.* I am beholden to Gérard Naddaf's translation of *Plato the Myth Maker* for the elucidation of this concept.—*Trans.*

6. *Phaedo* 60b1–61b7; cf. *Timaeus* 21c4–d3.

7. *Republic* II 377d4–6.

8. *Republic* II 373b6–8.

9. *Timaeus* 21 b1–7; *Critias* 108b3–7, cf. 108d3–6.

10. *Republic* II 377c2–4, 381e1–6; *Laws* X 887d2–3.

11. *Republic* II 377c2–4; *Laws* X 887d2–3.

12. *Gorgias* 527a5–6; *Republic* I 350e2–4.

13. *Laws* X 887d2–3; *Republic* II 377a6–7.

14. *Critias* 107a4–e3.

15. *Republic* III 392c6–393c7. On this topic, cf. R. Dupont-Roc, "Mimesis et énoncia-

tion," in *Ecriture et théorie poétique* (Paris: Presses de l'Ecole Normale Supérieure, 1976), 6–14.

16. *Republic* III 395b–397e.
17. *Republic* III 398c11–d10.
18. *Republic* III 399a5–c4.
19. *Laws* VII 814d7–815b3.
20. *Republic* III 395b8–d3.
21. *Laws* X 903a7–b3; *Phaedo* 114d1–7; cf. 77d5–78a2.
22. *Charmides* 156d3–157c6.
23. *Euthydemus* 289e1–290a4.
24. *Republic* III 415c7, X 621c1; *Phaedrus* 2266sb8; *Laws* VII 804e5, X887d2, XI 913c1–2, 927c7–8.
25. *Timaeus* 70d7–e5.
26. *Republic* II 377b6–6; *Statesman* 268e4–5.
27. *Laws* VIII 808c7–809a6.
28. *Timaeus* 43a6–44d2.
29. *Phaedrus* 276e1–3.
30. On this point, cf. Henry Fournier, *Les Verbes "dire" en grec ancien: Exemple de conjugaison supplétive* (Paris: Klincksieck, 1946).
31. *Sophist* 259d–264b.
32. *Sophist* 262a1.
33. *Sophist* 262a3–4.
34. *Sophist* 269c9–d7.
35. Cf. *Timaeus* 37c–38c.
36. *Sophist* 263b2–8.
37. *Sophist* 262e5–6.
38. *Sophist* 263e3–5.
39. *Sophist* 259d–264b.
40. *Sophist* 268c–d.
41. *Timaeus* 51d3–e6.
42. *Timaeus* 51e5–6.
43. *Republic* II 376e–III 403c.
44. W. Hirsch, *Platons Weg zum Mythos* (Berlin: de Gruyter, 1971).
45. *Statesman* 271a5–b3.
46. *Timaeus* 26c7–e5.
47. See chapter 1, section "The Critique of Poetical Discourse."
48. *Republic* II 376e6–377a8, 377d2–e3; III 386b8–c1; *Cratylus* 408b6–d4.
49. *Gorgias* 523a1–3, 527a5–8.
50. *Republic* II 378e7–379a4.
51. *Statesman* 269b5–c3; *Timaeus* 22c3–d3.
52. Vladimir Propp, *Morphologie du conte* [1928], followed by *Les Transformations des contes merveilleux* [1925], with an appendix title of *L'étude structurale et typologique du conte* [1969] by E. Meletinski, trans. Marguerite Derrida, Tzvetan Todorov, and Claude Kahn, Point 12 (Paris: Le Seuil, 1978). See also Claude Brémond's research in *Logique de récit* (Paris: Le Seuil, 1973).
53. *Statesman* 262a–264b.
54. *Statesman* 274e1–4.

55. *Statesman* 277a3–c6.

56. *Protagoras* 320c–324d.

57. *Protagoras* 324d–328d.

58. *Protagoras* 320c2–4.

59. *Protagoras* 324d6–7.

60. For a list, see Brisson, *Plato the Myth Maker,* appendix 3. The fact that Plato limits himself to allusions to all these characters shows the importance myth had at that time. When a narrative is known to all, elaboration is superfluous.

61. J. Tate, "Plato and allegorical interpretation," *Classical Quarterly* 23 (1929): 142–154.

62. *Republic* II 378d3–e3.

63. *Phaedrus* 229b4–230a6.

64. *Phaedrus* 237a9, 241e8.

65. *Theaetetus* 156c4, 164d9, e3; *Sophist* 242c8, d6.

66. *Timaeus* 26c8; *Laws* VI 752a2.

67. *Laws* VI 771 c7, 773b4; VII 790c3, 812a2; VIII 841c6.

68. *Timaeus* 29d2, 59c6, 68d2, 69b1.

69. *Timaeus* 29d2, 59c6, 68d2.

70. Gregory Vlastos, "The disorderly motion in *Timaeus,*" in *Studies in Plato's Metaphysics,* ed. R. E. Allen (London: Routledge and Kegan Paul / New York: Humanities Press, 1965), 383. On this same topic, see Pierre Hadot's article "Physique et poésie dans le *Timée* de Platon," *Revue de Théologie et de Philosophie* 115 (1983): 113–133. I only partially agree with Pierre Hadot's interpretation of the expression *eikōs logos* in this article. It seems to me problematic that, by using this expression, "Plato is explicitly thinking of a genre, a literary form" (p. 119).

71. *Timaeus* 30b7, 48d2, 53d5, 55d5–6, 56a1, 57d6, 90e8.

72. *Timaeus* 34c3, 44d1, 48c1, 49b6, 56d1, 72d7.

Chapter Three

1. Aristotle is quoted here in English, with occasional modifications, from *The Complete Works of Aristotle: The Revised Oxford Translation,* ed. Jonathan Barnes, 2 vols. (Princeton: Princeton University Press, 1984).—Trans.

2. *Methaphysics* A 2, 982b11–19.

3. Cf. Wilhelm Nestle, *Vom Mythos zum Logos: Die Selbstenfaltung des griechischen Denkens vom Homer bis auf die Sophistik und Sokrates* (Stuttgart: Kröner, 1940).

4. As Pierre Vidal-Naquet wrote in his "Préface à Sophocle, *Tragédies*" (Paris: Gallimard, 1972), 13.

5. Quotations from Aristotle's *Poetics* [in Brisson's work] came from *Poétique,* Greek text with French translation and notes by Roselyne Dupont-Roc and Jean Lallot, and preface by Tzvetan Todorov (Paris: Le Seuil, 1980). [English translation drawn from Barnes; see note 1 above.]

6. *Poetics* 9, 1451b19–26.

7. In order to understand what Aristotle means by "tragedy," I draw from the pertinent passages of Paul Ricoeur's *Poétique,* in the first essay in his book titled *La Métaphore vive* (Paris: Le Seuil, 1975), 51–61.

8. *Poetics* 6, 1450a9–10.

9. *Poetics* 6, 1449b36–1450a15.

10. *Poetics* 6, 1450b8–10; cf. 6, 1450a5–6.

11. *Poetics* 6, 1450b11–12; cf. 6, 1450a6–7.

12. *Poetics* 6, 1450b12–15.

13. *Poetics* 6, 1449b34–35.

14. *Poetics* 6, 1450b17; cf. 6, 1449b35–36.

15. *Poetics* 2, 1448a1 and 29.

16. *Poetics* 6, 1450a38–39.

17. *Poetics* 1, 1447a8–10.

18. *Poetics* 9, 1451b27–33.

19. *Poetics* 9, 1451b5–6.

20. *Poetics* 9, 1451b8–9.

21. *Poetics* 2, 1448a17–18; cf. 3, 1448b24–27; 5, 1449a32–34 and 1449b9–10.

22. *Poetics* 14, 1453b1–14.

23. *Rhetoric* III 12, 1413b12–13.

24. *Rhetoric* III 1, 1403b32–35.

25. See Paulette Ghiron-Bistagne, *Recherches sur les acteurs dans la Grèce antique* (Paris: Les Belles Lettres, 1976).

26. See Jean Pépin, *Mythe et allégorie: Les origines grecques et les contestations judéo-chrétiennes* [1958] (Paris: Les Etudes Augustiniennes, 1976).

27. Brisson speaks of "the French term 'allegory.'" Since the English cognate has the same meaning, I have omitted "French."—Trans.

28. In January 1962, during an archaeological dig at Derveni, north west of Salonika, in a gorge at the 10-kilometer marker on the road from Salonika to Langoza, a papyrus roll was discovered near a tomb belonging to a group of six. Like the B and C tombs, tomb A, where the papyrus roll was found, was the burial site of a soldier as evidenced by the remains of weapons discovered in it. In addition, tomb B, the richest of the group, contained, among other artifacts, a golden coin with Philip of Macedonia on it. The papyrus roll was found outside of tomb A, in the remains of a funerary pyre. It seems evident that it was intended to be burned. One of the ends of the roll escaped the flames, though it was carbonized, which prevented it from decaying and disintegrating. Opening the remains of this papyrus roll presented great difficulties because of its condition. The work was entrusted to Anton Fackelmann, conservator of the National Library of Vienna, who used static electricity to detach twenty-three columns of text and some fragments belonging to the four preceding columns. The roll must have originally been three meters long. The upper part of each column survives, that is, between 11 and 16 lines made up of 30 and 45 letters. But since it is impossible to know how many lines are lost, the width of the roll remains unknown.

29. I cited according to the numbering of the columns in the English translation and edition of this document by R. Janko, "The Derveni Papyrus: An Interim Text," *Zeitschrift für Papyrologie und Epigraphik* 141 (2002): 1–62; thereafter cited as DP. Janko's translation was not yet available at the time of publication of the French edition of the present book. For another English translation and commentaries, see *Studies on the Derveni Papyrus*, ed. André Laks and Glenn W. Most (Oxford: Clarendon Press, 1997). For a complete bibliography of works on the Derveni Papyrus up to 1994, see Maria Serena Funghi, "Esegesi di testi orfice," in *Corpus dei papiri filosofici greci et latini* III (Florence: Olschki, 1995), 565–585.

30. Walter Burkert has written three articles on the topic: "Orpheus und die Vorsokratiker: Bermerkungen zum Derveni-Papyrus und zur pythagoreischen Zahlenlehre," *Antike und Abendland* 14 (1968): 83–114; "Le genèse des choses et des mots: Le papyrus de Derveni entre Anaxagore et Cratyle," *Etudes philosophiques*, 1970, 21–32; "Heraclito nel pa-

piro di Derveni: due nuove testimonianze," *Atti del Symposium Heracliteum* 1981, a cura di Livio Rossetti, 37–72.

31. M. L. West, *The Orphic Poems* (Oxford: Clarendon Press, 1983). See also Luc Brisson, "Les théogonies orphiques et le papyrus de Derveni," *Revue de l'Histoire des Religions* 202 (1985): 389–420, reprinted in *Orphée et l'Orphisme dans l'Antiquité gréco-romaine* Collected Studies Series, CS 476 (Aldershot: Variorum, 1995).

32. αἰνίζεται; cf. DP XIII.6.

33. *logos,* cf. DP XXV.11.

34. I draw inspiration on this from Jeffrey S. Rusten, "Interim Notes on the Papyrus from Derveni," *Harvard Studies in Classical Philology* 89 (1984): 121–140.

35. πρόσθεν: DP XVII.2, 9; XVIII.11; XXI.13.

36. τὰ νῦν ἐόντα: DP XVI.2, 8; XVII.2, 8; XXI.9; XXV.3.

37. ἡ νῦν μετάστασις: DP XV.9.

38. κινεῖσθαι: DP XXI.2.

39. DP XV.2–3.

40. κρούεσθαι: DP XIV.4, 7; XV.1, 8.

41. μερίζεσθαι: DP XXI.2; XXV.2.

42. συνίστασθαι: DP IX.6; XVII.2, 8; XXV.9.

43. παγῆναι, DP XV.4 and συμπαγῆναι, DP IX.8.

44. DP IX.5–7; XV.1–4.

45. διαστῆναι, DP XV.2; διακριθῆναι, DP XXI.14; cf. χωρίζεσθαι, DP XIV.2; XV.2–3.

46. αἰωρέσθαι: DP XVII.9; XXV.4, 7; cf. ἴσχει, DP XV.4.

47. ἑκὰς ἀλλήλων, DP XXV.3–4; cf. διχ᾽ ἀλλήλων, DP XV.2.

48. ἀρχή, a word that also stands for the meaning of "beginning, principle."

49. DP XV.7 et seq.; see VIII.4–5.

50. Kronos's name is associated with κρούειν, DP XIV.7.

51. ἐκ τῶν ὑπαρχόντων τὰ νῦν ὄντα γίνεται, DP XVI.2.

52. Cf. DP XIV.

53. DP XV.

54. DP XIV.

55. DP XV. In the *Cratylus* (396c), Socrates argues that Ouranos's name is perfectly correct, since "we call 'celestial' (οὐρανία) the vision that rises upward, 'that sees things that are above' (ὁρῶσα τὰ ἄνω)." This vision also "produces a pure mind" (τὸ καθαρὸν τοῦ νοῦ), an expression that explains Kronos's name (*Cratylus* 396b [καθαρὸς νοῦς = Κρ . . . ό.ν.ο.ς]), the son produced by Ouranos.

56. DP XVII; XIX.2–4; XXIII.3–5. As in Diogenes of Apollonia, cf. Philodemus, *De pietate* c. 6b = DK 64 A 8 (this account will be cited below).

57. The translation is Janko's (see note 29), slightly modified.

58. DK 8 A 2 = Scholia B to *Iliad* III 67 = Porphyry, *Homeric Questions* I, p. 240. 14–241.12 Schrader; cf. DK 8 A 1 = Tatien, *Oratio ad Graecos,* chap. 31, p. 31. 4–18 Schwarz.

59. DK 59 A 1 = Diogenes Laertius II 1, 1.

60. DK 61 A 6 = Georges Syncellus, *Chronographia* 140c, p. 282. 19–21 Dindorf = p. 174.25–175.2 Mosshammer.

61. DK 64 A 8 = Philodemus, *De pietate* 6b.

62. DK 68 B 30 = Clement of Alexandria, *Protrepticus* 68, 5, cf. *Stromateis* V 14, 102, 1 [English translation, slightly modified, drawn from the G. W. Butterworth translation (New York: Putnam's Sons, 1919), 155–156.]

63. DK 68 A 33 = Diogenes Laertius IX 46.

64. Plato, *Protagoras* 316d.

65. DK 84 B 5 = Sextus Empiricus, *Adversus Mathematicos IX 18.*

66. DK 84 B 2 = *Memorabilia* II 1, 21–34.

67. For an edition, French translation, commentary, and index verborum of two famous allegorical texts attributed to Antisthenes, *Ajax* and *Ulysses,* see Marie-Odile Goulet-Cazé, "L'*Ajax* et l'*Ulysse* d'Antisthène," ΣΟΦΙΗΣ ΜΑΙΗΤΟΡΕΣ *"Chercheurs de sagesse": Hommage à Jean Pépin* (Paris: Etudes Augustiniennes, 1992), 5–36.

68. *SSR* VA 41 Giannantoni = *Memorabilia* VI 15–18.

69. *SSR* VA 194 Giannantoni = Dio Chrysostomus, *Orationes* LIII [36] 4–5.

70. *SSR* VA 94 Giannantoni = Plutarch, *De uitioso pudore* 18, *Moralia* 536b.

71. *SSR* VA 93 Giannantoni = Proclus, *In Alcibiadem,* p. 98. 14–16 Creuzer [Segonds].

72. *SSR* VA 92 Giannantoni = Eratosthenes, *Catasterismi* 40, p. 45.14–20 Olivieri.

73. *SSR* VA 188 Giannantoni = *Scholia to Odyssey* ψ 377 and ε 211, cf. η 257 = Porphyry, *Homeric Questions* II, p. 68. 23–70.16 Schrader.

74. *SSR* VB 340 Giannantoni = Stobaeus, *Eclogarum* III 29, 92.

75. *SSR* VB 583 = Dio Chrysostomus, *Orationes* VI [6]; SSR VB 584 = Dio Chrysostomus, *Orationes* VIII [7] 21, 24.

76. *Metaphysics* Λ 8, 1074b1–14.

77. On the allegorical interpretation of the Golden Chain, see Pierre Lévêque, *Aurea catena Homeri: Une étude sur l'allégorie grecque,* Annales littéraires de l'Université de Besançon, vol. 27 (Paris: Les Belles Lettres, 1959), 165–167.

78. Aristotle, *Movement of Animals,* 4, 699b32–700a6.

79. Aristotle, *Politics* B 9, 1269b27–31.

80. Aristotle, *Politics* Θ 6, 1341b2–8.

Chapter Four

1. The authoritative work is still Arthur Stanley Pease's edition, Marcus Tullius Cicero, *De natura deorum,* 2 vols. (Cambridge, MA: Harvard University Press, 1955–58). I have also used Martin van den Bruwaene's sometimes problematic edition, Cicéron, *De natura deorum,* which includes an introduction, the original text with a French translation, notes, a conclusion, and several appendixes. This work was published in four volumes in the series Latomus in Brussels: Introduction and book I, 1970 [= vol. 107 of the Latomus series]; book II, 1978 [= vol. 154]; book III, 1980 [= vol. 175]; conclusion, appendixes, 1986 [= vol. 192]. [English translations, slightly modified, drawn from Cicero, *The Nature of the Gods,* trans. P. G. Walsh (Oxford: Clarendon Press, 1997).]

2. C. Aurelius Cotta was a brilliant and skillful orator who loved scholarship and was attached to the Platonic succession, which was taken up by the Academy of Rome on the model of the Athens Academy. (On the general history of the New Academy, the authoritative work is still that of Victor Brochard, *Les Sceptiques grecs,* Paris: Vrin, 1981, reprint of the second edition of 1887). Cotta was to die in 73 B.C. from complications of an old wound. Returning from exile in 82, he became consul in 75. Since Cicero was absent from Rome until 77, the scene supposedly described in *De natura deorum* should be dated around 76. On the place and significance of *De natura deorum* in Cicero's work, see Carlos Lévy, *Cicero Academicus: Recherches sur les Académiques et sur la philosophie cicéronienne,* Collection de l'Ecole française de Rome 162 (1992), 557 et seq.

3. Cicero's choice of Cotta and the fictive date of the conversation recounted in *De*

natura deorum lead to the designation of C. Velleius as the representative of Epicureanism. Indeed, toward the end of Sulla's dictatorship, Velleius was the most prominent Epicurean.

4. Q. Lucilius Balbus was a professional philosopher. He was the disciple and friend of Posidonius, and attracted the flattering attention of Antiochus of Ascalon, the most famous member of the New Academy, who dedicated one of his works to him (*DND* I 16).

5. We know little about Phaedrus, a philosopher who may have been of Athenian origin and who lived between 140 and 70 B.C. He may have been the leader of the Epicurean school at Rome for a while.

6. Philo (born ca. 160 B.C.), when in Larissa, had been the disciple of Callicles, himself the disciple of Carneades. In 88, during Mithridates' wars against Rome, he left for Rome, where both Catulus the father and Catulus the son were among his disciples. He was embroiled in a controversy with Antiochus of Ascalon (see note 8 below). He died in Rome shortly after 79.

7. Zeno of Sidon, who is thought to have been born around 150 B.C. was the disciple of Apollodorus. He was the leader of the Epicurean school between Apollodorus and Phaedrus (see note 5 above).

8. Antiochus of Ascalon, thought to have been born between 130 and 120 B.C., was the disciple of the Academician Philo of Larissa and of the Stoic Mnesarchos in Athens. In 88, he accompanied Philo of Larissa to Rome, where he made the acquaintance of L. Lucullus. He distanced himself from the skepticism of Philo of Larissa and ended up adopting a more dogmatic Platonism marked by a strong Stoic influence. He is thought to have died around 68. See John Glucker, *Antiochus and the Late Academy,* Hypomnemata 56 (Göttingen: Vandenhoeck & Ruprecht, 1978).

9. Published by H. Diels in *Abhandlungen der Königl. Preuss. Adad. der Wiss.,* Phil.-Hist. Klasse [1915 nb. 4; 1916 nb 6 and 7], in Berlin in 1916 and in 1917, the Περὶ θεῶν is considered by Philippson (*RE* XIX, 2 [1938] 2460–2462) a possible source for the *De natura deorum.*

10. Philodemus, an Epicurean philosopher and poet, was a contemporary of Cicero, who himself was the student of Zeno of Sidon (see note 7 above). He worked on conceptual physics and expounded Epicurean theses; some of his writings have been found at Herculaneum. On this topic, see Marcello Gigante, *La bibliothèque de Philodème et l'Epicurisme romain,* preface by Pierre Grimal, Etudes anciennes 56 (Paris: Les Belles Lettres, 1987).

11. Edited by Th. Gomperz, Herkulaneische Studien II (Leipzig: Teubner, 1866), the Περὶ εὐσεβείας is also considered by Philippson a possible source for *De natura deorum* (*RE* XIX, 2 [1938], 2462–2463). And now, Philodemus, *On Piety, Part I: Critical Text with Commentary,* ed. Dirk Obbink (Oxford: Clarendon Press, 1996) (text and English translation on right-hand pages).

12. Panaetius of Rhodes (185–109 B.C.) was a Stoic philosopher, the disciple of Crates of Mallos in Pergamum and then, at Athens, of Diogenes of Babylon (see note 29 below), at that time leader of the Stoic school. In 144 he went to Rome, where he was a member of Scipio Aemilianus's circle. Between 140 and 138, he accompanied Scipio in his travels to the east, after which he lived alternatively in Rome and Athens. In 129 he succeeded Antipater as leader of the Stoic school.

13. Posidonius, born in Apamea around 135 B.C., is thought to have been the disciple of Panaetius of Rhodes (see note 12 above) at Athens. After traveling around the Mediterranean pursuing scientific aims, he settled in Rhodes. He arrived in Rhodes around 87 as ambassador to Marius. Posidonius was a prolific writer, but only fragments of his work survive.

14. See the texts and the bibliography in Walter Burkert, "Cicero als Platoniker und Skeptiker," *Gymnasium* 72 (1965): 178.

15. On the attitude of the Stoics, Epicureans, and Academicians toward allegory, see Pépin, *Mythe et allégorie.*

16. *Kreios* is probably linked to *kreiōn,* "sovereign."

17. *SVF* I n° 100 = *Schol. Hes. Theog.* 134.

18. *SVF* I n° 540 = Macrobius, *Saturnalia* I 17, 8.

19. *SVF* I n° 542 = incomplete citation from Macrobius in his *Saturnalia* I 17, 31; and *SVF* n°. 541 = Macrobius, *Saturnalia* I 17, 36.

20. *SVF* I n° 546 = Macrobius, *Saturnalia* I 18, 14.

21. *SVF* II n° 1084 = *Etymologicum Magnum,* s.v. Ῥέα.

22. *SVF* II n° 1094 = Plutarch, *In Amatorio* 13, *Moralia* 757b.

23. *SVF* II n° 1095 = incomplete citation of Macrobius in his *Saturnalia* I 17.

24. *SVF* II n° 1062 = Stobaeus, *Eclogarum* I 1, 26.

25. *SVF* II n° 1078 = Philodemus, *de Pietate* c. 13; cf. Cicero, *DND* I 41.

26. Commentary to the *Iliad* Λ 33, 828.39 sq. = III 144.7–22 van der Valk.

27. *Odyssey* III 1 et seq.; X 138 et seq.; Hesiod, *Theogony* 371 et seq.; 957 et seq.

28. Pseudo-Heraclitus, *Homeric Questions* 27.

29. Diogenes of Seleucia on the Tigris (240–152 B.C.) also called Diogenes of Babylon, is thought to have been the disciple of Chrysippus and to have succeeded to Zeno of Tarsus as leader of the Stoic school. He is thought to have gone to Rome in 156–155. His best-known disciple was Panaetius of Rhodes (see note 12 above).

30. The mythographical work attributed to him, titled Βιβλιοθήκη, dates from the first or even the second century A.D.

31. Macrobius, *Saturnalia* I 17, 19.

32. Athenaeus VII 126, 325a; 325b.

33. Cornutus, a Greek, arrived at Rome during Nero's reign, around A.D. 65 or 68, where he was the teacher of Persaeus and Lucan. Of his works, only a manual of allegorical interpretation has survived: Ἐπιδρομὴ τῶν κατὰ τὴν Ἑλληνικὴν θεολογίαν (or θεωρίαν) παραδεδομένων θεῶν.

34. Pseudo-Heraclitus was a Stoic of the first century B.C. Initially he wanted above all to defend Homer against his detractors. It was only later that he found allegorical interpretation to be the best strategy for this, as suggested in his Ὁμηρικὰ προβλήματα εἰς ἃ περὶ θεῶν Ὅμηρος ἠλληγόρησεν.

35. Lactantius, *Divinae institutiones* I 11, 33.

36. Quintus Ennius is thought to have lived between 239 and 179 B.C. He is the author of a substantial oeuvre, of which only fragments have survived; see *Remains of Old Latin,* ed. and trans. E. H. Warmington (London: Heineman; Loeb Classical Library. Cambridge, MA: Harvard University Press, 1935), 1: 1–465. He may be said to have been the point of encounter of three civilizations: Greek, Oscan, and Latin.

37. Sextus Empiricus, *On Atheism* 73–74.

38. Sextus Empiricus, *Adv. Math.* X 17; cf. IX 50 [English translation, with slight modifications, drawn from R. G. Bury, *Sextus Empiricus* (Cambridge, MA: Harvard University Press, 1960–1967)].

39. Lactantius, *De ira Dei* 11, 7–8.

40. Strabo I 1, 2.

41. See chapter 3, section on allegory.

42. Diagoras was a lyrical poet from Melos who is thought to have lived in the last quarter of the fifth century B.C. and was considered the typical atheist.

43. Carneades is thought to have been born in Cyrene around 219 B.C. His teacher was the Academician Hegesinos, whom he succeeded as leader of the Academy, and the Stoic Diogenes of Babylon (see note 29 above). Through the latter, he became imbued with Chrysippus's doctrine. In 156, along with Diogenes of Babylon and Critolaos, he was entrusted with an ambassadorial mission to Rome to have Athenians exempted from a fine following the sacking of Oropos. He died in 129 B.C. without having written anything.

44. On this topic, see François Guillaumont, *Philosophe et augure: Recherches sur la théorie cicéronienne de la divination* (Brussels: Collection Latomus, 1984).

45. *DND* III 5.

46. See Frag. 670 and 671 Ribbeck = frag. 14–15 Warmington. Born in 170 B.C., Accius is thought to have lived until 90 B.C. He was a poet who was inspired by the Greek models but whose vigorous and personal style makes for originality. *Remains of Old Latin,* ed. Warmington, 2: 325–594.

47. *DND* III 41.

48. *DND* III 43–44. [The parenthetical Latin is Brisson's clarification.]

49. See chapter 8, opening paragraph.

50. *DND* III 44.

51. See *DND* II 64.

52. See *DND* II 67.

53. *DND* III 62.

54. See I 3; II 63.

55. *DND* II 63.

56. A doxographer with Skeptic sensitivity.

57. *Adv. math.* I 280.

58. *Adv. math.* IX 29.

59. *Adv. math.* IX 39–41.

Chapter Five

1. Pierre Hadot, "Théologie, exégèse, révélation, écriture dans la philosophie grecque," in *Les Règles de l'interprétation,* Collection Patrimonie, ed. Michel Tardieu (Paris: Editions du Cerf, 1987), 14–23.

2. This is the opinion of J. P. Lynch, *Aristotle's School: A Study of a Greek Educational Institution* (Berkeley: University of California Press, 1972), 135–207, as well as that of John Glucker, *Antiochus and the Late Academy,* Hypomnemata 56 (Göttingen: Vandenhoeck & Ruprecht, 1978), 330–379.

3. See H. J. Krämer, "Die Ältere Akademie," in *Grundriss der Geschichte der Philosophie,* ed. F. Überweg, vol. 3, ed. H. Flashar (Basel-Stuttgart: Schwabe & Co., 1983), 161; and H. J. Mette, *Lustrum* 26 (1984), Frag. 8–14.

4. Proclus lists several responses to this question in his *Commentary on the Timaeus* III, 103, 19–104.22 Diehl.

5. John Dillon, *The Middle Platonists* (London: Duckworth, 1977), 114–183.

6. Luc Brisson, "Usage et fonction du secret dans le Pythagorisme ancien," in *Le Secret,* ed. Philippe Dujardin (Lyon: Presses Universitaires de Lyon, 1987), 87–101. Reprinted in *Orphée et l'Orphisme dans l'Antiquité Gréco-Romaine* (Aldershot: Variorum, 1995).

7. Brisson uses the French term *symbole.—Trans.*

8. Clement of Alexandria, *Stromateis* V 57, 1.

9. Plutarch, *De Iside et Osiride* 9–10, *Moralia* 354b–e.

10. See chapter 3, section on allegory.

11. *De audiendis poetis* 4, *Moralia* 19e. [English translation, slightly modified, drawn from *Plutarch's Moralia,* trans. Frank Cole Babbit (New York: G. P. Putnam's Sons, 1927).]

12. *De Pythiae oraculis* 30, *Moralia* 409d.

13. *De Iside et Osiride* 32, *Moralia* 363d and *De esu carnium* 7, *Moralia* 996b.

14. *Iliad* XXIII 652 and 795; *Odyssey* XIV 508; cf. also Aeschylus *Suppliants* 534, *Agamemnon* 1483.

15. Hesiod, *Works and Days* 202 (fable of the hawk and the nightingale).

16. *Odyssey* XXI 110.

17. Christoph Riedweg, *Mysterienterminologie bei Platon, Philon und Klemens von Alexandria,* Untersuchungen zur antiken Literatur und Geschichte, vol. 26 (Berlin: de Gruyter, 1987).

18. Georges E. Mylonas, *Eleusis and the Eleusinian Mysteries* (Princeton: Princeton University Press, 1961); Walter Burkert, *Antike Mysterien: Funktionen und Gehalt* (1987; 2d ed., Munich: C. H. Beck, 1991).

19. *Hymn to Demeter* I 478–479. [English translation drawn from *The Homeric Hymns,* trans. Charles Boer (Chicago: Swallow Press, 1970), 133.]

20. *Oedipus at Colonus* 1049–1054 [English translation drawn from *Oedipus at Colonus,* ed. and trans. H. Lloyd-Jones, Loeb Classical Library (Cambridge, MA: Harvard University Press, 1994).]

21. Scholia in the *Laurentianus* to *Oedipus at Colonus* 1051 p. 445.24–24 Papageorgius.

22. Here we are touching on a fundamental point, a formidable conceptual difficulty. If a thing is ineffable (ἀπόρρητος), if it is not possible to speak of it, why must its divulgation (ἀνέξοιστος) be forbidden? In fact, an answer to this question might pertain to the recognition of a semantic and lexicographic ambiguity. On this topic, see Jean Pépin, "L'arcane religieux et sa transposition philosophique dans la tradition platonicienne," in *La storia della filosofia come sapere critico: Studi offerte a Mario Dal Pra* (Milan: Franco Angeli, 1984), 18–35.

23. Riedweg, *Mysterienterminologie bei Platon, Philon und Klemens von Alexandria.*

24. Félix Buffière, *Les Mythes d'Homère et la pensée grecque* (Paris: Les Belles Lettres, 1956), 36–41.

25. *Phaedrus* 244a–245c; cf. 264c–265c.

26. Philo of Alexandria tells the developments of this expedition in the *De legatione ad Gaium;* see also Flavius Josephus, *Jewish Antiquities* XVII 81–84.

27. This dialogue comes to us in an Armenian version with a strong Hellenic coloration, dating from the fifth or sixth century, which itself was translated into Latin by J.-B. Aucher, a Mekhitarist monk of the Saint Lazarus monastery of Venice at the beginning of the nineteenth century. Several factors have led scholars to doubt its authenticity: *On Providence* remains silent about the Scriptures; it passionately defends the poets; it accepts the deification of the elements; and it places Greek philosophers above all else.

28. Apelles was a famous painter, originally from Colophon, thought to have lived in the fourth century B.C.

29. *De Providentia* II 40–41.

30. *De Providentia* II 42. The citation Philo introduces here is from *Phaedrus* 245a.

31. For a more balanced and complete point of view, see Pépin, *Mythe et allégorie,* 231–242; and Richard Goulet, *La philosophie de Moïse: Essai de reconstitution d'un commentaire philosophique préphilonien du Pentateuque* (Paris: Vrin, 1987). There is a very rich collection on the topic in *Philon d'Alexandrie,* Colloques Nationaux du C.N.R.S., Lyon, 11–15 septem-

bre 1966 (Paris: Editions du C.N.R.S., 1967), with articles by Jean Pépin, "Remarques sur la théorie de l'exégèse allégorique chez Philon," 131–137; Monique Alexandre, "La culture pro-fane chez Philon," 105–129; Pierre Boyancé, "Echo des exégèses de la mythologie grecque chez Philon," 169–189; and Marguerite Harl, "Cosmologie grecque et représentations juives dans l'oeuvre de Philon d'"Alexandrie," 189–203.

32. See Plutarch, *Oeuvres morales,* vol. 1, part I (Paris: Les Belles Lettres, 1987), vii–ccxxvi; for his life, xii–lix.

33. *De Pythiae oraculis* 24, *Moralia* 406f.

34. *De Pythiae oraculis* 25, *Moralia* 406f–407b.

35. *De Pythiae oraculis* 24, *Moralia* 406e.

36. *De Pythiae oraculis* 30, *Moralia* 409c–d.

37. *De Pythiae oraculis* 25–26, *Moralia* 406f–407f.

38. Daniel Babut, *Plutarque et le Stoïcisme* (Paris: Les Belles Lettres, 1969).

39. Jean Hani, *La Religion grecque dans la pensée de Plutarque* (Paris: Les Belles Lettres, 1976).

40. *De Iside et Osiride* 10, *Moralia* 354e. [English translation, slightly modified, drawn from Plutarch, *De Iside et Osiride,* ed. and trans. J. Gwyn Griffiths (Cardiff: University of Wales Press, 1970). Greek words are in Brisson's text.]

41. Yvonne Vernière, *Symboles et mythes dans la pensée de Plutarque: Essai d'interprétation philosophique et religieuse des Moralia* (Paris: Les Belles Lettres, 1977).

42. Same warning in 358e–f.

43. Greek words are in Brisson's text.—Trans.

44. *De Iside et Osiride* 11, *Moralia* 355b–d.

45. Plutarch was writing to his wife about the death of their daughter while he was away. The young child was called Timoxena like her mother.

46. *Consolatio ad uxorem* 10, *Moralia* 611d. [Translations from Moralia, with the excep-tion of the quotes from *De Iside and Osiride,* are drawn with slight modifications from *Plutarch's Moralia,* trans. Philip H. de Lacy and Benedict Einarson (Cambridge, MA: Har-vard University Press, 1959). Greek words are in Brisson's text.]

47. *De Iside et Osiride* 35, *Moralia* 364d–e.

48. *Isis et Osiris,* Plutarque, *Oeuvres morales* V, 2, trans. Christian Froidefond (Paris: Les Belles Lettres, 1988); Plutarch, *De Iside et Osiride,* ed. and trans. J. Gwyn Griffiths; Plutarch, *Über Isis und Osiris,* ed. and trans. Theodor Hopfner [1940–1941] (Darmstadt: Wis-senschaftliche Buchgesellschaft, 1967).

49. *De Iside et Osiride* 12–19, *Moralia* 355c–358e.

50. *De Iside et Osiride* 57, *Moralia* 374b–c.

51. *Symposium* 203b.

52. *De Iside et Osiride* 57, *Moralia* 374c–e.

53. This festival was celebrated in numerous Greek towns around the winter solstice, during the longest nights. Its main theme seems to have been the mystery of the death and resurrection of Dionysos.

54. *De Iside et Osiride* 35, *Moralia* 364f.

55. See Brisson, *Plato the Myth Maker,* 129–30.

56. See Pierre Thévenaz, *L'Ame du monde: Le devenir et la matière chez Plutarque* (Neufchâtel: Paul Attinger, 1938).

57. *De Iside et Osiride* 20, *Moralia* 358f–359a.

58. Cf. *De Iside et Osiride* 58, *Moralia* 374e.

59. *De Iside et Osiride* 22, *Moralia* 359d–e.

60. *De Iside et Osiride* 23, *Moralia* 359f–360a.

61. *De Iside et Osiride* 25–31, *Moralia* 360d–363d.

62. Guy Soury, *La Démonologie de Plutarque: Essai sur les idées religieuses et le mythes d'un platonicien éclectique* (Paris: Les Belles Lettres, 1942).

63. *De Iside et Osiride* 25, *Moralia* 360d–e.

64. *De Iside et Osiride* 25, *Moralia* 360e–f.

65. *De Iside et Osiride* 26, *Moralia* 361c.

66. *De Iside et Osiride* 32–44, *Moralia* 363d–368f.

67. *De Iside et Osiride* 32, *Moralia* 363d–364a.

68. *De Iside et Osiride* 33–40, *Moralia* 364a–367d.

69. *De Iside et Osiride* 41–44, *Moralia* 367c–368f, and, more particularly, 365f–366a.

70. *De Iside et Osiride* 70, *Moralia* 378f–379b.

71. *De Iside et Osiride* 71, *Moralia* 379b–e.

72. *De Iside et Osiride* 45–64, *Moralia* 369a–377a.

73. *Laws* X 896d et seq. Cf. *De Iside et Osiride* 45–48, *Moralia* 369a–371a.

74. *De Iside et Osiride* 56, *Moralia* 373e.

75. *De Iside et Osiride* 49–64, *Moralia* 371a–377a.

76. *De Iside et Osiride* 20, *Moralia* 358f–359a.

77. *De Iside et Osiride* 3–4, *Moralia* 352b–c.

78. *De Iside et Osiride* 9, *Moralia* 354b–c.

79. *De Iside et Osiride* 67, *Moralia* 377e–378a.

80. *De Iside et Osiride* 9, *Moralia* 354b–c.

81. *De Iside et Osiride* 68, *Moralia* 378a–d.

82. *De Iside et Osiride* 77, *Moralia* 382d–e.

83. In *The Middle Platonists* (London: Duckworth, 1977), 362 and 379–380, John Dillon agrees to identify this Cronius with the Cronius to whom Lucian addresses *The Death of Peregrinus*, written in A.D. 165 in these words Λουκιανὸς Κρονίῳ εὖ πράττειν. On the expression εὖ πράττειν as a typically Platonic expression, see Plato, *Lettres,* ed. and trans. Luc Brisson, GF 466 (Paris: Flammarion, 1987) 10–11, n. 2.

84. John Lydus (*De mens.* IV 80 = frag. 57 des Places) calls him "Numenius the Roman." But it is impossible to know if this account is limited to a reference to a more or less lengthy stay of Numenius in Rome.

85. Numenius, *Fragments,* ed. and trans. E. des Places (Paris: Les Belles Lettres, 1973). [English translation drawn, with modifications, from *The Neoplatonic Writings of Numenius,* comp. and trans. Kenneth Guthrie (Lawrence, KS: Selene Books, 1987).]. On the significance of Numenius, the main authority on Platonism in the third century A.D., see H. D. Saffrey, "Un lecteur antique des oeuvres de Numénius: Eusèbe de Césarée," in *Forma futuri: Studi in onore del cardinale Michele Pellegrino* (Turin: Bottega d'Erasmo, 1975), 145–153.

86. Frag. 1a des Places = Eusebius, *Praeparatio Evangelica* IX 7, 1.

87. Frag. 1b des Places = Origines, *Contra Celsum* I 15.

88. Frag. 30 des Places = Porphyry, *The Cave of the Nymphs* 10. [English translation, slightly modified, drawn from *Porphyry: The Cave of the Nymphs in the Odyssey,* trans. John M. Duffy et al. Arethusa Monographs (Buffalo, NY: State University of New York at Buffalo, 1969). Greek words are in Brisson's text.]

89. Frag. 23 des Places = Eusebius, *Praeparatio Evangelica* IX 7, 1. [= Fragment 41 in Guthrie.]

90. Frag. 37 des Places = Proclus, *In Timaeum* I, 76.30–77.24 Diehl.

91. A certain Telephus of Pergama (second century A.D.) is thought to have written an Περὶ τῆς Ὁμήρου καὶ Πλάτωνος συμφωνίας.

92. Frag. 35 des Places = Proclus, *In Remp.* III 128.26–130.14; 130.15–16; 131.8–14.

93. The idea of "revealed truth" underlies several works of the time: *Chaldaic Oracles, Corpus Hermeticum,* and Gnostic *Apocalypses* by Nag-Hammadi. All this literature added to Christian and Jewish literature unavoidably influenced philosophers' perception of Greek myths.

94. On Plotinus's interpretation of myths, see Pépin, *Mythe et allégorie,* 190–209; and Robert Lamberton, *Homer, the Theologian. Neoplatonist Allegorical Reading and the Growth of the Epic Tradition* (Berkeley: University of California Press, 1986), 83–107.

95. *LP* [Porphyry's *Life of Plotinus*] 3.44–45.

96. *LP* 14.12.

97. *LP* 17.1–2, 17.18, 18.3, 21.4.

98. *LP* 17.5–6.

99. *LP* 20.74, see Porphyry's commentary in 21.5–9.

100. *Enn.* III 5 [50], 9.24–26 [English translations, slightly modified, drawn from Plotinus, *The Enneads,* trans. Stephen Mackenna, 4th ed. rev. B. S. Page (London: Faber and Faber, 1969). Greek words are in Brisson's text.]

101. *Enn.* III 5 [50], 9.26–28.

102. *Enn.* IV 3 [27], 9.15–20.

103. *Enn.* III 5 [50], 9.28–29.

104. Hesiod, *Theogony,* 126–210; 453–506; 617–735.

105. *Republic* II 377e–378b.

106. On the terms σιγᾶσθαι and δι᾽ ἀπορρήτων and the mention of the sacrifice of a pig, see earlier in this chapter, section "A New Way of Interpreting Myths."

107. Frag. 21 des Places = Proclus, *In Tim.* I 303.27–304.7 Diehl.

108. On this topic, see Pierre Hadot, "Ouranos, Kronos and Zeus in Plotinus's Treatise against the Gnostics," in *Neoplatonism and Early Christian Thought: Essays in Honour of A. H. Armstrong,* ed. H. J. Blumenthal and R. A. Markus (Aldershot: Variorum, 1981), 124–137.

109. *Enn.* III 8 [30], 11.33–45.

110. "Intellectual-Principle" in the MacKenna translation.—Trans.

111. *Enn.* V 1 [10], 4.9–10.

112. *Enn.* V 1 [10], 7.30–35.

113. *Enn.* V 8 [31], 13.1–11.

114. *Enn.* V 1 [10], 7.35–36; see also V 5 [32], 3.20–24.

115. *Enn.* IV 4 [28], 9.1–1.8.

116. *Enn.* IV 4 [28], 10.1–4; see also 10.4–29.

117. *Enn.* IV 3 [27], 12.6–19.

118. *Enn.* IV 3 [27], 12.1–4.

119. Jean Pépin, "Plotin et le miroir de Dionysos (*Enn.* IV 3 [27], 12.1–2," *Revue Internationale de Philosophie,* 1972, 304–320.

120. *Enn.* III 6 [26], 19.25–41.

121. Cf. *Enn.* V 1 [10], 7.30–35, passage quoted above in text at note 112.

122. Cf. Lucretius, *De natura rerum* II 614–617, and Augustinus, *De civite dei* VII, chap. 24–25.

123. Περὶ ἀγάλματων, frag. 8. Bidez = 379f Smith = Eusebius, *Praeparatio Evangelica* III 1, 42.

124. *Theol. Graec. Comp.*, p. 23.16–22 Lang.

125. *Enn.* III 6 [26], 14.10–12.

126. *Enn.* III 5 [50], 2.

127. *Enn.* III 5 [50], 3.

128. *Enn.* III 5 [50], 4.

129. *Enn.* IV 9 [9], 9.28–34.

130. *Enn.* II 3 [52], 15.9–12; cf. Hesiod, *Theogony* 904–905.

131. *Enn.* V 5 [32], 6.27–28; cf. *Cratylus* 404e–406a.

132. *Enn.* IV 4 [28], 27.16–17.

133. *Enn.* IV 3 [27], 14.

134. On Heracles in Plotinus, see Jean Pépin, "Héraclès et son reflet dans le Néoplatonisme," in *Le Néoplatonisme,* Colloques internationaux du C.N.R.S., Royaumont, 9–13 June 1969 (Paris: Editions du C.N.R.S., 1971), 167–192.

135. *Enn.* IV 3 [27], 27; 32.24–4.1.

136. *Republic* X 611d.

137. On Narcissus, see Pierre Hadot, "Le mythe de Narcisse et son interprétation par Plotin," *Nouvelle Revue de Psychanalyse* 13 (1976): 81–108.

138. See previous paragraph.

139. On Calypso, see F. Buffière, *Les Mythes d'Homère et la pensée grecque* (1956), 461–464.

140. *Enn.* I 6 [1], 8.6–21.

141. *VP* 15.1–6.

142. See earlier in this chapter, section "A New Way of Interpreting Myths."

143. Herodotus VII 153; Lysias, *Contra Andocides* [VI] 1; Isaeus, *The Succession of Apollodorus* [VII] 9; Plutarch, *Alcibiades* 13.

144. George E. Mylonas, *Eleusis and the Eleusinian Mysteries* (Princeton: Princeton University Press, 1961), 229–230.

145. Mylonas (see note 144 above) expresses great doubts on this, however.

146. *In Tim.* I 49.12–16 Diehl, commenting on *Timaeus* 18c–d by referring to the passage in *Republic* (VIII 546a–c) on the "nuptial number."

147. *In Tim.* I 450.20–22; III 248.30–249.5 Diehl, which O. Kern classifies under number 163 of *Orphicorum Fragmenta.*

148. Frag. 15 Heinze = frag. 213 Isnardi Parente = Aetius, *Placita* I 7, 30 = Stobeus *Ecl.* 162.

149. For a general presentation of this metaphysical system, see Pierre Hadot, "La métaphysique de Porphyre," in *Porphyre,* Entretiens sur l'Antiquité Classique n° 12, Vandoeuvres-Genève, 30 August–5 September 1965 (Fondation Hardt, 1966), 125–157.

150. This text was translated into French first by F. Buffière, in an appendix to his book *Les Mythes d'Homère et la pensée grecque* (1956), 595–616, from a text established by W. Nauck, *Porphyrii philosophiae platonicae Opuscula selecta* (Leipzig: Teubner, 1886), 53–83; then by Yann le Lay from the original translation by Pierre Quillard, preceded by "La philosophie de Porphyre et la question de l'interpretation" by Guy Lardreau (Paris: Verdier, 1989) from a newly established text: Porphyry, *The Cave of the Nymphs in the Odyssey,* a revised text with translation by Seminar Classics 606 (J. M. Duffy, Ph. F. Sheridan, L. G. Westerink, and J. A. White), State University of Buffalo, Arethusa Monograph, 1969. A more recent edition of *The Cave of the Nymphs* is that of L. Simonini (Milan: Adelphi, 1986). See also Jean Pépin, "Porphyre, exégète d'Homère," in *Porphyre* (see note 149 above), 231–266.

151. *Cave of the Nymphs* 71.1, 55.17, 56.7 Nauck.

152. Fragm. 53 Bidez = 372 F Smith = Stobeus, *Ecl.* II 1, 32.

153. *Od.* XIII 102–112 [English translation drawn from Porphyry, *The Cave of the Nymphs in the Odyssey* (see note 150 above).]

154. Jean Pépin, "The Platonic and Christian Ulysses," in *Neoplatonism and Early Christian Thought,* ed. Blumenthal and Markus, 3–18 and 234–239.

155. To quote the famous sentence in the *Statesman* 273d–e.

Chapter Six

1. Plato is the one who unveils the objects of philosophy, as the hierophant, in the mysteries, unveils sacred objects. Incidentally, Plotinus was the first to claim to be only an exegete of Plato (*Enn.* V 1 [10] 8, 12).

2. *Platonic Theology* 1, p. 6.16–7.8 Saffrey-Westerink. [English translation, slightly modified, drawn from the 1816 translation by Thomas Taylor (Kew Gardens, NY: Selene Books, 1985), 2. Greek terms and phrases are in Brisson's text.]

3. On this topic, see H. D. Saffrey and L. G. Westerink, "Introduction à Proclus," in *Théologie platonicienne I* (Paris: Les Belles Lettres, 1968), xxvi–xlviii. See also Daniela Patrizia Taormina, *Plutarco di Atene: L'Uno, l'Anima, le Forme,* text, translation, and commentary, Symbolon 8 (Catania: Università di Catania, 1989).

4. See chapter 5, section "A New Way of Interpreting Myths."

5. See Saffrey and Westerink, "Introduction à Proclus," lxxv–lxxxix. See also H. D. Saffrey, "La *Théologie platonicienne* de Proclus, fruit de l'exégèse du *Parménide*," *Revue de Théologie et de Philosophie* 116 (1984): 1–12.

6. *In Parm.* 613.15–633.12.

7. *In Parm.* 633.13–635.27.

8. *In Parm.* 635.25–638.14.

9. *In Parm.* 638.14–640.16.

10. *In Parm.* 640.17–643.5.

11. *In Parm.* 1054.37–1055.17.

12. *In Parm.* 1057.5–1058.2.

13. *Platonic Theology* I 12.

14. *Platonic Theology* I 10.

15. *Platonic Theology* I 6.

16. *Platonic Theology* I 7.

17. *Platonic Theology* I 4.

18. On this topic, see *Platonic Theology* I 4, p. 19.23–20.25; *In Parm.* 646.21–647.24.

19. From the article by Luc Brisson, "Proclus et l'Orphisme," in *Proclus: Lecteur et interprète des Anciens,* Colloques internationaux du C.N.R.S. (Paris: Editions du C.N.R.S., 1987), 46; reprinted in *Orphée et l'Orphisme dans l'Antiquité gréco-romaine.* (Aldershot: Variorum, 1995).

20. *In Parm.* 801.22–23.

21. See Anne D. R. Sheppard's analyses in *Studies on the 5th and 6th Essays of Proclus' "Commentary on the Republic,"* Hypomnemata 61 (Göttingen: Vandenhoeck & Ruprecht, 1980), 145–161.

22. There are some useful comments on this topic in Robert Lamberton, *Homer the Theologian: Neoplatonic Allegorical Reading and the Growth of the Epic Tradition* (Berkeley: University of California Press, 1986), 164–174.

23. *Life of Proclus,* chap. 18.

24. On the meaning of this account, see Clemens Zintzen, "Die Wertung von Mystik und Magie in der neuplatonischen Philosophie," *Rheinisches Museum* n.s. 108 (1965): 71–100. See also A. J. Festugière, "Proclus et la religion traditionelle" [1966], in *Etudes de Philosophie grecque* (Paris: Vrin, 1971), 575–584; and "Contemplation philosophique et art théurgique chez Proclus" [1968], ibid., 585–596. See especially Jean Trouillard, "Le merveilleux dans la vie et la pensée de Proclos," *Revue Philosophique* 163 (1973): 439–452; and *La Mystagogie de Proclos* (Paris: Les Belles Lettres, 1982).

25. *Life of Proclus,* chap. 20.

26. Thus, 1, 120 [70 × 16] pages.

27. *Life of Proclus,* chap. 26.

28. English translation, slightly modified, drawn from *Marinos of Neapolis, the Extant Works, or The Life of Proclus and the Commentary on the Dedomena of Euclid,* ed. A. N. Oikonomides; *Life of Proclus,* trans. Kenneth Sylvan Guthrie (Chicago: Ares Publishers, 1977), 63.—Trans.

29. S.v. Συριανός in the *Suda* vol. IV, p. 479, 1–2 Adler; s.v. Πρόκλος, vol. IV, p. 210.12–13 Adler.

30. K. Praechter, "Das Schriftenverzeichnis des Neuplatonikers Syrianos bei Suidas," *Byzantinische Zeitschrift* 26 (1926): 253–264.

31. *Platonic Theology* IV 23, 69.12.

32. *In Tim.* I 315.1–2.

33. See Photius, *Bibliotheca,* codex 214, 173a.

34. *Suda* s.v. Ἡραΐσκος, vol. II p. 580.5–6 Adler 5.

35. *Suda,* s.v. Σαραπίων, vol. IV, p. 324.17–28 Adler.

36. Damascius, *Life of Isidore,* § 126, p. 170.1–6 Zintzen = Photius, *Bibliotheca,* codex 242, 344a–b.

37. For text and translations of the *Chaldean Oracles,* see *Oracles chaldaïques,* ed. and trans. Edouard des Places (Paris: Les Belles Lettres, 1971; new ed. 1989); and *The Chaldean Oracles,* ed. and trans. Ruth Majercik (Leiden: Brill, 1989). For a general interpretation, see Hans Lewy, *Chaldaean Oracles* [1956], rev. ed. under the direction of Michel Tardieu (Paris: Les Etudes Augustiniennes, 1978).

On the influence of the *Chaldean Oracles* on the Neoplatonists I drew essentially from the three articles by H. D. Saffrey, "Les Neoplatoniciens et les Oracles chaldaïques," *Revue des Etudes Augustiniennes* 27 (1981): 209–225; "La Théurgie comme phénomène culturel chez le Néoplatoniciens (IVème–Vème siècles)," *Koinonia* 82 (1984): 161–171; "Proclus, diadoque de Platon," in *Proclus: Lecteur et interprète des anciens,* Actes du Colloque international du C.N.R.S., Paris, Oct. 2–4, 1985, ed. Jean Pépin and H. D. Saffrey (Paris: Edition du C.N.R.S., 1987), xi–xxviii, particularly xix–xxviii.

38. This text was published by C. Sathas in *L'Annuaire pour l'encouragement des Etudes Grecques en France* (1875), 215–219, and translated by P. Lévêque in *Aurea Catena Homeri: Une étude sur l'allégorie grecque* (Paris: Les Belles Lettres, 1959), 78–81.

39. *De myst.* II 7, p. 83.9–84.20.

40. Cf. Luc Brisson, "Amélius: Sa vie, son oeuvre, sa doctrine, son style," *ANRW* II 36, 2: 811.

41. See chapter 5 above, section on Plotinus.

42. Cf. Luc Brisson, "Orphée et l'Orphisme dans l'Empire romain, de Plutarque jusqu'à Jamblique," *Aufstieg und Niedergang der römischen Welt,* pt. 2, vol. 36.4 (1990): 2867–3931.

Reprinted in *Orphée et l'Orphisme dans l'Antiquité gréco-romaine* (Aldershot: Variorum, 1995).

43. *De princ.*, Ruelle I, 123, 317.13–14 = Combès-Westerink, III 159. 17–18.

44. See Luc Brisson, "Le corps 'dionysiaque': L'anthropogonie décrite dans le *Commentaire sur le Phédon de Platon* (1, par. 3–6) attribué à Olympiodore—est-elle orphique?" ΣΟΦΙΗΣ ΜΑΙΗΤΟΡΕΣ *"Chercheurs de sagess." Hommage à Jean Pépin*. Collection des Etudes Augustiniennes. Série Antiquité–131 (Paris: Institut d'Etudes Augustiniennes, 1992), 481–499; reprinted in *Orphée et l'Orphisme dans l'Antiquité gréco-romaine.*

45. *OF* 54 (Damascius), *OF* 57 (Athenagoras), *OF* 60 (Damascius), *OF* 64 (Damascius), *OF* 65 (*Suda*, Georgius Cedrenus, John Malalas), *OF* 66a (Proclus, Syrianus), *OF* 68 (Proclus Syrianus), *OF* 70 (Damascius). Moreover, as M. L. West rightly notes in *The Orphic Poems* (Oxford: Clarendon Press, 1983), 200, n. 78, there is no valid reason to believe that the source of the scholia to Apollonius of Rhodes (III 26 = *OF* 37) is the *On the gods* by Apollodoro of Athens. Even more telling, Χρόνος is a correction proposed by Zoega for Κρόνος.

46. For a general presentation, see Robert-Alain Turcan, *Mithra et le mithriacisme,* Que sais-je? n° 1929 (Paris: Presses Universitaires de France, 1981); *Mithras platonicus: Recherches sur l'hellénisation philosophique de Mithra,* EPRO 47 (Leiden: Brill, 1975); and *Les Cultes orientaux dans le monde romain* (Paris: Les Belles Lettres, 1989), 193–241. See Luc Brisson, "La figure de Chronos dans la théogonie orphique et ses antécédents iraniens," in *Mythes et représentations du temps* (Paris: Editons du C.N.R.S., 1985), 37–55; reprinted in *Orphée et l'Orphisme dans l'Antiquité gréco-romaine.*

47. *In Tim.* II 290 et seq.

48. See *OF* 156, and *In Tim.* I 118–25–26.

49. *In Tim.* III 255.10–19.

50. *In Tim.* III 255.20–21.

51. See item 3 in the list above.

52. See item 1 in the list above.

53. For an inventory, see *In Remp.* I 154.12–159.6.

54. *In Temp.* I 202.17–205.23.

55. Jean Trouillard "L'activité onomastique selon Proclos," *De Jamblique à Proclus,* Entretiens sur l'Antiquité classique, n° 21 Hardt Foundation (Geneva: Vandoeuvres-Genève, 1974), 239–251.

56. A. R. Sheppard, *Studies on the 5th and 6th Essays of Proclus' "Commentary on the Republic,"* 145–161.

57. *In Remp.* I 74, 16–30.

58. *In Remp.* I 85.16–26.

59. *In Remp.* I 178.6–179.32.

60. This section owes much to Jean Bouffartigue, "Représentations et évaluations du texte poétique dans le *Commentaire sur la République* de Proclos," in *Le Texte et ses représentations,* Etudes de littérature ancienne 3 (Paris: Presses de l'Ecole Normale Supérieure, 1987), 129–143; the table is on p. 132.

61. *In Remp.* I 177.15–23.

62. *In Remp.* I 198.13–19.

63. For Daemonology in Plutarch, see chapter 5 above text at note 61.

64. *Od.* VIII 266–367.

65. *In Remp.* I 141.1–143.19.

66. *Il.* XIV 346–351.

67. *In Remp.* I 133.19–133.17.

68. *In Remp.* I 137.2–139.17.

69. *In Remp.* I 136.15–137.2.

70. *In Remp.* I 139.20–140.6.

71. *In Remp.* I 135.17–136.14.

72. See chapter 5 above, section on Porphyry.

73. *In Remp.* I 177.23–178.2.

74. *In Remp.* I 179.13–15; 186.24–25; 193.4–8.

75. *In Remp.* I 179.10–13; 186.26–28.

76. *In Remp.* I 178.2–5.

77. *In Remp.* I 194.18–26, cf. *Od.* III 267–268.

78. *In Remp.* I 192.15–17; 192.28–193.4.

79. *In Remp.* I 179.19, 32; 192.18; 72.18.

80. *In Remp.* I 195.22.

81. *In Remp.* I 195.13.

82. Sheppard, *Studies on the 5th and 6th Essays of Proclus' "Commentary on the Republic,"* 175–176.

83. Luc Brisson, "Le discours comme univers et l'univers comme discours: Platon et ses interprètes néo-platoniciens," in *Le Texte et ses représentations,* 211–218; see also James A. Coulter, *The Literary Microcosm: Theories of Interpretation of the Later Neoplatonism* (Leiden: Brill, 1976).

84. According to Chiara Faraggiana di Sarzana, "Le commentaire à Hésiode et la *paideia* encyclopédique de Proclus," in *Proclus, lecteur et interprète des anciens,* 22–41, this commentary may be a marginal note on Plutarch's commentary on Hesiod's *Works and Days.* See also, by the same author, "Il commentario procliano alle *Opere e Giorni* I: Plutarco fonte di Proclo," *Aevum* 52 (1978): 17–40; *Aevum* 55 (1981): 22–29. For the text itself, see *Scholia vetera in Hesiodi Opera et Dies,* ed. A. Pertusi (Milan: Pubblicazioni dell'Università Cattolica del S. Cuore, n.s. 53, 1955).

85. *In Tim.* III 249.17.

86. On the character of Phorkys, see *In Tim.* III 186.23–25.

87. *In Remp.* II 208.2–4.

Chapter Seven

1. Discussed later in this chapter.

2. N. Festa, *Theodori Ducae Lascaris epistolae* (Florence, 1898), 310.

3. Michael Psellus, *Chronographia* VI 61.

4. *Iliad* III 156–157: "Surely, there is no reason to (οὐ νέμεσις) blame the Trojans and strong-greaved Achaians / if for a long time they suffer hardship for a woman like this one." [English translation, with slight modification, drawn from *The Iliad of Homer,* trans. Richmond Lattimore (Chicago: University of Chicago Press, 1970).]

5. From a historical perspective, it appears that the starting point of the Byzantine era should be May 11, 330, the day when Constantine solemnly inaugurated the new capital of the Empire on the shores of the Bosphorus and the end point should be May 29, 1453, when the last Byzantine emperor was killed while defending the city from the Turks, who entered it on that day. But in the context of the present book, it seems pertinent to take as point of departure the closing of the school of Athens by Justinian in 529. This said, the last three

chapters of this book will cover a millennium in the East and West. So I claim only to provide a few reference points to help readers orient themselves.

6. The first part of this chapter owes much to Robert Browning, "Homer in Byzantium," *Viator* 6, 1975: 15–33; Nigel G. Wilson, *Scholars of Byzantium* (Baltimore: Johns Hopkins University Press, 1983); Paul Lemerle, *Le premier humanisme byzantin: Notes et remarques sur enseignement et culture à Byzance des origines au Xème siècle* (Paris: Presses Universitaires de France, 1971); and C. N. Constantinides, *Higher Education in Byzantium in the Thirteenth and Early Fourteenth Centuries (1204–ca. 1310),* Texts and Studies in the History of Cyprus 11 (Nicosia: Cyprus Research Center, 1982). For a more general view, see Herbert Hunger, *Die Hochsprachliche profane Literatur der Byzantiner,* 2 vols. (Munich: Beck, 1978). See also Louis Bréhier's three-volume work [1946–1950] *Le Monde byzantin,* now published in the series L'évolution de l'humanité: n°13, *Vie et mort de Byzance* (new ed., February 1992, with preface by Gilbert Dagron); n° 20 *Les Institutions de l'Empire byzantin;* n° 21, *La Civilisation Byzantin.* And, finally, *The Oxford Dictionary of Byzantium,* 3 vols. (Oxford: Oxford University Press, 1991).

7. Henri-Irénée Marrou, *Histoire de l'éducation dans l'Antiquité* [1948] (Paris: Le Seuil, 1967), 485–489.

8. *In Arist. Eth. Nicom.* [X 10 1180b10–13], *CAG* 20, 1892, p. 613.3–6 Heylbut.

9. In *Bibliotheca graeca medii aevi* V, ed. G. Sathas (Paris: Maisonneuve, 1876), 14.

10. G. W. Bowersock, *Greek Sophists in the Roman Empire* (Oxford: Clarendon Press, 1982).

11. *Cod. Theod.* XIV 9, 3.

12. See section "The Transmission of Texts," later in this chapter.

13. Paul Lemerle goes so far as to speak of the "myth" of the Patriarchal Academy for the period prior to the twelfth century.

14. Many manuscripts were illustrated with mythological motives. See Kurt Weitzmann, *Greek Mythology in Byzantine Art,* Studies in Manuscript Illumination 4 (Princeton: Princeton University Press, 1951).

15. For a description, see L. G. Westerink, "La collection philosophique," in Damascius, *Traité des premiers principes: De l'ineffable et de l'Un,* vol. 1, ed. L. G. Westerink, trans. J. Combès (Paris: Les Belles Lettres, 1986), lxxiii–lxxx.

16. For a general description, see Wilson, *Scholars in Byzantium,* 120–135. The most important surviving manuscript of his library is the E. D. Clark 39, which includes twenty-four of Plato's dialogues, all the most important ones except for the *Republic, Timaeus,* and *Laws.*

17. On the title, date, and content of this "formidable" encyclopedia, see A. Adler, in *RE* II, 4, 1931, s.v. Suidas, 675–717.

18. Paul Lemerle, "Le gouvernement des philosophes: l'enseignement, les Ecoles et la culture," *Cinq études sur le XIème siècle byzantin* (Paris: C.N.R.S., 1977), 193–248.

19. *PG* 120, 1156b.

20. Published by G. Sathas, in *Bibliotheca graeca medii aevi* V (Paris: Maisonneuve, 1876), 142–167.

21. On Psellus, see esp. E. Kriaras, in *RE,* Suppl. XI (1968), s.v. Psellos, 1124–1182.

22. These texts attributed to Isaac Comnenus were published by Daniel Isaac as an appendix to Proclus, *Trois études sur la Providence* I (1977), 153–223; II (1979), 109–169; III (1982), 129–200.

23. Here are a few numbers to give an idea of the size of these commentaries. In the Berlin edition, the commentary on the *Iliad* (4 volumes published between 1827 and 1830)

is made up of more than 1,555 pages; and the commentary on the *Odyssey* (2 volumes published between 1825 and 1826) is almost 800 pages long.

24. See Pépin, *Mythe et allégorie*, 247–274. Discussing the diversity of Christian attitudes toward allegory, Pépin divides these attitudes into four groups: "Some of these authors, the first when taken in chronological order, took their very faithful inspiration from allegorical interpretation such as we have just seen at work in the New Testament, without owing anything important to the figurative exegeses of paganism. This was the case with the *Epistle of Barnabas* and Hippolytus of Rome. Others, among whom Clement of Alexandria is the best example, appeared, on the contrary, to be well versed in pagan allegorism, and made much use of its techniques and lessons in their own explanations of the Bible. Their insightfulness and the loftiness of their views kept them from discrediting the sources from which they were drawing. A third category, much more numerous, would be made up of writers who, without themselves making use of an allegorical interpretation of the Bible, showed an often strong hostility toward pagan allegory. This frankly negative attitude was that of the author of the pseudo-Clementine writings, of the various Greek apologists, and of several Latin polemicists such as Tertullian, Arnobius, Lactantius, and Firmicus Maternus. However, this logic of negation did not come into play for the authors of the fourth category, in whom the sometimes extravagant practice of biblical allegory was combined with an effort to disqualify the same exegetic technique when pagans applied it to their own texts. This inconsistent attitude is found in Origen and his disciple Eusebius, and, in the West, in Augustine" (260–261).

25. On the interpretation of Homer by Eustathius and by Tzetzes in general, see C. Matzukis, "Homer within the Byzantine framework," *Akroterion* 27 (1992): 2–5.

26. See Pierre Lévêque, *Aurea catena Homeri: Une étude sur l'allégorie grecque,* Annales littéraires de l'Université de Besançon 27 (Paris: Les Belles Lettres, 1959).

27. *Iliad* VIII 17–27 [English translation drawn from *The Iliad of Homer,* trans. Richmond Lattimore (Chicago: University of Chicago Press, 1951).]

28. On this topic, see H. Erbse, *Beiträge zur Überlieferung der Iliasscholien,* Zetemata 24 (Munich: Beck, 1960), 123–173; Marchinus van der Valk, *Researches on the Text and Scholia of the Iliad,* 2 vols. (Leiden: Brill, 1963–1964). For an edition of the text, see Eusahii *Commentarii ad Homeri Iliadem, pertinentes ad fidem codicis Laurentiani,* 4 vols., ed. Marchinus van der Valk (Leiden: Brill, 1971–1987).

29. *Comm. ad Iliadem* II, 514.25–515.3 van der Valk.

30. *Comm. ad Iliadem* II, p. 515.3–7.

31. See *SVF,* n° 1076, p. 315.4 von Arnim = Philodemus, *De piet.* chap. 11.

32. *Theaetetus* 153c–d.

33. *Comm. ad Iliadem* II, p. 515.7–8 van der Valk.

34. *Comm. ad Iliadem* II, p. 515.8–11 van der Valk.

35. See Seneca, *Naturales questiones* III 29, 1.

36. *Comm. ad Iliadem,* II, p. 515.11–18 van der Valk.

37. *Comm. ad Iliadem* II, p. 515.18–21 van der Valk.

38. Georges Dumézil, *Les Dieux Souverains des Indo-européens* (Paris: Gallimard, 1977), which repeats *Mitra-Varuna* [1941, 1948] and *Jupiter, Mars, Quirinus* [1941, 1948].

39. On this topic, see G. Morgan, "Homer in Byzantium: John Tzetzes," in *Approaches to Homer,* ed. C. A. Rubino and C. W. Shelmerdin (Austin: University of Texas Press, 1983), 165–188.

40. See note 28 above.

41. *Der unbekannte Teil der Ilias-Exegesis des Iohannes Tzetzes,* ed. Anastasios Lolos, Beitr. zur klass. Philol. 130 (Königstein: Hain, 1981).

42. *Allegories of Homer* [on the *Iliad* and the *Odyssey* 1–13], published by P. Matranga, in *Anecdota graeca* I (1850), 1–295; then by J. F. Boissonnade, Tzetzae *Allegoriae* Iliadis (Paris, 1851); and finally by H. Hunger, *Byzantinische Zeitschrift* 49 (1956): 249–310 (on the *Odyssey* 1–12) and ibid. 38 (1955): 4–48 (on the *Odyssey* 13–24).

43. Johannes Tzetzes, "Allegorien aus der *Verskronik,*" Kommentierte Textausgabe, ed. Herbert Hunger, *Jahrbuch der Österreichischen Byzantinischen Gesellschaft* 4 (1955): 13–49; see also Hunger, "Allegorische Mythendeutung in der Antike und bei Johannes Tzetzes: Unter Heranziehung bisher unbekannter Tzetzes-Texte aus *Vindob. phil. gr.* 118 und *Vat. Barb. gr.* 30, ibid. 3 (1954): 35–54.

44. Since Herodotus, Egypt had been considered the source of civilization.

45. An oxymoron.

46. *Allegories of Homer,* v. 1–11.

47. See also Isaac Sebastocrator, text at note 22 above.

48. Published by H. Hinck, in *Polemonis Declamationes* (Leipzig: Teubner, 1873), 59–88.

49. See IV 4, 5.

50. Nicetas's Eulogy, published by G. Sathas, in *Bibliotheca Graeca medii aevi* V (Paris: Maisonneuve, 1876), 88.

51. Published by Sathas, in *Bibliotheca graeca medii aevi* V, 256.

52. For an edition of these texts with a selection of ancient commentaries, see *Oracles chaldaïques,* ed. and trans. E. des Places (Paris: Les Belles Lettres, 1971).

53. Under the title *Magic Oracles of the disciples of Zoroaster:* Μαγικὰ Λογία τῶν ἀπὸ Ζωροάστρου Μάγων.

54. As Charles Zervos argues in his *Un philosophe néoplatonicien du XIme siècle, Michel Psellos: Sa vie, son oeuvre, ses luttes philosophiques, son influence* (Paris: Leroux, 1919), 168–182.

55. In Tzetzae *Allegoriae* Iliadis accedunt Pselli allegoriae quarum una inedita, curante, J. Fr. Boissonade (Paris, 1851), 343–352.

56. English translation, slightly modified, drawn from Euripides, *Orestes,* trans. John Peck and Frank Nisetich (Oxford: Oxford University Press, 1995), 21.— *Trans.*

57. In Tzetzae, *Allegoriae Iliadis,* ed. Boissonnade, 352–354.

58. Text edited by G. Sathas, in *L'Annuaire de l'Association pour l'Encouragement des Etudes Grecques en France* V (1875), 215–219; see Pierre Lévêque, *Aurea Catena Homeri: Une étude sur l'allégorie grecque,* Annales Littéraires de l'Université de Besançon 27 (Paris: Les Belles Lettres, 1959); 78–81. New edition in Psellus, *Opera philosophica. Minora* I, ed. J. M. Duffy and D. J. O'Meara (Leipzig: Teubner, 1992), op. 46, 164–168.

59. In Tzetsae *Allegoriae Iliadis,* ed. Boissonade, 363–365.

60. *Iliad* IV 1–4. Text edited by G. Sathas, in *L'Annuaire* (see note 58 above), 210–215. [English translation drawn from Lattimore (see note 27 above).]

61. In Tzetzae *Allegoria Iliadis,* 363–365.

62. See Dominic J. O'Meara, *Pythagoras Revived: Mathematics and Philosophy in Late Antiquity* (Oxford: Clarendon Press, 1989), chap. 3 and appendix I.

63. The table is drawn from François Masai, *Pléthon et le Platonisme de Mistra* (Paris: Les Belles Lettres, 1956), 224.

64. Plethon, *Traité des Lois,* ed. C. Alexandre, trans. A. Pellissier (Paris: Didot, 1858), 256.

Chapter Eight

1. See chapter 4, in extract beginning, "If the gods exist, . . ."

2. On the *Ghaya,* cf. note 22 below.

3. I drew inspiration for this chapter from Jean Seznec, *La survivance des dieux antiques: Essai sur le rôle de la tradition mythologique dans l'humanisme et dans l'art de la Renaissance,* Studies of the Warburg Institute 11 (1940); 2d ed. with revised bibliography, Collection Idées et Recherches (Paris: Flammarion, 1980). The Middle Ages in the West can be said to begin in 476, when Odoacer, the leader of the German tribes, overthrew the last Augustus of the West, Romulus Augustulus, and it can be said to end on October 7, 1571, with the victory of the Spanish, Venetian, and Genovese forces over the Turks at Lepanto. Again, it must be remembered that these few pages only allow a bird's-eye view of this millennium.

4. Henri-Irénée Marrou, *Histoire de l'éducation dans l'Antiquité* [1948] (Paris: Le Seuil, 1967), 490 et seq.

5. Paul Lemerle, *Le premier humanisme byzantin: Notes et remarques sur enseignement et culture à Byzance des origines au Xᵉᵐᵉ siècle.* Bibliothèque Byzantine, Série Etudes 6 (Paris: Presses Universitaires de France, 1971).

6. See chapter 4 above, section "The Stoic Doctrine on the Gods in *De natura deorum.*"

7. *Octavius.*

8. *De idolorum vanitate.*

9. *De idolatria. Ad nationes. Apologelicum.*

10. *Adversus nationes.*

11. *Instructiones adversus gentium deos.*

12. *Divinarum institutionum libri* VII.

13. *De erroribus profanarum religonum.*

14. John Daniel Cooke, "Euhemerism: A mediaeval interpretation of classical paganism," *Speculum* 2 (1927): 396–410; V. Alphandéry, "L'Evhémérisme et les débuts de l'histoire des religions au Moyen âge," *Revue de l'Histoire des Religions* 109 (1934): 1–27.

15. See chapter 4 above, section "The Extensions of This Doctrine."

16. Orosius, *Histoires (Contre les païens),* Greek text and French translation, 3 vols. (Paris: Les Belles Lettres, 1990–1991). See also Hans-Werner Goetz, *Die Geschichtstheologie des Orosius,* Impulse der Forschung (Darmstadt: Wissenschaftliche Buchgesellschaft, 1980).

17. In chapter XI of book VII. On this topic, cf. Katherine Nell MacFarlane, *Isidore of Seville on the Pagan Gods* (*Origines* VIII 11), Transactions of the American Philosophical Society, vol. 70, p. 3 (1980).

18. *De sex aetatibus mundi, PL* CXXIII, III 35.

19. See extract above, beginning, "Tradition tells us that . . ."

20. Jean Pépin, "La lecture du *De antro nympharum* de Porphyre en Occident" [1974], reprinted in *La tradition de l'allégorie: De Philon d'Alexandrie à Dante,* II: *Etudes historiques* (Paris: Etudes Augustiniennes, 1987), 81–90.

21. Franz Boll, *Sternglaube und Sterndeutung: Die Geschichte und das Wesen der Astrologie,* with Carl Bezold, ed. W. Gundel (Leipzig: Teubner, 1931).

22. Maslama ibn Ahmad al-Magritti, the supposed author of *Picatrix* [= *Ghayat al-Hakim*]: vol. 1, Arabic text, Studien der Bibliothek Warburg 12 (Leipzig, 1933); vol. 2, German translation, Studies of the Warburg Institute 27 (London, 1962); vol. 3, Latin version, Studies of the Warburg Institute 39 (London, 1986).

23. See chapter 4 above.

24. Gregory the Great, *Expositio in librum Job sive moralium libri* XXXV.

25. Fulgentius Planciades, *Opera,* ed. R. Helm (Leipzig: Teubner, 1898), completed by J. Préaux in 1970.

26. Theodulphi *Carmina, PL* CV, 331–332.

27. *Moralis philosphia de honesto et utili, PL* CLXXI, 1007. This work has also been attributed to William of Conches.

28. John of Salisbury, *Entheticus major et minor,* 3 vols., ed. and trans. Jan Van Laarhoven (Leiden: Brill, 1987).

29. *Entheticus* V, 185–188.

30. F. Ghisalberti, "Un cultore di Ovidio nel secolo XII," *Memorie del R. Istituto Lombardo di Scienze e Lettere,* 1932, 157–232.

31. *The Parisiana Poetria of John of Garland,* ed. with introd., translation, and notes by Traugott Lawler (New Haven: Yale University Press, 1974).

32. *Ovide moralisé,* critical edition, introd. C. de Boer (Amsterdam: North-Holland, 1954).

33. Jean Pépin, "Dante et la tradition de l'allégorie" [1970], in *La Tradition de l'allégorie: De Philon d'Alexandrie à Dante,* II: Etudes historiques (Paris: Etudes Augustiniennes, 1987), 251–320.

34. Hans Liebeschütz, *Fulgentius Metaforalis: Ein Beitrag zur Geschichte der antiken Mythologie im Mittelalter,* Studien der Bibliothek Warburg 4 (Leipzig: Teubner, 1926), 65–114.

35. Petrus de Alliaco, *Imago mundi,* Latin text and French translation and notes by Edmond Buron (Paris, 1930).

36. Alexander Neckham, *De natura rerum* libri duo, ed. T. Wright (London: Longman, 1865).

37. For a list and descriptions of the manuscripts that include the astrological part of this treatise, see the work of Fritz Saxl, *Verzeichnis astrologischer und mythologischer illustrierter Handschriften des lateinischen Mittelalters,* 2 vols. (Heidelberg: C. Winter, 1915–1927).

38. See chapter 7, note 14.

39. Albricus, *Allegoriae poeticae seu de veritate ac expositione poeticarum fabularum* libri IV (Paris, 1520); Robert Raschke, *De Alberico mythologo,* diss. (Breslau 1913).

40. *Libellus de deorum imaginibus,* in Liebeschütz, *Fulgentius Metaforalis,* 117–128.

Chapter Nine

1. By limiting the Renaissance to a period extending from the end of the fourteenth century to the end of the sixteenth in Europe we neglect the fact that the renewal at that time manifested itself in various ways and took on different forms in the different regions of Europe that were affected. There were even some eighteenth-century authors who remained Renaissance people.

2. As shown in chapter 8.

3. This chapter, therefore, resembles a bibliographical index file. It owes a great deal to the book by Don Cameron Allen, *Mysteriously Meant: The Rediscovery of Pagan Symbolism and Allegorical Interpretation in the Renaissance* (Baltimore: Johns Hopkins University Press, 1970). For given names, readers should refer, whenever possible, to *Dizionario biografico degli Italiani* (Istituto della Enciclopedia italiana, 1960). I would like to thank Sylvain Matton for carefully reading the present chapter and making a number of suggestions that prevented many mistakes; I am solely responsible for any remaining ones.

4. Printing takes over during the second half of the fifteenth century.

5. Printed as a separate work in Venice in 1471 and in 1508, and in Lyon in 1541.

6. See chapter 8, text at note 39.

7. See chapter 8, text at note 32.

8. Published at Ulm, 1473 = *De la ruyne des nobles hommes et femmes* (Bruges, 1476).

9. See chapter 8, text at note 40.

10. See chapter 1, section "The Communication of the Memorable in an Oral Civilization."

11. Ernst von Leutsch, "Homeros im Mittelalter," *Philologus* 12 (1857): 366–368.

12. F. Bertini, "Interpreti medievali di Virgilio: Fulgencio e Bernardo Silvestre," *Sandalion* 7–8 (1983–1984): 151–164.

13. Statius Publius Papinius, *Operum,* 3 vols. (Leipzig: Teubner, 1898–1926). For the *Thebaid,* see Roger Leseur's edition and translation, 3 vols. (Paris: Les Belles Lettres: 1990–1991).

14. Dictys Cretensis, *Ephemeridos belli troiani libri sex,* ed. F. Meister (Leipzig: Teubner, 1872). See also M. Ihm, "Der griechische und lateinische Dictys," *Hermes* 44 (1909).

15. Dares Phrygius, *De excidio Troiae historia,* ed. F. Meister (Leipzig: Teubner, 1873). See also O. Schissel von Fleschenberg, *Dares-Studien,* Halle, 1908.

16. Benoît de Sainte-Maure [or More], *Le roman de Troie,* 6 vols., compiled from all known manuscripts by Léopold Constant (Paris: Didot, 1904–1912).

17. Guido delle Colonne, *Historia destructionis Troiae,* trans. and ed. M. E. Meet, Mediaeval Academy of America Publications 36 (Bloomington: Indiana University Press, 1974).

18. This text can be found in *Poetae latini minores,* ed. E. Baehrens (Leipzig: Teubner, 1881), 8–59.

19. On this translation, which was never published, see Agostino Pertusi, *Leonzio Pilato fra Petrarca e Boccacio: Le sue versioni omeriche negli autografi di Venezia e la cultura greca del primo Umanesmo,* Civiltà Veneziana, Studi 16 (Venice and Rome, 1965).

20. Georg Finsler, *Homer in der Neuzeit* (Leipzig: Teubner, 1912).

21. Pierre de Nolhac, *Pétrarque et l'Humanisme* (Paris, 1892).

22. Moreno Morani, "Per una storia delle versioni italiane dell' *Iliade,*" *Orpheus* 10 (1989): 261–310.

23. The work discussed in chapter 4, section "The Extensions of This Doctrine."

24. This was a late work, originating in Byzantium, published in Greek in 1531 by V. Opsopaeus (Haganoae), and translated into Latin (*Moralis interpretatio errorum Ulyssis Homerici,* Tiguri) by C. Gesner in 1542. It was edited by J. Colombus and published in Stockholm in 1678 and in Leiden in 1745.

25. Antenor was a Trojan elder and an adviser to Priam. He advocated a peaceful solution to the conflict, which led to his being spared by the Greeks when they took Troy. After the sack of the city, he left for Thrace along with his sons, and from there he set out for the north of Italy. This is why he is thought to be the ancestor of the Veneti.

26. In his *Historia Julia, sive syntagma heroicus* (Helmstadt, 1593).

27. In his *Geographia sacra seu Phaleg et Chanaan* (Caen, 1646).

28. In *La istoria universale provata con monumenti e figurata con simboli de gli antichi* (Rome, 1697).

29. In his *Aenigmata prisci orbis: Jonas in luce, in historia Manassis et Josiae, ex eleganti veterum Hebraeorum stilo solutum aenigma. Aenigmata Graecorum et Latinorum ex caligine Homeri, Hesiodi, Orphei . . . enodata* (Helmstadt, 1723).

30. *Noctes solitariae sive de iis quae scientifice scripta sunt ab Homero in Odyssea* (Venice, 1613).

31. *De theologia Homeri* (Leipzig, 1689).

32. *De philosophia Homeri* (Wittenberg, 1704).

33. *Vera historia Romana, seu origo Latii vel Italiae ac Romanae urbis* (Rome, 1655).

34. In his *Homerus Hebraizon: sive comparatio Homeri cum scriptoribus sacris quoad normam loquendi* (Oxford, 1658).

35. In his *Homeri gnomologia* (Cambridge, 1660).

36. Edited by Francesco Sbordone *Hieroglyphica* (Naples: Loffredo, 1940); English translation by George Boas, *Hieroglyphica,* Bollingen series 22 (New York: Pantheon Books, 1950).

37. Oliver Masson and Jean-Luc Fournet, "A propos d'Horapollon, l'auteur des *Hieroglyphica,*" *Revue des Etudes Grecques* 105 (1992): 231–236.

38. We know nothing about the owners of this table before the sixteenth century. It could be seen at Cardinal Bembo's residence, which is why it was called "Bembine." According to some, the cardinal had bought it from a locksmith who had seized it during the sack of Rome by the high constable of Bourbon in 1527. According to others, he received it from Pope Paul III. Whatever the case may be, as soon as it was discovered, it made a splash in the world of scholarship. A famous engraver of Parma, Aeneas Vico, made a careful engraving of it and published the engraving in Venice in 1559. There was also an engraving made by J. Franco and brought up to date in 1600. After Cardinal Bembo's death, the table became the property of the dukes of Mantua; it remained in their gallery until 1630, the year when Mantua was taken by the imperial troops. The table then disappeared, but reappeared later in the treasury of the archives of Turin. It is still in the royal gallery of that city.

39. In his *Vetustissimae tabulae aenae sacris Aegyptiorum simulachris coelatae accurata explicatio, in qua antiquissimarum superstitionum origines . . . enarrantur* (Venice, 1605).

40. See note 38 above.

41. *Hieroglyphica sive de sacris Aegyptiorum litteris commentarii* (Basel, 1556), a folio of almost a thousand pages that was reissued seven times before its last printing in 1678. It was translated into French in 1576 and 1615, and into Italian in 1602. An edition that came close to being a paperback one was published in 1592 by Heinrich Schwalenberg and was reprinted a number of times.

42. Giovanni Polara, "La fortuna di Virgilio," *Coronide Virgiliana,* a cura di Marcello Gigante, Pubb. del Bimillenario Virgiliano no 8 (Naples: Giannini, 1988), 13–42. See also "Vie et mort de l'allégorie dans les commentaires des Bucoliques à la Renaissance," *Hommages à Henry Bardon,* ed. M. Renard and P. Laurens (Latomus: Brussels, 1985), 10–40.

43. Donatus, *Interpretationes virgilianae,* ed. H. Georg (Leipzig: Teubner, 1905). On the historical problem raised by this book, see "Is Donatus' commentary on Virgil lost?" *Classical Quarterly* 10 (1916): 158–164.

44. Fabius Planciades Fulgentius.

45. *Commentum super sex libros Eneidos Virgili.* Cf. F. Bertini, "Interpreti mediaevali di Virgilio: Fulgencio e Bernardo Silvestre," *Sandalion* 7–8 (1983–1984): 151–164.

46. For a general approach, see Sebastiano Timparano, *Per la storia della filologia Virgiliana antica,* Quaderni di Filologia Critica 6 (Rome: Salerno, 1986).

47. The title may be explained as follows. The work is supposed to be an account of the discussions that were held in the monastery of Camaldoli in 1468. At the end of each of the

daily discussions, the abbé Mariotto Allegri invited the participants to dinner. The main interlocutor and the discussion leader was the famous scholar, philosopher, and architect L. B. Alberti. Alberti's comments were regularly interrupted by Lorenzo de Medici, asking a question or making a comment, thus providing transitions. Alberti, who mentions that he has read Ficino's treatises on the immortality of the soul, which were not yet published at the time, is supposed to express the ideas of his teacher up to a certain point. Giuliano de Medici, Marco Parenti, Pietro and Donato Acciaioli, Alamanno Rinuccini, Antonio Canigione, Piero Landino, and even Marsilio Ficino are riveted to his words but remain silent.

48. *De civili et bellica fortitudine liber ex mysteriis poetae Vergilii nunc primum depromptus* (Rome, 1526).

49. In his *In primum* Aeneidos *Virgilii librum ex Aristotelis de arte poetica et rhetorica praeceptis explicationes* (Bologna, 1563).

50. Such as *L'Opere di Virgilio Mantoano* (Venice, 1576), which provides a text surrounded by commentaries in Italian.

51. *Ovid Renewed: Ovidian Influences on Literature and Art from the Middle Ages to the Twentieth Century,* ed. Charles Martindale (Cambridge: Cambridge University Press, 1988).

52. See chapter 8, section "Moral Interpretation."

53. *Metamorphoseos libri XV. In eosdem libros Raphaelis Regii luculentissime enarrationes. Neque non Lactantii et Petri Lavinii commentarii non ante impressi* (Venice, 1540).

54. *The Fable of Ovid treting of Narcissus* (London, 1560).

55. *In omnia P. Ovidii Nasonis opera observationes* (Antwerp, 1575).

56. *Symbolorum libri XVII,* 1599; *Metamorphoseon libris XV* (Antwerp, 1610).

57. P. Ovidii Nasonis Metamorphoseon *plerarumque historica naturalis moralis ekphrasis* (Frankfurt, 1619).

58. *The Third Part of the Countesse of Pembroke Yuychurch* (London, 1592).

59. Ghislaine Amielle, *Recherches sur les traductions françaises des* Métamorphoses *d'Ovide illustrées et publiées en France à la fin du XVᵉᵐᵉ et au XVIᵉᵐᵉ siècle,* Coll. Caesarodunum, Textes et images de l'Antiquité n° 1 (Paris: Touzot, 1989).

60. *Les* Métamorphoses *d'Ovide, traduittes en prose Francoise . . . Avec XV discours contenans l'explication morale des fables.*

61. *Les* Metamorphoses *d'Ovide en latin et françois: Avec les nouvelles explications historiques, morales et politiques sur toutes les fables, chacune selon son sujet.*

62. *Les Métamorphoses,* edited and translated (Amsterdam, 1732).

63. Since the list of all these authors would be too long here, see the relevant pages in Don Cameron Allen, *Mysteriously Meant: The Rediscovery of Pagan Symbolism and Allegorical Interpretation in the Renaissance* (Baltimore: Johns Hopkins, University Press 1970), 201–214.

64. This major repertory of the first half of the fourteenth century went into eight editions.

65. In 1532 Pictor published his *Theologia mythologica* (Antwerp), and in 1558, he published his *Apotheseos tam exterarum gentium quam Romanorum deorum libri tres* (Basel).

66. The *Historia de deis gentium* (Basel, 1548), by Lilio Gregorio Giraldi; the *Delle imagini de gli dei de gli antichi* (Venice, 1556) by Vincenzo Cartari, and the *Mythologiae sive explicationis fabularum libri decem* by Natale Conti (Venice, 1568).

67. Some minor works, however, can be cited: *The Golden Boke of the Leaden Gods* (London, 1577) by Stephen Batman; the *Mystagogus poeticus* (London, 1647) by A. Ross; and *L'his-*

toire poétique pour l'intelligence des poètes et auteurs anciens by Pierre Gautruche, published in Caen in 1673, and translated into English by M. Assigny in London in 1672.

68. The *Tableaux du temple des Muses* (Amsterdam, 1655) by the abbé Michel de Marolles; the *Pantheum mythicum, seu fabulosa deorum historia* (Amsterdam, 1659; translated into English by Andrew Tooke, and known under the title of *Tooke's Pantheon of the Heathen gods and Illustrious Heroes* (London 1698).

69. In the sixteenth century, Father Lubin was the name given to naive or stupid monks. Rabelais applies it here to the Dominican Thomas of Wales, whose allegorical interpretations of Ovid were famous at the time. In fact, the *Metamorphosis Ovidiana moraliter a magistro Thoma Walleys . . . explanata,* published in Paris in 1509 and in 1511, then in Lyon in 1513, had been written in the fourteenth century by Pierre Bersuire (see this chapter, section "The Persistence of the Middle Ages").

70. [English translation drawn from François Rabelais, *The Histories of Gargantua and Pantagruel,* trans. J. M. Cohen (Harmondsworth, U.K.: Penguin Books, 1955), 38.]—Trans.

71. D. Martin Luther, *Werke, Kritische Gesamtausgabe,* Band 43 (Weimar: Böhlaus, 1912).

72. Ioannis Calvini, *Sermon 146* ["On the Book of Job"], in *Opera quae supersunt omni,* ed. G. Baum, E. Gunitz, and E. Reuss, vol. 35 (Brunschwig, 1887).

73. In his *Ecclesiastae sive de ratione concionandi libri quatuor.*

74. C. W. Lemmi, *The classical Deities in Bacon* (Baltimore, 1933); and "Mythology and alchemy in the wisdom of the ancients," in *Essential Articles for the Study of Francis Bacon,* ed. Brian Vickers (Hamden, CT: Archon Books, 1968), 51–92.

75. Francis Bacon, *The Advancement of Learning and New Atlantis* (London: Oxford University Press, 1951), 99.

76. Arrian I 11, 55; VI 9, 3; Diodorus of Sicily XVII 17–18; Justinian XI 5, 12; Plutarch, *Life of Alexander* 15.

77. On the Bembine Table, see above, section "The Egyptians."

78. *Le imagini con tutti i reversi trovati et le vite degli* [XII] *imperatori tratte dalle medaglie et dalle historie degli antichi* (Venice 1548); *Discorsi sopra le medaglie degli antichi* [Da Marzia sino a Domizia] (Venice, 1555); *Le imagini delle donne auguste* (Venice, 1557).

79. *Discours de la religion des anciens romains* (Lyon, 1556).

80. Gabriele Simeoni published *Le présage du triomphe des Gaulois* (Lyon, 1555); *Les illustres observations antiques* (Lyon, 1558); *Dialogo pio et speculativo con diverse sentenze latine et volgari* (Lyon, 1560).

81. *Discorso sopra le medaglie de gli antichi* (Venice, 1559).

82. *In veterum numismatum Romanorum miscellanea explicationes* (Lyon, 1560).

83. *C. Julius Caesar, sive Historiae imperatorum Caesarumque Romanorum ex antiquis numismatibus restitua liber primus* (Bruges, 1563).

84. *Discours sur les medalles et graveures antiques principalement romaines* (Paris, 1579).

85. *Diálogos de las medallas,* published in 1587; translated into Italian in 1592, and into Latin in 1617.

86. *Introductio ad historiam numismatum* (Amsterdam, 1683).

87. *Thesaurus numismatum Romanorum* (Amsterdam, 1608).

88. *Imperatorum Romanorum numismata aurea* (Antwerp, 1615).

89. *Dissertationes de praestantia et usu numismatum antiquorum* (Rome, 1664).

90. Alciati, *Emblemata* (Paris, 1531).

91. *De urbis antiquitatibus libri quinque,* published in Rome around 1527 and translated into Italian by Paolo Rosso, *L'Antichità di Roma* (1543).

92. *Symbolarum epistolicarum liber primus* (Padua, 1628).

93. *De pictura veterum libri tres* (Amsterdam, 1630).

94. *Commentariolus in veterem picturam Nymphaeum referentem* (Rome, 1676).

95. *Sculpturae veteris admiranda* (Nuremberg, 1680).

96. Text by Giovanni Pietro Bellori and drawings by Pietro Sante Bartoli (Rome, 1680; new edition with 35 new illustrations, 1691).

97. *Historia utriusque belli Dacici a Traiano Caesare gesti ex simulacris quae in columna ejusdem Roma visuntur collecta* (Rome, 1576).

98. *Colonna Traiana* (Rome, 1673).

99. *De columna Traiani syntagma* (Rome, 1683).

100. *Dell'antichità di Roma* (Rome, 1554).

101. *Antiquaria urbis* (Rome, 1513).

102. In *Antiquae tabulae marmoreae solis effigie symbolisque exculptae, accurata explicatio* (Rome, 1616; Paris, 1617).

103. *Inscriptiones antiquae totius orbis Romani* (Heidelberrg, 1602–1603).

104. *Syntagma inscriptionum antiquarum* (Leipzig and Frankfurt, 1682).

105. *Inscriptionum antiquarum explicatio* (Rome, 1699).

106. *Roma sotterranea* (Rome, 1632).

107. *Le gemme antiche figurate* (Rome, 1657).

108. *Commentaires historiques contenants en abrégé les vies, éloges, et censures des empereurs . . . jusques à Pertinax* (Paris, 1635).

109. Notably with his *Hieroglyphica, sive antiqua schemata gemmarum anularium quaesita, moralia, politica, historica, medica, philosophica et sublimiora explicata* (Padua 1653), dedicated to Queen Christina of Sweden.

110. In the *Odyssey* X 302 et seq., Hermes, who wants to enable Odysseus to resist Circe's spells, gives him a plant with magical properties that the gods call μῶλυ.

111. *Antiquitatum variarum volumina* XVII (Paris, 1512).

112. In his *Illustrations de Gaule et singularitez de Troye* (Paris, 1512).

113. *An historical treatise of the travels of Noah in Europe* (London, 1601).

114. Cologne, 1605.

115. London, 1652.

116. In his *De descensu domini nostri Iesu Christi ad inferos,* published in London in 1611 by Bishop Parker.

117. *De profanis Aegyptiorum, Romanorum et sacris Christianorum ritibus libri tres* (Rome, 1681).

118. *Conformité des cérémonies chinoises avec l'idolâtrie grecque et romaine* (Cologne, 1700).

119. *De papatu per ethnicismum impraeganto* (Frankfurt, 1634).

120. *De origine idolatriae apud gentiles et Christianos* (Leiden, 1708).

121. *The original idolatries, or the birth of heresies* (London, 1624).

122. *Dissertationes de origine ac progressu idolatriae et superstitionum* (Amsterdam, 1696).

123. *De theologia gentili et physiologia christiana, sive de origine ac progressu idololatriae* (Frankfurt, 1668).

124. *Geographia sacra seu Phaleg et Chanaan* (Caen, 1646).

125. *"Theologoumena pantodapa," sive de natura ortu, progressu, et studio verae theologiae libri sex* (Oxford, 1661).

126. *Origines sacrae, or a rational account of the grounds of christian faith, as to the Truth and divine authority of the Scriptures* (London, 1662).

127. *The court of the Gentiles; or, A discourse touching the original of human literature both philologie and philosophie from the Scriptures and Jewish Church* (Oxford, 1669, 1671, 1678).

128. *De religione Gentilium errorumque apud eos causis* (Amsterdam, 1663).

129. *De oraculis veterum ethnicorum dissertationes duae* (Amsterdam, 1683); *De origine ac progressu idololatriae superstitionum* (Amsterdam, 1696).

130. *Pensées diverses écrites à un docteur de Sorbonne à l'occasion de la comète qui parut au mois de décembre 1680* (Rotterdam, 1683).

131. *Histoire des oracles* (Paris, 1686).

132. *An historical dissertation on idolatrous corruptions in religion* (London, 1734).

133. *Demonstratio evangelica* (Paris, 1679); *Altnetanae quaestiones de concordia rationis et fidei* (Paris, 1690).

134. The section owes much to the article by François Secret, "Alchimie et mythologie" in *Dictionnaire des Mythologies,* ed. Yves Bonnefoy (Paris: Flammarion, 1981) [*Mythologies,* trans. under the direction of Wendy Doniger (Chicago: University of Chicago Press, 1991).] See also Secret, "Notes sur quelques alchimistes italiens de la Renaissance," *Rinascimento,* series 2, XIII (1973): 197–217. See also Sylvain Matton, "L'herméneutique alchimique de la fable antique," introd. to reissue of *Les Fables égyptiennes et grecques dévoilée et réduites au même principe avec une explication des hiéroglyphes et de la guerre de Troie,* by Dom Antoine Pernety (Paris, 1786, 2 vols.): Joachim Telle, "Mythologie und Alchemie: Zum Fortleben der antiken Götter in der Frühneuzeitlichen Alchemieliteratur," *Humanismus und Naturwissenschaften,* ed. Rudolf Schmitz und Fritz Krafft, Beiträge zum Humanismusforschungen 35, (Boppard am Rhein: Boldt, 1980), 135–154.

135. Marcelin Berthelot, *Collection des anciens alchimistes grecs,* 3 vols. (Paris, 1887–1888).

136. Marcelin Berthelot, *Histoire des sciences: La chimie au Moyen âge,* 3 vols. (Paris, 1893); W. Ganzenmüller, *Die Alchemie im Mittelalter* (Paderborn: Bonifacius, 1938).

137. *Suda,* s.v. δέρας (dealing with the golden fleece), vol. II, 24.21–26 Adler.

138. *Prezioza margarita novella,* edizione del vulgarizzamento, introduzione e nota a cura di Chiari Crisciani (Florence, 1976).

139. Philippe Eléphant, of English origin, was professor of medicine at the University of Toulouse at the height of his career in 1355–1356. His works seem to have preceded this date; three treatises have been preserved: *Mathematica, Alquimia,* and *Ethica.* The three treatises appear to be organized along a similar numerical structure with symbolic value involving, at each level, known mythological figures. On this author, see the entry by Guy Beaujouan and Paul Cattin in *Histoire Littéraire de la France,* vol. 41 (Paris, Imprimerie Nationale, 1981), 265–363.

140. *Chrysopeiae libri III et Gerontico liber primus* (Verona, 1491).

141. On Psellus, see chap. 7, sections "The Transmission of Texts" and "Psellos."

142. On this event, see François Secret, "Gianfracesco Pico della Mirandola, Lilio Gregorio Giraldi et l'alchimie," *Bibliothèque d'Humanisme et Renaissance* 38 (1976): 93–108.

143. The French reads, "d'un oeil 'chymique.'"—Trans.

144. Cf. Paul Kuntze, *Le grand Olympe, eine alchimistische Deutung von Ovids Metamorphosen* (Halle, 1912).

145. It was published in 1544 in Venice (reprinted three times: 1551, 1551, and 1562), and there were two Latin translations in 1548 and a third one in 1671. It is to Geber (Abu 'Abd Jabir ibn Hayyan al Sufi), king of the Arabs and prince of philosophers, that Arab alchemy

owed its extraordinary fame throughout of the Middle Ages. The uncertainty in the attribution of these works is linked to the obscure beginnings of a chain under "saintly gnostic
patronage." It has been supposed that Jabir, whose birth and death may have occurred between 730 and 804, was the name chosen by the Ikhwan al Safa, that is, the "Brothers of Pu-
rity and Loyalty" who had their center in Basra and wrote an encyclopedia there in the tenth
century. Translated into Persian and Turkish, the encyclopedia had a considerable influence
on Islamic thinkers and mystics. In fact, the Geber mentioned by Bracesco was the one to
whom Paul of Tarentum attributed the *Summa Perfectionis* in the fourteenth century.

146. These folios are known under the title of *Commentaria symbolica in duos tomos dis-
tincta, in quibus explicantur arcana pene infinita ad mysticam, naturalem et occultam rerum
signifcationem attinentia, quae nempe de abstrusione omnium prima adamica lingua: tum de
antiquissima Aegyptiorum coeterarumque gentium orphica philosophia, tum ex sacrosanta veteri mosaica et prophetica, nec non coelesti nova christiana, apostolica et sanctorum patrum evangelica theologia depromta sunt. Praeterea quae etiam celeberrimorum vatum fragmentis et
denique in chymistarum secretissimis involucris continguntur* (Venice, 1591).

147. The author of *Mysticae numerorum significationis liber* (Bergamo, 1583–84).

148. In his translations of the thirteenth book of *Amadis de Gaule* (Paris, 1563–1564) and
of *Poliphile* (Paris, 1546), and in *La Fontaine périlleuse . . . contenant la stéganographie des mys-
tères secrets de la science minérale* (Paris, 1572), in which he cites Roger Bacon among others.

149. Vigenère, 1523–1596, published notably *Les images ou tableaux de platte peinture de
Philostrate* (Paris, 1578).

150. Nuysement, c. 1560–1624, published *Le poème philosophic sur l'azoth des philosophes.
Les douze clefs de la philosophie* (Paris, 1620); *Traitez de l'harmonie et constitution générale du
vray sel, secret des philosophes* (Paris, 1621).

151. *Aenigmata . . .* (Paris, 1533).

152. Morisot, 1592–1661.

153. Maier's hypotheses and program are set forth in the *Arcana arcanissima, hoc est Hieroglyphica Aegyptio-Graeca vulgo necdum cognita, ad demonstrandam falsorum apud antiquos
deorum, dearum, heroum, animantium et institutorum pro sacris receptorum originem, ex uno
Aegyptiorum artificio, quod aureum animi et corporis medicamentum peregit, deductam, unde
tot poetarum allegoriae, scriptorum narrationes fabulosae, et per totam encyclopaediam, errores
sparsi clarissima veritatis luce manifestantur, quaeque tribui singula restituuntur, sex libris ex-
posita* (Oppenheim, 1614).

154. Pernety, *Dictionnaire mytho-hermétique, dans lequel on trouve les allégories fabuleuses
des poètes, les métaphores, les énigmes et les termes barbares des philosophes hermétiques* (Paris,
1758).

155. Trismosin, *Aureum Vellus* (Rorschach am Bodensee, 1598–1599).

156. Tollius, *Fortuita, in quibus praeter critica nonnulla, tota fabularis historia graeca, aegyptiaca ad chemiam pertinere asseritur* (Amsterdam, 1687).

157. Raymond Marcel, *Marsile Ficin (1433–1499)* (Paris: Les Belles Lettres, 1958).

158. There is not enough space and time here to discuss the main stages of the specula-
tive movement known as hermeticism. For this information, see François Secret's article
"Hermétisme: Quelques fables et quelques symboles des XVIᵉᵐᵉ et XVIIᵉᵐᵉ siecles," in *Dictionnaire des Mythologies* (see note 134 above).

159. *In Platonicam Theologiam: De animorum immortalitate*, text established and translated by Raymond Marcel, 3 vols. (Paris: Les Belles Lettres, 1964–1970).

160. Marsile Ficin, *Sur le Banquet de Platon ou de l'amour*, ed. and trans. Raymond Mar-

cel (Paris: Les Belles Lettres, 1956). See also André-Jean Festugière, *La philosophie de l'amour de Marsile Ficin, et son influence sur la littérature française au XVIème siècle,* Etudes de philosophie médiévale 31 (Paris: Vrin, 1941).

161. *De vera religione* IV 7; *Confessiones* VI 9, 13; *De civitate dei* VIII 9–10; X 19, 1, cited in the prologue to the *Platonic Theology.* [English translation drawn from Ficino, *Platonic Theology,* 2 vols., trans. Michael J. B. Allen with John Warden, Latin text ed. James Hankins with William Bowen (Cambridge, MA: Harvard University Press, 2001), 1: 11.]

162. English translation from *Platonic Theology,* 1: 295.—Trans.

163. *Hymn* XXXIV 16–17.

164. English translation from *Platonic Theology,* 1: 273.—Trans.

165. Agostino Steuco de Gubbio was a polyglot and a polymath. In 1535, he published in Lyon the *Cosmopoeia vel de mundano opificio,* and still in Lyon in 1540 the *De perenni philosophia libri X,* which was reprinted many times.

166. Stefano Convenzio's *De ascensu mentis in Deum ex Platonica et Peripatetica doctrina* was published in Venice in 1563.

167. Crispo, *De ethnicis philosophis caute legendis disputationeum ex propriis cujusque principiis quinarius primus* (Rome, 1594).

168. In Pansa's work titled: *De osculo seu consensu ethnicae et Christianae philosophiae tractatus* (Chieti, 1601).

169. Paris, 1606.

170. Galanti, *Christianae theologiae cum Platonica comparatio quin imo cum tota veteri sapientia ethnicorum, Chadaeorum nempe, Aegyptiorum et Graecorum* (Bologna, 1627).

171. Halloix, *Illustrium ecclesiae orientalis scriptorum qui sanctitate iuxta et eruditione . . . vitae et documenta* (Douai, 1633).

172. On the Cambridge Platonists in general, see C. A. Patrides, ed., *The Cambridge Platonists* (London: Arnold, 1969); Rosalie L. Coli, *Light and Enlightenment: A Study of the Cambridge Platonists and the Dutch Aminians* (Cambridge: Cambridge University Press, 1957).